Watermarks 1450–1850

Library of the Written Word

VOLUME 98

The Handpress World

Editor-in-Chief

Andrew Pettegree (*University of St. Andrews*)

Editorial Board

Ann Blair (*Harvard University*)
Falk Eisermann (*Staatsbibliothek zu Berlin – Preußischer Kulturbesitz*)
Shanti Graheli (*University of Glasgow*)
Earle Havens (*Johns Hopkins University*)
Ian Maclean (*All Souls College, Oxford*)
Alicia Montoya (*Radboud University*)
Angela Nuovo (*University of Milan*)
Helen Smith (*University of York*)
Mark Towsey (*University of Liverpool*)
Malcolm Walsby (*ENSSIB, Lyon*)
Arthur der Weduwen (*University of St. Andrews*)

VOLUME 78

The titles published in this series are listed at *brill.com/lww*

Watermarks 1450–1850

A Concise History of Paper in Western Europe

By

Frans Laurentius and Theo Laurentius

BRILL

LEIDEN | BOSTON

Cover illustration: A ream wrapper with Fortuna, made probably in the Veluwe area for the trader P. Koumans Smeding, c. 1820 (see also Fig. 13).

The Library of Congress Cataloging-in-Publication Data is available online at https://catalog.loc.gov
LC record available at https://lccn.loc.gov/2023937095

Typeface for the Latin, Greek, and Cyrillic scripts: "Brill". See and download: brill.com/brill-typeface.

ISSN 1874-4834
ISBN 978-90-04-50683-1 (hardback with dustjacket)
ISBN 978-90-04-50684-8 (e-book)

Copyright 2023 by Koninklijke Brill NV, Leiden, The Netherlands.
Koninklijke Brill NV incorporates the imprints Brill, Brill Nijhoff, Brill Hotei, Brill Schöningh, Brill Fink, Brill mentis, Vandenhoeck & Ruprecht, Böhlau, V&R unipress and Wageningen Academic.
All rights reserved. No part of this publication may be reproduced, translated, stored in a retrieval system, or transmitted in any form or by any means, electronic, mechanical, photocopying, recording or otherwise, without prior written permission from the publisher. Requests for re-use and/or translations must be addressed to Koninklijke Brill NV via brill.com or copyright.com.

This book is printed on acid-free paper and produced in a sustainable manner.

Contents

List of Figures   VII

Introduction   1

1 **The History of Paper in Europe**   3
   Italy   5
   France   7
   Germany   10
   Switzerland   12
   The Netherlands   13
   Belgium   16
   England   18
   Scandinavia   19
   Spain   20
   Portugal   20

2 **Different Aspects of Paper**   22
   Quality and Raw Material   22
   Coloured Paper   24
   Decorated Paper   25
   Formats   26
   Ream Wrappers   28
   Wove Paper   30
   Special Watermarks   30
   Watermarks Encountered   30

Index of Watermark Types   43

Index of Letters and Monograms   44

Index of Names and Words   47

Bibliography   49

Table of Watermarks   53

Catalogue   91

Figures

1 Map of Western Europe with the main centres of paper production between 1550 and 1850 4
2 Papermaking, etching by an anonymous German engraver, *c.*1800 5
3 A depiction of a small Hollanderbeater, engraving from "Versuch de Ursprung der Spielkarten …", by J. G. I Breitkopf, 1784 6
4 The complete production line of a papermill in the 19th century, wood engraving from "De voornaamste uitvindingen", Leiden, *c.*1860 7
5 Two ream wrappers from the Lizonne area for the Dutch market, *c.*1655 9
6 A view of the Gleismühle, Woodcut to "Weltchronik", by Hartmann Schedel, 1493 10
7 A ream wrapper for "Rögemer Schlangen Papier" made in the Würtemberg area, *c.*1700 11
8 A detail of a map of Basle with the location of the papermills. Engraving by Gabriel Bodenehr, 1720 13
9 A depiction of a papermill in the vicinity of Strasbourg, etching by Jacob van der Heyden, ca. 1630 13
10 A depiction of a Hollander beater, wood engraving from "De voornaamste uitvindingen", Leiden, *c.*1860 14
11 A ream wrapper for Pro Patria paper by the Van der Ley family, c. 1760 15
12 View of a papermill near Vaassen in Gelderland, drawing by Gerrit Hulseboom, *c.*1800 16
13 A ream wrapper with Fortuna, made probably in the Veluwe area for the trader P. Koumans Smeding, *c.*1820 17
14 A ream wrapper for paper with Arms of England watermark, traded by H. F. de Charro from The Hague, *c.*1850 18
15 Titlepage to J. C. Schäffer's book with experiments from 1770 23
16 Detail of a ream wrapper with the description Supra fine fine, *c.*1815 24
17 Detail of a French ream wrapper printed on very crude material, *c.*1700 25
18 Detail of a Brocade paper, printed in Nurnberg, 1720 26
19 Three details of different marbled papers, dating from 1630 to 1750 27
20 Detail of a so-called "Hernhutter"paper, decorated with starch paint, *c.*1750 28
21 Detail of a printed, decorated paper, *c.*1770 28
22 Depiction of a complete ream wrapper from the Honigh family, *c.*1820 29
23 Depiction of a classic ream wrapper for (L) paper with Arms of Amsterdam watermark, *c.*1700, and (R) a ream wrapper for paper in use during the Kingdom of Holland, 1806–1810 29
24 A ream wrapper for Foolscap paper, probably from the Veluwe area, *c.*1660 35
25 Depiction of two ream wrappers for paper with horn watermark (L) German paper, *c.*1820 and (R) paper made by Jean Villedary in France for the Dutch market, *c.*1680–1700 37
26 A ream wrapper for Phoenix paper, *c.*1655, collection Zeeland Archives, Middelburg 40
27 A ream wrapper for Seven Provinces paper, *c.*1653, Collection Zeeland Archives, Middelburg 41

Introduction

Academic interest in watermarks in laid and wove paper has grown notably over the course of the twentieth century. Our research for this book was driven by the search for information on the original place of production and dating of papers we encountered, and the related economic and historical aspects of the paper trade. Data on and images of watermarks have sporadically been published already from the mid-nineteenth century.[1] However, in almost all cases, these early researchers only noted where the paper in question was found (in a city archive, for example), the location the mark was used, and the date on the document.

In 1907, Charles-Moise Briquet was one of the first to include in his introductions a short overview of the possible origin of the paper for each type of watermark. This marked the start of an entirely new approach to research. For example, it became possible to study the trade routes between paper mills and users, leading to a better insight in the economic history of paper. As a result, in the twentieth century several important watermark studies appeared, often published by the Paper Publication Society. An important example of these was the study by Edward Heawood published in 1950. Heawood examined many atlases, which would prove useful to our research for this book as well.

In our previous watermark catalogues from 2007, 2008, 2016 and 2018, we have also tried to ascertain as much information as possible on the origins of the specimens we examined.[2] However, we found that for many regions, there has not yet been any research on local paper production. In countries like Germany, Italy and Belgium, there has only been fragmentary research on post-medieval paper, which means that further research can still be very rewarding. In some cases it turned out to be close to impossible to make a more precise identification of a watermark.

This catalogue is based on specimens that we gathered over the past ten years, in addition to our work on our various research projects. As in our previous books, we have used soft X-ray radiography to obtain images of the watermarks.[3]

In this study, we discuss specimens dated between 1470 and 1850. The research pool was very diverse: individual documents from archives, prints, maps, letters from Western Europe and books. Conditions for inclusion in this study were rarity of the mark, whether the mark was dated and clarity of the mark. In some cases, a watermark offered all three, but often a mark was only dated, or only clear. We did not strive for any form of completeness. Our initial preference was for archived specimens, since these usually meet all three of the abovementioned criteria. A good example of these are the Portuguese watermarks. For this section, we could draw from an archive we obtained from Lisbon. Given our interest in various paper sizes, we researched a lot of maps. Several private collectors from Europe and America made available to us items from their own collections, as did a number of cartographic antiquarians. Apart from these sources, over the past thirteen years there have been many scattered occasions where a specimen with an interesting watermark happened to cross our path, often prints that we encountered in our antiquarian work. The reason for inclusion of these specimens was usually their unique properties and clarity. In addition, out of our own interest we have built a sizeable private collection, reflecting all aspects of paper, which has also regularly been a source of interesting material. Many of the objects used to illustrate the text in this book are drawn from our own collection.

Due to the large gaps in the records on watermarks, especially post-medieval watermarks, we felt it made sense to publish our findings. In some occasions, the specimens could be identified using older reference works, but in other cases they remained a mystery. Since we feel that the questions they pose are still of interest, and in order to set a starting point for further research, we included these specimens and provided as much background information on them as possible.

As mentioned above, we researched a lot of maps. Apart from their international character, these gave us some insights into paper in large formats. Since we had previously mainly researched double folio writing paper, this seemed a meaningful addition. As it turned out, the watermarks in paper in large formats had their own

---

1 Th. & F. Laurentius, *Watermarks 1600–1650, found in the Zeeland Archives* (Houten: Hes & De Graaf, 2007), p. vi for an extensive overview of these publications.
2 See Th. & F. Laurentius, *Watermarks 1600–1650*, Th. & F. Laurentius, *Watermarks 1650–1700, found in the Zeeland Archives* (Houten: Hes & de Graaf, 2008), Th. & F. Laurentius, *Italian watermarks 1750–1860* (Leiden: Brill, 2016), Th. & F. Laurentius, *Watermarks in paper from the South-West of France, 1560–1860* (Leiden: Brill, 2018).
3 Jan van Aken, 'An improvement in Grenz radiography of paper to record watermarks, chain and laid lines', in *Studies in conservation*, 48, 2 (2003), pp. 103–110.

characteristics. We have attempted to gather watermarks from as many different atlases and maps from about 1480 to 1825 as possible. Of course, our collection is far from complete, but it did offer us a wealth of new information on editions, paper use and dating. For the work of a map publisher like Petrus Kaerius, it is now possible to order different editions chronologically based on their watermarks. The same goes for the work of for example Willem Blaeu, Ortelius and even incunabula like the Rome editions of Ptolemy's *Cosmography* published between 1478 and 1508.

As it turns out, paper is an extremely convenient aid in determining the place and date of publication of maps. Parisian publishers appear to have had a habit of using paper from the Auvergne, specifically from the paper mills around Rioms. And oddly enough, the absence of a mark can also be useful information. We have determined that maps published in the Netherlands between approximately 1670 and 1700 only very rarely have a watermark. It was also interesting to find that some publishers were involved in paper production themselves. Kaerius turned out to have been a member of the *Compagnie van Duytsche Papieren*. We encountered a publication by publisher Fricx from Brussels using paper with his own name as a watermark, and we found the same for the publishers Covens & Mortier.

In addition, a lot of scattered specimens were recorded in prints, documents, books and blank paper. We had access to a private collection of archived material and blank paper from Portugal. As we were working on all this material, we came to the remarkable conclusion that almost no 'old' paper was used. An argument we heard regularly was that of course, some paper remained on the shelf, to be used at some later date. However, over the course of our entire research, we only found one example of this.[4] Another category of interesting research material are the early examples of wove paper. However, because of its smoother, more uniform quality, wove paper also results in less clear watermark pictures. Despite this handicap, we did our best to gather representative examples.

We want to hereby express our thanks to Jaap van den Bovenkamp, Leen Helmink, Maarten van der Steeg, Robert Peerlings, Franz Gittenberger and many others for the ample opportunities they offered us to study the material in their collections. We hope that this collection of watermarks from five centuries of paper use in Western Europe will prove to be of use, and will also serve to encourage others to study this material in archives, libraries and print rooms, because a lot of work still remains to be done in this area.

---

4   See no. 29 in this catalogue; this was a print engraved around 1660, printed on older, heavier and larger-sized paper, probably due to the engraving's irregular dimensions.

CHAPTER 1

The History of Paper in Europe

The history of paper in Europe starts between 1000 and 1200, when paper was introduced in Spain and Italy through these countries' trade relations with North Africa.[1] The art of paper making had originally been invented in China.[2] The appearance of paper must have been an impressive innovation in the Western world. Until that point, materials to write on, like parchment, had been in limited supply.

Spain was ruled by the Moors at the time, who decided to keep the secret of paper making strictly to themselves. This meant the technique could not spread to other places outside of Spain. Italy was a different story. Entrepreneurial merchants from Lombardy in Northern Italy eagerly embraced the trade in paper. They took their paper products to Switzerland, Austria, France and Germany, where they not only sold the end product, but also introduced the techniques for producing it. Over a century later, local production in these countries grew to a point that the Italian influence started to wane.

From the fourteenth century onwards, paper production could be found all over Europe. An essential factor for the spread and popularisation of paper was the invention of the printing press in the fifteenth century. It could be argued that without paper, the printing press would never have taken off as it did, and conversely, that paper would not have grown to be such a fundamental presence without the printing press. Once printing became more and more popular in the second half of the fifteenth century, paper became even more indispensable. An almost insatiable demand for paper came into existence, a demand that can be seen to this day. The paper trade became a market involving huge economic interests. Bulk traders, such as the Dutch in France in the seventeenth century, were involved in all aspects of the industry, from supply of raw material (rags), to infrastructure (mills, mill races), to transport and financing.[3] The importance of the paper trade was so great, that the Amsterdam stock exchange had a designated section for it. The retail trade was conducted by notaries and booksellers, but also by pharmacists, since they sold related products such as sealing wax and ink.[4] (Fig. 1)

Over the course of the time period covered in this book, a number of crucial were introduced in the paper industry. A very early innovation was the transition from bamboo moulds to copper wire. In Spain in the twelfth and early thirteenth century, a change occurred in paper production technique. Until that time, the usual Arabian method for making a sheet of paper involved a floating mould. This mould was constructed from thin strips of bamboo, held in place by irregularly knotted threads made of plant fibers placed perpendicular to the bamboo. The bamboo mould was put into a large water vat, in which it floated. Paper pulp was poured into the mould and spread out evenly. The paper was then dried. Using this method, fairly large sheets of paper could be produced. Around 1250, a new type of mould was developed, probably because of a shortage of bamboo. This new mould was made of copper wire, surrounded by a wooden deckle. Since this new construction did not float, its size was reduced so the mould could be dipped into the vat of water and pulp by hand. This was the birth of laid paper. (Fig. 2)

This invention also resulted in the so-called watermark. With thin copper wires, an image could be knotted into the stiff copper mesh. After drying, the image would appear as lighter lines in the paper. This had never been possible with bamboo sieves. Apart from the watermark, the structure of the copper mesh was also visible in the sheet of paper. This was the origin of the well-known pattern of laid lines and chain lines seen in laid paper.

In the late seventeenth century, Dutch makers in the Zaan region invented a machine called the Hollander beater, which provided them with a faster method of beating rags, also resulting in better-quality paper pulp. This will be discussed further in the section on the Netherlands. (Fig. 3)

Another essential invention made around 1700 was the use of slightly thicker copper wires placed slightly wider apart in the mould. This allowed the water to drain faster, speeding up the production process.

Of major importance was James Whatman's invention of wove paper around 1756. In a sense, this smoother paper

---

1 H. M. Fiskaa, 'Das eindringen des Papiers in die Nordeuropäischen Länder im Mittelalter', *Papiergeschichte*, 3–4 (1967), pp. 28–29.
2 Henk Voorn, *De papiermolens in de provincie Noord Holland* (Haarlem: Stichting voor het onderzoek van de geschiedenis van de Nederlandse papierindustrie, 1960), pp. 3–4.
3 Gabriel Delâge, *L'Angoumois au temps des marchands Flamands* (Paris: Libraire Bruno Sepulchre, 1990), pp. 117–120. This book provides an overview of the Dutch influence in the Angoumois.
4 P. F. Tschudin, *Schweizer Papiergeschichte* (Basel: Basler Papier-Mühle, 1991), p. 17.

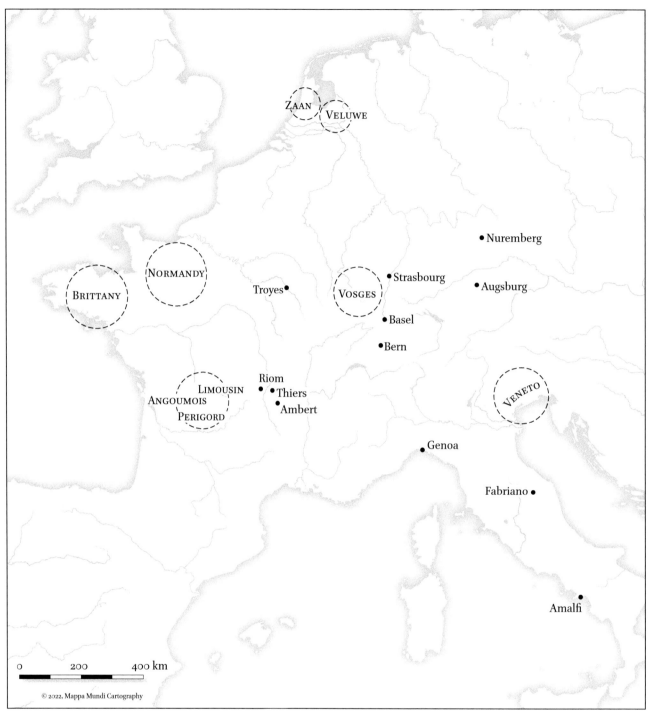

FIGURE 1   Map of Western Europe with the main centres of paper production between 1550 and 1850

FIGURE 2 Papermaking, etching by an anonymous German engraver, c.1800

hailed the beginning of the Industrial Revolution. The invention of the paper machine by Nicolas-Louis Robert in 1798 can be regarded as the start of modernisation and the end of paper production by hand.[5] However, it would take until at least 1840 for this production technique to become commonplace. In this book, we have taken the mid-nineteenth century as our endpoint, because of the major changes in the character of paper. Mechanisation and new types of raw material made this paper less suitable and less interesting from the point of view of our research. In practice, we also found that the industrially produced paper from the second half of the nineteenth century is extremely difficult to identify, because of its lack of watermarks and information on paper makers. (Fig. 4)

Italy

By the thirteenth century, paper making had become a well-known process in Italy. The oldest mills, in Fabriano, date from 1276. The technique quickly spread through all of Italy. Merchants from Lombardy in the North especially were essential to the sale and distribution of paper through Western Europe in the fourteenth century. The conditions necessary for the production process were amply present and as a result, an almost fully self-sufficient system emerged. When in the fifteenth century other European countries started building their own mills, export of paper decreased. However, the Italian centres of production in Lombardy, the Veneto region, Fabriano, Amalfi and the area between Genoa and Bologna remained in business, especially after the introduction of the printing press.[6] Paper was also still being exported to Turkey, Spain and Portugal. During the seventeenth century, Italian paper arrived in the Netherlands through the Mediterranean trade. During our research, we regularly found Italian papers in the Zeeland archives.[7]

---

5 Dard Hunter, *Papermaking, the history and technique of an ancient craft* (New York: Dover Press, 1978), pp. 341–349.

6 The paper consumption in Florence was already vast by the 15th century. Print shops bought large batches of paper, for example from Brescia.

7 Laurentius, *Watermarks 1600–1650*, nos. 78–86, 88–91, 236–242, 259–262, 404–412 are some good examples. Most of the Italian paper in the Northern Netherlands appears to originate from Genoa, Liguria and Veneto. This fits very well with the discovery of Italian ceramics in the Netherlands dating from the same period. See Nina Linde Jaspers, *Schoon en werkelijk aangenaam, Italiaanse importkeramiek uit de 16e en 17e eeuw in Nederlandse bodem*, MA thesis (Amsterdam: Universiteit van Amsterdam, 2007), pp. 27–36.

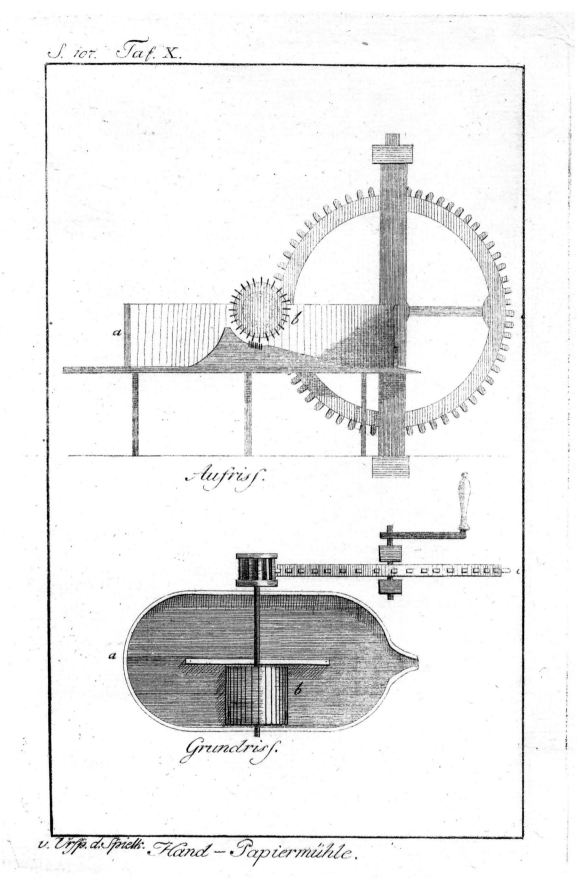

FIGURE 3   A depiction of a small Hollanderbeater, engraving from "Versuch de Ursprung der Spielkarten ...", by J. G. I Breitkopf, 1784

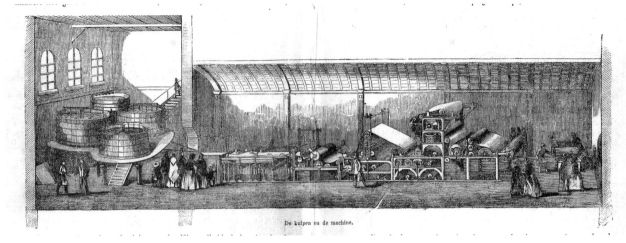

FIGURE 4   The complete production line of a papermill in the 19th century, wood engraving from "De voornaamste uitvindingen", Leiden, c.1860

Much as in for example Germany, the lack of political unity was a cause of great diversity in local mills and their individual watermarks. Only very little has been published on the sixteenth, seventeenth and eighteenth centuries with regard to this subject.[8] This often makes identification of these watermarks very difficult. However, their typical iconography makes these Italian watermarks easily recognisable. In order to shed more light on this subject, we have attempted to gather as much dated material as possible.

France

France appears frequently in our research, as it produced and exported a very large amount of paper. The presence of solid historical research in France on this industry is a happy bonus. In our work on our earlier books on watermarks, we found that identifying the French marks and monograms was an easy task. When Italian paper merchants started travelling to France from the thirteenth century, they journeyed westward, through the Languedoc, and reached the foothills of the Pyrenees.[9] However, their main route was along the Rhône to the North, bringing them as far as Geneva.

The oldest mills in France were most likely built and run by Italians. Over the course of the fifteenth century, paper making activities became fully French-owned. Large paper centres developed in several places. In the Auvergne, the number of mills grew to the point that the region became the main supplier of paper to Paris.

The towns of Riom, Thiers and Ambert developed into well-known centres for the paper industry.[10] The mills were often owned by large families who ran them for many generations. Well-known names included Cusson, Colombier, Richard de Bas, Clouvet, Artand, Bégou and Du Puy. In our research, we very regularly found watermarks from this area in books from Paris. This catalogue offers a range of examples from the seventeenth and eighteenth centuries, including a group of marks for paper in large formats.

In the Champagne, the city of Troyes became the centre of a sizeable local paper production industry. In the sixteenth century, it grew to be the main supplier of paper to the Northern Netherlands. Some of the best-known paper makers in this region were the Le Bé, Denise, Gouault, Nivelle, Pinette, De Garoys and Journeé families.[11] Troyes is also a good example of a center that stagnated because of historical developments. Its flourishing industry closed down after the fall of Antwerp in 1585. The trading routes towards the Northern Netherlands were blocked, and as a direct result Troyes paper production came to an almost complete halt. Many of the above-mentioned paper makers moved east and settled in the Vosges region, Franche-Comté and the Alsace. Troyes would never recover from this economic setback.

In the Alsace and the Vosges region, a paper industry emerged quite early, with one Strasbourg mill already

---

8   Laurentius, *Italian Watermarks*, p. 6.
9   Laurentius, *Watermarks in paper*, p. 3.
10 Elie Cottier, *L'Histoire d'un vieux métier* (Clermont Ferrand: Edition Mont-Louis, 1938), pp. 37–38.
11 Louis Le Clert, *Le papier, recherches et notes pour servir à l'histoire du papier, principalement à Troyes et aux environs depuis le quatorzième siècle* (Paris: A l'Enseigne de Pegase, 1926), volume II offers an extensive overview of the participants in the Troyes paper industry.

in operation in 1415. In the sixteenth century, the developments around Troyes helped this region grow into an important area with strong connections to paper makers in and around Basel, with Strasbourg as main staple town and junction. One of the best-known paper makers in this city around 1600 was Wendelin Riehel. He frequently included his monogram, WR, in his watermarks. It became a mark of quality, and as a result, other producers started to adopt it as well. They continued using the mark well after Riehel's death.[12] A sizeable amount of this paper was sold to Antwerp. In addition to the paper industry, a printing industry also developed in the Vosges region. Especially Epinal grew to be a large centre for all kinds of cheap printed material, including catchpenny prints and decorated paper.[13]

Normandy and Brittany also had a fairly large paper industry in the seventeenth century. A lot of the paper produced in this area was exported to England.[14] Paper was also sold to Paris and to the Netherlands.[15] Most of the mills were located near the towns of Vire, Tinchebray and Sourdeval.[16] Well-known paper makers in this area were the Danguy, Rondel, Lemoine, Vaullegeard, Lentaigne, Cosnard, Homo and Louvrier families.[17] In the mid-nineteenth century, many of the paper mills, fallen out of use after the mechanisation of the paper making process, were converted to die-cutting mills, producing spoons and forks.

France was also home to many small paper mills with a strongly local character. The Bordeaux-Toulouse-Pyrenees area is a good example of this.[18] The modes of paper production in this area remained unchanged for a long time, and as a result, the local products sometimes are very archaic in character. More local mills could be found in the Provence and further north along the Rhône. A well-known paper-making family were the Montgolfiers from Vidalon in the Ardèche. In 1782, two Montgolfier brothers even invented a paper hot air balloon. Their paper mill would later develop to become the large paper factory Canson & Montgolfier.

The largest active paper-making area was in the triangle of Limousin, Angoumois and Périgord in central-western France. From the beginning of the seventeenth century, Dutch merchants tried to procure paper from this area.[19] During the Twelve Years' Truce (1609–1621), several Dutch factors used the open borders to establish contacts in France. These activities had a major impact on paper use in the Northern Netherlands. After the Peace of Münster in 1648, the foundations laid in 1618–1620 would expand to large-scale export of the production of this area to the Netherlands. An early and notable example is the paper in large formats ordered from Saint-Junien in the Limousin through the Dutch entrepreneur Pieter Haack, which was then used in Amsterdam to print the famous Blaeu atlas.[20] This meant that a small town near Limoges was home to a mill that had the specific knowledge necessary to produce these large papers. This way, a steady export stream of paper to the Netherlands was started.[21] The paper was transported down the Charente river on barges to the Tonnay-Charente harbour, from where it was shipped to the Netherlands. Especially after the 1648 Peace of Münster, production and trade in this area expanded enormously, helped by sea transport being once again safe.

It is no surprise that by the second half of the seventeenth century, a large number of Dutch merchants or factors was operating in this part of France. They bought the product and financed the rag buying, and sometimes even the entire mill. (Fig. 5) Furthermore, they were involved in infrastructure, such as the construction of mill races and levees, the organisation of shipments and the trade in wine from the Cognac region.[22] Some of the well-known Dutchmen who settled in this area were Dirk and Abraham Janssen, the three Van Gangelt

---

12 The WR monogram still regularly appears in the 18th and early 19th century, combined with a crest showing a French lily. By this time, the original name has long since lost its significance.

13 Elly Cockx-Indestege, T. C. Greve, C. H. Porck, *Sierpapier & Marmering* (The Hague / Brussel: Koninklijke Bibliotheek, 1994), p. 40 and Hunter, *Papermaking*, p. 247, fig. 154.

14 Alexander Globe, *Peter Stent, London printseller 1642–1665* (Vancouver: University of British Columbia, 1985), app. C with examples of several watermarks, all originating from Normandy. Marie-Jeanne Villeroy, 'Papiers et papetiers dans le Bocage sous l'ancien Régime, seconde partie', *Le Pays Bas-Normand, revue trimestrielle*, 1 (2004), pp. 146–148.

15 See Laurentius, *Watermarks 1600–1650*, nos. 193, 194, 282, 385, 386, 387, 390 and 724–729, some common examples of Norman/Breton paper appearing on the Dutch market. Many of the watermarks common in the Angoumois/Limousin/Perigord area were copied by Norman papermakers, often surprisingly sloppily. See also Laurentius, *Watermarks 1600–1650*, p. VIII.

16 Jacques Duval, *Moulins à papier de Bretagne d XVIe au XIXe siècle* (Paris: L'Harmattan, 2005), pp. 45–137.

17 Villeroy, *Papiers*, vol. II, pp. 47–54.

18 Laurentius, *Watermarks in paper*, pp. 3–4.

19 Laurentius, *Watermarks 1600–1650*, p. xi and Laurentius, *Watermarks 1650–1700*, pp. vi–viii.

20 E. Heawood, *Watermarks* (Hilversum: Paper Publications Society, 1950), nos. 1362–1363.

21 Laurentius, F. & Roos, M. J., *Met veele schoone Figueren verciert* (Middelburg/Ijmuiden: Laurentius & Roos, 2012), pp. 27–30 for a number of watermarks from this region used in the late 1630s.

22 Delage, *Moulins à papier*, pp. 188–197.

FIGURE 5   Two ream wrappers from the Lizonne area for the Dutch market, c.1655

brothers, Francois and Pierre van Tongeren, Jacques Bos, Laurent van Ravestein, Francois le Bleu, Abraham van Wesel, Egbert Graafland, Paul van de Velde, Pierre Bosch, Anthonie Allard, Jean Boener, Pieter Haeck, Gerard Verduin, Ysbrand and Levinus Vincent, Jacob van Speeck and Gillis van Hoven.[23]

Important paper makers who often worked for the Dutchmen included Pierre Debenat, Francois Chatonnet, Claude de George, Pierre Clauzure and Jean Villedary.[24] The echo of especially that last name could still be discerned long after. His monogram IV stood for high-quality paper, and as a result, it was used as a mark of quality well into the eighteenth century. During the second half of the seventeenth century, various political and religious difficulties affected the export of paper to the Netherlands. In 1672, the Northern Netherlands banned the import of French paper. This was circumvented by merchants importing French paper through Hamburg, and then transporting it overland to the Netherlands with falsified ream wrappers.[25] From about 1675, this region would encounter more and more competition from the growing paper production industry in the Dutch Zaan region. The trade ended in 1685 with the Revocation of the Edict of Nantes, which forced the protestant Dutch paper merchants to leave France. The export of paper declined rapidly, and over the course of the eighteenth century even reversed, to France importing Dutch paper. The Angoumois would eventually develop a cigarette paper industry.

France would become one of the first countries on the continent to get involved in the production of wove paper. Examples of this production appear from about 1780. A good example of an early product is no. 497, a paper from the Papeterie du Marais, belonging to De la Garde Ainé et Compagnie, who as early as 1797 was even making wove paper in large formats.[26]

---

23 Laurentius, *Watermarks 1600–1650*, p. VII.
24 Ibid., p. VIII.
25 For such a ream wrapper, see Th. & F. Laurentius, *Vijftig historische riemkappen* (Middelburg: Laurentius, 2015), pp. 7–8.
26 Heawood, *Watermarks*, no. 3384 and Raymond Gaudriault, *Filigranes et autres caracteristiques des papiers en France au XVII et XVIII siècles* (Paris: CNRS Editions, 1995), p. 19.

FIGURE 6   A view of the Gleismühle, Woodcut to "Weltchronik", by Hartmann Schedel, 1493

Germany

Unlike France and the Netherlands, Germany did not have a consolidated economic or political structure until the nineteenth century. The country was divided into principalities, duchies and counties connected by complicated family ties, each with their own power and their own laws. This structure was an obstacle to the growth of a more nationally organised paper industry, and as a result, the production of the many paper mills had a strongly local character.

The oldest-known German mill stood near Nuremberg (Fig. 6) and was built by Ulman Stromer (1329–1407). Stromer was an enterprising man. He gathered his knowledge during his journeys to Barcelona, Genoa, Milan and Cracow. In addition, he ran a trade company. Travelling Lombardian paper makers taught him the secrets of papermaking. Stromer signed a work contract with some of them and around 1389, and converted the *Gleismühle* grain mill, east of the Nuremberg city wall, into a paper mill. The mill's name was later changed to *Hadermülle*. Subsequently, paper mills appeared all over the country, in towns like Chemnitz (1398), Ravensburg (1402), Augsburg (1407) and Lübeck (1420) in the north. The first mills in Kempten, which would later become a centre of paper making, were built in 1468. A century after the start of the first mill, about 200 small mills were operating in Germany. As in France, a number of areas proved to be especially suitable for paper-making because of the presence of fast-running streams and clean water. Naturally, paper mills concentrated there. The number of mills outside Nuremberg soon grew to twenty. Just to the south, Augsburg developed along a similar path, and eventually, the area expanded with a large number of mills in Kempten and even across the Austrian border.[27]

As in France, the introduction of the printing press was an important accelerator of the growth in German paper production. In the second half of the fifteenth century, several important printing centres developed. Cities like Nuremberg and Augsburg feature here as well. Both cities were home to a flourishing combination of paper production and printing activities until well into the nineteenth century.[28] Augsburg produced a never-ending supply of printed matter from about 1670. In the eighteenth century,

---

27   Friedrich von Hössle, *Geschichte der alten Papiermühlen im ehemaligen Stift Kempten und in der Reichstadt Kempten* (Augsburg: Jos. Rösselschen Buchhandlung, 1900), pp. 13–19.

28   Edmund Marabini, 'Die Papiermühlen im ehemaliger Burggrafenthum Nürnberg', *Bayerische Papiergeschichte*, 2 (1896), pp. 5–12 and Hössle, *Geschichte*, p. 9.

FIGURE 7   A ream wrapper for "Rögemer Schlangen Papier" made in the Würtemberg area, *c*.1700

production must have run into hundreds of thousands of copies.²⁹ To the west, in Baden-Württemberg, a similar growth in the number of mills could be seen. (Fig. 7) This development was linked to the paper production in the Swiss city of Basel. The towns of Maulburg, Lörrach and, to the east, Ravensburg also took part in this industry. This growth was strongly stimulated by exports to the Northern Netherlands in the first half of the seventeenth century.³⁰ A large portion of the paper produced was also bought by Dutch traders at the annual Frankfurt Fair.³¹ The German paper industry was strongly affected by the Thirty Years' War (1618–1648). Many mills were burned and ruined in this destructive conflict. In the Aachen-Maastricht-Liège triangle, paper mills were established as well, starting in the late sixteenth century.³² These mills were located near tributaries of the Meuse, with Düren as the central clearing house for the area.³³ Although this paper production centre was not as big as the centres mentioned earlier, it, too, was a supplier to the Northern Netherlands. Watermarks with the Aachen city crest or a one-headed eagle with the letters ACH appear regularly.

An interesting technological development is the introduction of Dutch windmill technology in Northern Germany in the early eighteenth century.³⁴ Wove paper was also produced in Germany from about 1782. Since only a small proportion of the post-medieval German paper has been examined, identification can be very difficult.³⁵ We have by now succeeded in compiling a representative group of examples of Augsburg paper.

Switzerland

The oldest paper in Switzerland was imported by Italian merchants. French paper appeared in the late fourteenth century and German from the fifteenth. The first paper mill in Switzerland was most likely located in Marly, near Freiburg. In the archives of this town, the 1394 *Bürgerbuch* includes several paper makers. From about 1400, mills were established in Western Switzerland on the Basel-Bern-Geneva axis, in Belfaux, La Glâne and Pays-de-Gex. Over the course of the fifteenth century, mills appeared in Basel itself as well. The best-known and most important entrepreneur involved in the production of paper was Heinrich Halbysen the Elder († 1451). Despite the sometimes tumultuous political developments, the Basel industry grew to become the largest concentration of mills in Switzerland. Most of the production was located in the St. Alban quarter, within the city walls. The print shops established after 1450 of course further stimulated these developments. As in other countries, most mills were owned by families, who were often active in the industry for many generations. Apart from the Albysens, we can find the Gallizianis, the Dürrs, the Dürings and the Heusslers.³⁶ Basel grew to become an important centre, as did Bern. (Fig. 8)

After a period of decline, around 1590 the Northern Netherlands became an important booster of the Swiss industry. Following the loss of Troyes as a supplier, Dutch merchants looked for new sources and found the Swiss and Swiss-German paper production industry, with Strasbourg as its hub. (Fig. 9) This area was known as the *Bovenlanden* or Upper regions. The ample paper supply, paired with the Rhine river offering a safe alternative to the Spanish blockade of the Southern Netherlands, made it the ideal supplier. From then on, large amounts of so-called *Bovenlands* paper were exported to the Netherlands. The main Dutch paper trader involved in this trade was Cornelis van Lokhorst, who in 1595 established the *Compagnie van Duytsche papieren*, with agents in Strasbourg and Basel.³⁷ During the entire first half of the seventeenth century, the export of paper from Switzerland to the Netherlands flourished. The trade only ended with the Peace of Münster in 1648, which reopened all European borders. Dutch traders then once again turned their attention to centres in France. It is likely that this was partly because in the *Bovenlanden*, the

---

29 Schmidt, Friedrich, 'Papierherstellung in Augsburg bis zum Frühindustrialisierung' in Gier, Helmut & Janota, Johannes (eds.), *Augsburger Buchdruck und Verlagswesen* (Wiesbaden: Harassowitz, 1997), pp. 587–590.

30 Laurentius, *Watermarks 1600–1650*, p. XI.

31 I. H. van Eeghen, *De Amsterdamse boekhandel 1680–1725* (Amsterdam: Scheltema & Holkema NV, 1978), vol. IV.

32 Jaak Nijssen, 'Die Papiermühlen im Maastricht-Aachener Raum (ca. 1570–1640), insbesondere in Schoppen ('s-Gravenvoeren)', *IPH Yearbook*, 8 (1990), p. 96.

33 In the 16th and 17th century, this area was also a centre for ceramics. Ceramics and paper appear together in other places as well, likely because of geographical factors. An interesting example are the ceramics from the Limousin and Limoges, which were transported to the harbour town of La Rochelle along the same routes as the paper, to be shipped to the Netherlands.

34 Klaus B. Bartels, *Papierherstellung in Deutschland*, (Berlin-Brandenburg: Be.Bra wissenschaft Verlag, 2011), pp. 91–92.

35 Laurentius, *Watermarks 1600–1650*, nos. 225, 226, 268, 271, 278 and 285; and Laurentius, *Watermarks 1650–1700*, no. 186.

36 W. Fr. Tschudin, *The ancient papermills of Basle and their marks* (Hilversum: Paper Publications Society, 1958), pp. 39–41.

37 Laurentius, *Watermarks 1600–1650*, p. X. Also see Voorn, 'Uit de oudste geschiedenis', p. 303.

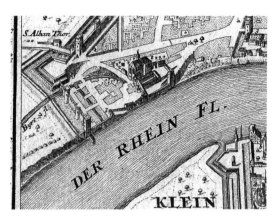

FIGURE 8   A detail of a map of Basle with the location of the papermills. Engraving by Gabriel Bodenehr, 1720

FIGURE 9   A depiction of a papermill in the vicinity of Strasbourg, etching by Jacob van der Heyden, ca. 1630

Dutch could only buy the end product and had no influence over the full process. Swiss production was greatly reduced, and the industry went on to produce mainly paper for local use. Basel and Bern did remain true centres of paper making until well into the eighteenth century, in addition to a large number of small local mills.[38] Interestingly, there was a small revitalisation of exports to the Netherlands when around 1690–1700, Dutch factors once again started buying Swiss paper. This was a result of the War of the Spanish Succession, which closed the borders with France, blocking imports.[39]

The Netherlands

Until the seventeenth century, the Netherlands was dependent on foreign suppliers for most of its paper needs. Lacking strong energy sources to power water mills, it had to import almost everything. The earliest paper mill one could point to as Dutch was built in 1428 near Gennep, but since this town was German territory until the nineteenth century, it cannot be considered Dutch in that sense.[40] In the fifteenth and sixteenth centuries, a lot of paper was

---

38   P. F. Tschudin, *Schweizer Papiergeschichte*, pp. 57–66.
39   In our research, we also noted an odd peak in the use of Swiss and Swiss-German paper in the Netherlands around 1700.

40   Henk Voorn, *De papiermolens in de provincie Zuid-Holland* (Wormerveer: Stichting voor het onderzoek van de geschiedenis van de Nederlandse papierindustrie, 1973), p. 52. However, the mill was built by Dutchman Willem Boye from Nijmegen.

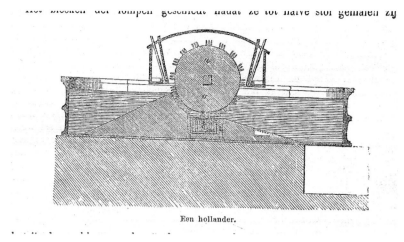

FIGURE 10 A depiction of a Hollander beater, wood engraving from "De voornaamste uitvindingen", Leiden, c.1860

imported from the Champagne, with the city of Troyes as staple town: for this reason, in contemporary sources the product was called *Troois* paper. Italian and Norman paper was also used, as were other imports.

Major changes occurred after the fall of Antwerp in 1585. The separation of the Northern and Southern Netherlands brought the trade to a sudden halt, resulting in an immediate and urgent paper shortage in the Northern part. Various initiatives to produce paper domestically, such as a tide mill near Zwijndrecht, did not last.[41] The solution was found in Switzerland. More viable projects appeared on the borders of the Veluwe area in the central Netherlands. Artificial water courses were constructed, to obtain a gradient sufficient to power the blades of a mill. An important entrepreneur in this field was Martin Orges.[42] By the mid-seventeenth century, a considerable number of mills had been established in this area and production met a large proportion of the national paper needs. However, the quality of the Veluwe paper was uneven; the paper was often brownish, meaning that much of it could only be used in printing offices. Important names in this industry included Andries Bergheyck, Schut and Wolvers. Veluwe production of laid paper continued well into the nineteenth century. Important paper makers from this era were Pannekoek, Hessels, Hummen and Oorspronk.

From about 1660, windmill technique had advanced to the point that it could also be used in the paper industry. An important windmill park developed west of Amsterdam. The large, flat area, with ample clean water, lots of wind, and the Zaan river as a nearby waterway, proved to be very suitable to the paper industry.[43] In addition to the technical improvements to windmills, another invention improved the preparation of raw material for the paper production. Up until that point, paper makers all over Europe used stamp mills to pound rags into pulp. Around 1673, the Hollander Beater or Hollander was invented. (Fig. 10) This machine cut up the rags with rotating knives and could produce high-quality paper pulp faster than before. The inventor of this machine was most likely Pieter van der Ley. Within a comparatively short time, the Hollander was put to use in all Zaan windmills, giving the Zaan region a major advantage over other European paper makers.[44] Several limiting factors, including war, blocked the import of foreign paper, just around the time the abovementioned technological innovations appeared. Combined, this greatly stimulated the industry in the Zaan region.

In the eighteenth century, the Zaan region was extraordinarily important as a centre of paper production. Here as well, some families were active over a long period of time. Well-known names include Honigh, Blaauw, Kool, Rogge, Gerrevink, Van Huysduynen and Van der Ley. (Fig. 11)

Home to over a hundred mills in the eighteenth and nineteenth centuries, the Zaan region would continue to be of great importance to the Dutch and the international market. With its combination of quality, innovation and mass production, it would eventually decisively outcompete French paper imports. Of course, this means many

---

41 Ibid., pp. 52–53. This mill was built in 1586 by Nicolaes van Aelst, a refugee from the Southern Netherlands. Another initiative started in 1586 was a mill near Alkmaar, established by Jean du Bois.

42 Henk Voorn, *De papiermolens in de provincie Gelderland* (Haarlem: Stichting voor het onderzoek van de geschiedenis van de Nederlandse papierindustrie, 1985), p. 133.

43 Voorn, *De papiermolens in de provincie Noord-Holland*, p. 4.

44 It would take at least another 150 years before the Hollander would be used throughout Europe. For more information on this, see Laurentius, *Watermarks in paper*, p. 4.

FIGURE 11 A ream wrapper for Pro Patria paper by the Van der Ley family, c.1760

FIGURE 12 View of a papermill near Vaassen in Gelderland, drawing by Gerrit Hulseboom, c.1800

examples of Zaan paper can be found in this catalogue. However, as a result of this strong position, Zaan producers failed to adopt the technical innovations developed in Europe after 1750, such as the invention of wove paper. This new technique was introduced only in 1807.[45] In the nineteenth century, this was the cause of many Zaan mills disappearing, while some of the smaller and less sophisticated mills in the Veluwe still survived. (Fig. 12) Apart from these large players, in towns like Groningen, Waddinxveen and Boxtel, smaller mills producing handmade paper continued to operate until the Industrial Revolution. (Fig. 13)

Belgium

Paper production in Belgium started in the late fourteenth century. The oldest known mill is in Houplines, dating from 1389.[46] Here as well, the first paper mills were introduced by Italian merchants. Paper making never became a major industry. A large proportion of the paper from the late fifteenth and sixteenth centuries was imported from the Champagne. After political complications in the late sixteenth century, import shifted to Eastern France. In the books published in Antwerp between about 1590 and 1620, we often found Lotharingian paper.

Over the course of the seventeenth century, the number of local Belgian paper mills steadily increased.[47] Mills were mainly located in the area around Brussels, in towns like Dendermonde and Lier. Some of the most important paper producers in this area in the seventeenth and eighteenth centuries included Bauwens, Van Langenhoven, Foppens and Fricx.[48] Fricx is especially interesting: he

---

45   Voorn, *De papiermolens*, pp. 59–60.

46   Inge van Wegens, 'The Duchy of Brabant claims its place in the European paper history', *IPH Congressbook*, 11 (1996), p. 174.

47   Jos de Gelas, 'The making of paper in Brabant', *IPH Yearbook*, (1990), pp. 46–49, pp. 80–82 en Wegens, *The Duchy of Brabant*, p. 174.

48   De Gelas, *The making*, p. 4.

FIGURE 13   A ream wrapper with Fortuna, made probably in the Veluwe area for the trader P. Koumans Smeding, c.1820

ran both a print shop, producing prints and books, and his own paper factory. In the eastern part of the country, paper mills appeared along the Voer river.[49] With their production, they linked themselves to the mills of the Maastricht-Aachen-Liège triangle mentioned earlier.

Despite these efforts, the local paper industry was never large enough to meet demand. The Del Marmol archives show that in the seventeenth century, a large proportion of paper was imported from Italy, France and Spain.[50] In the eighteenth century, a lot of paper came from the Netherlands as well.

It proved quite difficult to find local Belgian paper to examine. However, we did succeed in finding several identifiable Belgian watermarks. A good example is no. 162, a paper from the Dendermonde paper mill.

England

For a long time, England lagged behind the rest of Europe in developing its own paper industry.[51] The oldest known mill, built by John Tate in Stevenage, was established around 1494. Its paper was coarse and of uneven thickness, but still suitable for printing books. The next mention of a paper mill is from 1588, almost a century later. It was built in Dartford, near Kent, by entrepreneur John Spielman.[52] But the bulk of paper was imported from Italy, Normandy and Brittany. Later in the seventeenth century, Dutch traders like Abraham Janssen and Gillis van Hoven started to import large amounts of paper from the Angoumois. This paper had English watermarks, such as the London city crest, the English coat of arms and the Bristol city crest.

FIGURE 14 A ream wrapper for paper with Arms of England watermark, traded by H. F. de Charro from The Hague, c.1850

49 Nijssen, *Die Papiermühlen*, p. 96.
50 F. del Marmol, *Dictionnaire des filigranes* (Namur/Paris: Marchal et Billard, Jacques Godenne, 1900), nos. 16, 17, 89–96, 99, 102–112.
51 Richard L. Hills, *Papermaking in Britain 1488–1988* (London: Athlone Press, 1988), p. 5.
52 Ibid., pp. 50–51.

But we found only one example of local production from this era: a horseman with a horn. We encountered this watermark in the Zeeland archives in a letter from Oliver Cromwell. The mark is so distinctive that there is a real possibility this was a local English product.[53]

It was only after the Revocation of the Edict of Nantes in 1685 that a large group of Protestant paper makers from France made the crossing to England. A good example from this group is the Frenchman Henri de Portal.[54] He started out in 1711 with a few mills in Hampshire, in the south of England, and eventually even supplied paper to the Bank of England. The English paper industry developed swiftly in the eighteenth century. An important English paper maker and innovator was James Whatman.[55] This paper maker from Maidstone in Kent was responsible for the invention of wove paper around 1756, a technical innovation that came about after a request from printer and typesetter John Baskerville (1706–1775).[56] Because of its greatly superior quality, wove paper conquered almost all of Western Europe in the second half of the 18th century, giving England a prominent position in the international paper industry. With its early industrialisation, in the nineteenth century England would end up being the leading country in paper production. (Fig. 14)

Scandinavia

From archival sources, we know that small amounts of paper were imported into Scandinavia as early as the mid-fourteenth century.[57] Local production started relatively late. Among the first paper makers were Sten Bille and his famous nephew Tycho Brahe.[58] They established their mills in the second half of the sixteenth century, in Scania, the southernmost province of Sweden, then under Danish rule. Bille's project was supported by the Danish king Frederick II, who also requested him to build a paper mill between Copenhagen and Helsingør. These early Danish mills ran into many problems: they faced a lack of trained personnel and had to build up an extensive system for rag collection. In the end, most of the paper workers were recruited from Germany. The first mill in Aarhus in Jutland was only built in 1637. Later in the seventeenth century, more mills were built near Copenhagen, the best-known of which was the *Strandmøllen*. Near the end of the seventeenth century, this mill came into the hands of the German Johann Drewsen. He was very successful and his descendants continued to be well-known paper makers until well into the nineteenth century.[59]

In Norway, Ole Bentsen became the best-known paper maker.[60] From about 1680, he ran the Bentse Brug mill near Christiania. He had prepared himself by spending considerable time working in the Dutch Zaan region, learning the trade. Bentsen hired Dutch paper makers to get his Norwegian mill off the ground. He, too, encountered problems starting up: the rags supply turned out to be an issue as was financing the project. In 1716, this resulted in a lawsuit involving the investors.[61] The mill continued to operate, but ownership changed hands several times in the subsequent years. Over the course of the eighteenth century, business improved. The company was eventually disbanded in 1898.

The Dutch entrepreneur Louis de Geer (1587–1652), originally a trader in copper and iron, deserves our special attention. He had started his career in Dordrecht in 1611, but soon moved to Amsterdam. Since he also traded in weapons and ammunition, his company grew quickly. The Swedish king Gustav II Adolph was De Geer's main arms buyer, as a result of the former's activities in the Thirty Years' War. However, De Geer could sell more wares than could actually be produced. For this reason, he tried to stimulate foreign industries, specifically in Sweden. When he was not sufficiently successful at this working from a distance, De Geer moved to Sweden in 1627, where he became the country's largest iron producer.[62] This allowed him to finance the king and the nobility, and to assemble a private fleet to secure the Sound. In addition to all these activities, he also found time to establish a paper mill in Norrköping in 1633, employing the Dutchman Emmerick and his two sons to run it. The sons, Abraham and Isaac,

---

53 Laurentius, *Watermarks 1650–1700*, no. 696.
54 Hills, *Papermaking*, pp. 37–38.
55 J. N. Balston, *The elder James Whatman, England's greatest papermaker (1702–1759)* (West Farnleigh, Kent: J. N. Balston Publisher. 1992), pp. 254–255.
56 Hills, *Papermaking*, pp. 68–69 en D. C. Coleman, *The British paper industry, 1495–1860* (Oxford: Clarendon Press, 1958), pp. 118–119. Baskerville had designed a font that was too delicate to be printed on the regular laid paper. Whatman solved this problem by using a woven cover on his mould, resulting in a much smoother and more even surface. Wove paper was more costly, however, because the dipping process was more time-consuming.
57 H. M. Fiskaa & O. K. Nordstrand, *Paper and watermarks in Norway and Denmark* (Amsterdam: Paper Publications Society, 1978), pp. 293–299.
58 Henk Voorn, *The papermills of Denmark & Norway and their watermarks* (Hilversum: Paper Publications Society, 1959), p. 14.

59 Ibid., pp. 28–29.
60 Ibid., pp. 33–37.
61 Ibid., p. 34.
62 Henk Voorn, 'De papiermolen van Louis de Geer', *De papierwereld*, XVII (1962), p. 139.

bought the necessary rags in the Netherlands and transported them to Sweden in ships from De Geer's fleet. From 1634, most of the paper produced was then exported to the Netherlands again.

Still, the total number of Scandinavian paper mills remained small in the seventeenth and eighteenth centuries. The industry flourished only when in the nineteenth century the paper machine was introduced, paired with the steam engine and wood pulp. Especially the new pulp was a determining factor: these countries had an abundant supply of wood. Over the course of the nineteenth century, the number of paper factories grew, giving Scandinavia a prominent position in the international paper industry.

Spain

The southern part of Spain was under Arabian rule from the eighth century onwards. Intellectual life was well-developed among the Moorish populace, and as part of this, the art of paper-making had been brought over from North Africa. Paper was made with the use of a floating mould. In this period, the industry was concentrated around Xàtiva in the province of Valencia. The oldest mention of the activities of a Spanish paper mill date from 1056.[63] After 1238, Christians took over power in this region. From the thirteenth century, paper making based on the innovation of the use of copper wires developed along the entire Mediterranean coast. The oldest known watermark from southern Spain dates from 1303, though Oriol Valls i Subira assumes this paper could also have been imported from Italy. In the late Middle Ages, Moorish and Jewish merchants traded the Spanish paper all across the Mediterranean region.[64] Their trade was limited to the coastal areas, especially when political complications caused a ban on export to the French interior after 1274. Around 1500, competition by Italian paper makers, Turkish influence in the eastern part of the Mediterranean region, and Catalonia implementing measures against the aforementioned Moorish and Jewish traders caused this trade to decline sharply. As a result, export to the rest of Europe ended almost completely. Catalan paper makers even copied Italian watermarks. The production slowly started to shift its focus to Spanish-speaking areas, such as the New World colonies in Argentina and Brazil.

With the rise of a local printing industry and its accompanying demand for paper, combined with the growing export to the various Spanish-speaking countries, a local, almost completely autonomous paper industry took shape.[65] It consisted mainly of the Catalan paper makers, whose business expanded greatly in the seventeenth and eighteenth century and who delivered outstanding quality. An interesting example of the local production is the Picador watermark, as can be seen in no. 371, with its distinctive local theme. The various interior wars in the early nineteenth century and the introduction of the paper machine would eventually end the production of handmade paper.

Portugal

Portugal developed a local paper industry relatively late, with its first mill established in Leiria in 1411. Until that point, the country had been dependent on imports from Spain and Italy. In the second half of the fifteenth century, the number of mills slowly started to climb, stimulated by the introduction of the printing press and the establishment of the universities of Lisbon and Coimbra. An economic climate emerged that made a local paper industry viable.[66] Many of the mills and print shops were Jewish-owned, and many of the books that appeared were in Hebrew. Around 1500, the Portuguese authorities implemented a number of drastic measures to reduce Jewish influence. Many of the mills and print shops then fell into Christian, and often German, hands.[67] The oldest Portuguese watermark dating from after this change is from 1536. But national paper production remained very limited, and almost stopped completely around 1700. Until the eighteenth century, Portugal had to import the bulk of its paper. Most of it came from Italy, mainly from the area between Genoa and Bologna; some was imported from the south-west of France through the Bayonne harbour.[68] The French paper makers often used Italian watermarks, adapting to the situation as it was.

In the early eighteenth century, the situation started to change with the arrival of several paper makers from

---

63 Oriol Valls i Subira, *Paper and watermarks in Catalonia* (Amsterdam: Paper Publications Society, 1970), pp. 3–8.
64 Ibid., p. 11.
65 See Laurentius, *Watermarks in paper*, no. 130 and p. 4 for an example of paper from Teruel in Aragon region.
66 Henk Voorn, 'Early papermaking in Portugal', *The Papermaker*, 30 (1961) and A. F. de Ataide e Melo, *O papel como elemento de identificaçâo* (Lisboa: Oficinas Graficas da Bibliotheca Nacional, 1926), pp. 25–30.
67 Alegre Ribeiro, 'La fabrication du papier au Portugal', IPH *Yearbook*, 10 (1994), p. 91.
68 Laurentius, *Watermarks in paper*, p. 3.

Genoa, like the Ottone family, active from about 1708. In 1715, the Ottones ran the Engheno de papel do Penedo mill in Lousã, in the district of Coimbra. The high quality of their paper attracted several print shops. Other well-known Italians who participated in paper making in Portugal include Caneva, Buzano and Thomate.[69] The Thomate family was especially active in this industry until well into the nineteenth century. Apart from the Italians, the German Erso family and the French Lambert family also worked in the town of Lousã. When the paper machine was introduced, their trade developed into a strong industry.

---

69   Bandeira, 'Paper manufacture in the district of Coimbra', p. 137.

CHAPTER 2

Different Aspects of Paper

In this chapter, we have gathered various aspects of paper that we noticed over the course of our years of research. These are aspects related to types and quality, colours, decorated paper, ream wrappers, formats, and individual elements like lines, decorative watermarks and official papers.

Quality and Raw Material

We have noticed a great variety in the quality of paper produced over the past centuries. The large demand, combined with an unstable supply of raw material, meant that paper makers were sometimes forced to adapt their production process to changing circumstances. In the ideal situation, there was sufficient supply of fine white rags to produce beautiful white printing and writing paper. However, due to shortages, high costs of raw material and historical factors, differences were inevitable.[1] As a result, from the sixteenth century on, we see more and more variety in quality. There was demand for various types of paper, such as sturdy packing paper, material for book bindings, paper for cheap products like children's books, and wallpaper.

The manufacturing of these products was partly determined by the raw materials available. While white rags were used for high-quality printing and writing paper, the abovementioned coarser types were made out of coloured rags, sailcloth and rope. Recycled printed paper, damaged books or forbidden books could also be re-used.[2] A good example are the papers used in Augsburg and Nuremberg in the eighteenth century. No. 439 in the watermark catalogue shows a good example of the flocky quality of this paper. Despite the abundance of research material, it proved extremely difficult to find a sheet of this paper where we could take a good, clear X-ray. The consistency of the paper was extremely flocky, almost resembling papier-mâché.

Most likely, the rags used as raw material were supplemented with old paper sent back to the mill. No wonder there were regular disputes over the paper delivered.[3] In our experience, most of the Italian paper is of high quality – Italy must have had a fairly consistent supply of high-grade raw material. The same can be said for material from the Angoumois and the Limosin produced for the Dutch market. The Dutch factors in these area were deeply involved in paper production, including the rags supply. The first selection was made in the paper mill. France in the eighteenth century already used no fewer than five different quality levels.[4] During transport, the choice of packaging could also cause a decrease in quality. In the 18th century, the ongoing shortage of good-quality rags prompted makers to start searching for alternative raw materials, mainly using plant material in their experiments. However, this never moved beyond the experimental stage. The experiments were in themselves successful, but there was insufficient raw material to scale up production. A practical alternative would be found with wood pulp only in the early nineteenth century.

Still, it is worthwhile to look a little closer at a few of these efforts. Some early experiments were undertaken by Edward Lloyd in 1684 and the asbestos paper made by the German professor Franz Ernst Brückmann in 1727. In France, Jean Etienne Guettard (1715–1786) conducted some interesting experiments with plants, including stinging nettles. But the most important French paper maker was Pierre-Alexander Léorier de l'Isle (1744–1826). His research was carried out in the paper mill in Montargis in the department of Loiret.[5] His main goal was to manufacture wallpaper. Most of the wallpaper had been imported from England, but the Anglo-French War (1778–1783) caused a shortage in France. Another French experiment carried out around 1800 was the use of the Conferva plant. But here as well, a shortage of resources proved limiting, so Voorn is quite correct when he remarks that the time had come for a more suitable raw material: wood and straw.[6] In the early nineteenth century, the English paper

---

1 For restrictions on and the economic value of rags and other raw materials, see Voorn, *De papiermolens van Gelderland*, pp. 23–27.
2 Voorn, *De papiermolens in de provincie Noord Holland*, p. 19. During the Reformation, in the Northern Netherlands many Catholic books were sent to the paper mills for repulping. The end product was called *monnikegrauw* (monk gray). As the examples show, this process still continued until the nineteenth century.
3 See Van Eeghen, *De Amsterdamse boekhandel*, 1978, volume IV, p. 197. Paper merchant Thomas Barst declared in 1701 that he had received a batch of paper made of 'decayed' (paper) fabric of very bad quality. Page 198 mentions the merchant Simon Bosboom, who rejected several batches of paper from France on account of its poor quality. This chapter mentions more instances of such disagreements.
4 See Voorn, *De papiermolens in de provincie Noord Holland*, p. 13.
5 Ibid., pp. 41–49.
6 Ibid., p. 53.

FIGURE 15   Titlepage to J. C. Schäffer's book with experiments from 1770

maker Matthias Koops switched to more modern methods for the preparation of raw materials.[7]

One of the best-known researchers was the scholar Jacob Christian Schäffer, born in the German town of Querfurt.[8] Schäffer initially studied theology, but had a great interest in nature, experimenting with different types of plants in his search for a suitable replacement for making paper. He made the pulp at home, using products like lye, and succeeded in several instances at making a product resembling paper. Schäffer published his findings in Regensburg in 1765, exciting so much interest that his work was published in several volumes in Amsterdam in 1770. (Fig. 15) Every volume contained a few of the papers he had manufactured. Although Schäfer's experiments resulted in unique papers, they did not provide a solution to the larger problem at hand.

There are various contemporary indications for paper quality. A useful source for these terms is the packaging of a stack of paper, known as the ream wrapper. We will elaborate on this later in this chapter. In many cases, the ream wrapper not only showed the maker and place of production, but also an indication of quality. (Fig. 16) We often see the indication 'super fine', referring to writing paper. Cheaper paper (usually intended for printing) was

---

7   Hunter, *Papermaking*, pp. 76–80.
8   Henk Voorn, *Rondom J. Chr. Schäfer* (Amsterdam: De Papierwereld, 1950), p. 27.

FIGURE 16   Detail of a ream wrapper with the description Supra fine fine, c.1815

given only the indication 'fine'. Occasionally, one can see a 'super fine fine' and even 'fine fine *très excellent*', which must have referred to writing paper of the very best quality. Especially in the eighteenth century, publishers' catalogues offered material on different types of paper. Terms like *grauw* (brownish) or *vael* (greyish) indicated inferior wares.[9] Sometimes, the material is described as cartridge paper.[10]

Coloured Paper

This generic term encompasses a broad group of papers, often in large formats, made of coloured rags or other coarse material, resulting in a range of colours and thickness. The paper is often of heavy quality and sometimes has a mushy structure. Sailcloth, rope and old paper were the raw materials for these greyish and brownish papers. Ream wrappers were also made of this material. Many coloured rags were processed into blue paper, used, for example, as filling in art albums. It is interesting to note that artists sometimes preferred the blue and brown paper for the specific possibilities it lent to their drawings. Thinner folio varieties were used for catchpenny prints, proclamations and as base for decorated paper. In the Netherlands, a large proportion of this paper was made in the Veluwe, where makers sometimes let the rags rot to make them easier to process into paper, part of the reason the paper turned out greyish and flocky.

Makers were not particular about their raw materials, as is clear from a ream wrapper of a paper which appears to be partly made out of straw, giving the paper a very brittle and inferior quality. (Fig. 17)

Coloured paper was often sold per thousand sheets; the thinner blue paper even per two thousand.

Notable is the almost complete absence of watermarks in brown, grey and blue paper. In these products, we found marks only very sporadically.[11] It appears that the quality of the paper was such that the makers did not deem it necessary to mark.

---

9   Frans Laurentius, 'Clement de Jonghe (ca. 1624–1677), kunstverkoper in de Gouden Eeuw', *Bibliotheca Bibliographica Neerlandica*, vol. X (Houten: Hes & De Graaf, 2010), p. 117.

10 As early as 1625, in the Resolutions of the States-General a patent for the production of *grauw papier* is awarded to one Mr. Nollinck. This resolution also shows the importance and value of the raw materials necessary for the manufacturing process. To give one example, it refers to old fishnets as a raw material.

11 From the marks we did find, we could see that this paper was made in all the major centres in Europe. Apart from white paper mills, it is likely there was always a mill for this product present as well.

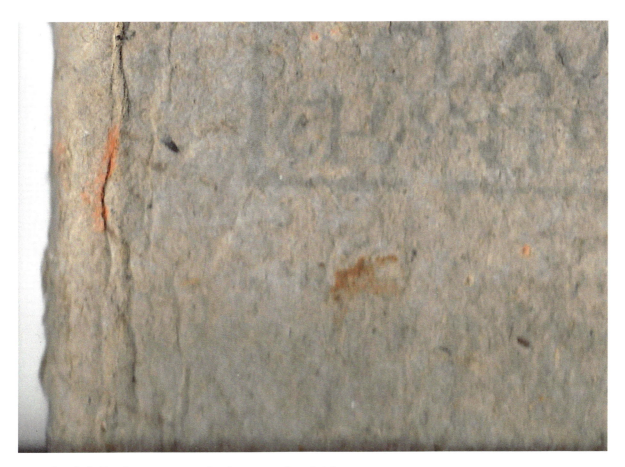

FIGURE 17 Detail of a French ream wrapper printed on very crude material, c.1700

Decorated Paper

An important and large industry was the production of decorated paper, which was used for book bindings, backs of playing cards, covers, wallpaper and shelf paper. This industry originates in Germany and Switzerland. Later on, the material was produced in the Netherlands, France and Italy as well, but Germany would remain the largest producer, with large centres in towns like Nuremberg and Aschaffenburg. decorated paper can be roughly separated into four categories: Chintz paper: paper printed in colour or with a bronze medium, using a wooden block or a copper plate. (Fig. 18) Marbled paper: paper decorated using the marbling technique. (Fig. 19) Painted paper: paper coloured with a brush. Paste paper or *Hernhutter Papier*: paper decorated with a mixture of paste and dye that was either painted or stamped onto the sheet. (Fig. 20)

Chintz paper originated in the textile industry. From the late fifteenth century, we find papers printed with wooden blocks that were also used on fabrics.[12] Over the course of the sixteenth century, a full-blown industry developed that printed patterns in one or more colours, originally using wooden blocks, but later also using copper plates. In addition to printing colours, makers in the seventeenth century developed printing with a bronze medium. The papers decorated in this method were called brocade paper. An interesting variety is velvet or *velours* paper: Using paste and a block, a pattern was printed on the paper, which was then dusted with textile floss.[13] The most common examples show a large variety in geometric and floral patterns. (Fig. 21)

Marbled paper was originally invented in Turkey in the late fifteenth century, hence its early name of *Turkisch marmor*. It was made in a container filled with water with a coagulant, in which water-based colours were dripped. This floating layer of paint could be further manipulated using combs and other instruments, resulting in a broad range of patterns.[14] Based on watermarks, we were able to

---

12 Albert Haemmerle, *Buntpapier* (München: Georg D. W. Callwey, 1961), fig. VI.

13 Large sheets were also used as wallpaper.

14 See J. F. Heijbroek & T. C. Greven, *Sierpapier, marmer-, brocaat- en sitspapier in Nederland* (Amsterdam: De Buitenkant, 1994), p. 21 for different varieties and typology.

FIGURE 18 Detail of a Brocade paper, printed in Nurnberg, 1720

determine that these papers were also manufactured in Europe as early as the late sixteenth century.

Painted paper is likely the simplest method of making decorated paper. Such paper is found uninterrupted since the fifteenth century. Double folio sheets were painted with a brush, using water-based paints, often in bright colours.[15] This was often done very swiftly, meaning the brushstrokes remained visible. These sheets were sometimes also used as base for brocade paper.

Paste paper, also known as *Hernhutter Papier* is closely related to painted paper, the difference lying in the type of paint. In this case, the dye is mixed with paste, a medium offering interesting possibilities in applying shadow effects and use of blocks and combs. This technique was especially popular in the eighteenth and nineteenth centuries.[16]

Formats

Formats are a complicated matter. Paper formats were standardised only in the nineteenth century, and even then, many variant sizes still appeared. Until this standardisation, a great and confusing variety of indications was used, often based on the watermark, but sometimes also using specific format indications. However, it is very difficult to assign consistent modern measurements to all these formats. In addition, in our research we noticed that even in non-bound sheets, such as letters, the deckle edges had often been removed. Finding a deckle edge is relatively rare.[17]

Paper formats were a subject of debate as early as the fifteenth century. In Bologna, a stone was used to list the format indications for different types of paper.[18] Labarre

---

15 Ibid., p. 11.
16 Ibidem, pp. 30–31.
17 Henk Voorn, *Old Ream Wrappers* (North Hills, Pa: Bird & Bull Press, 1969), p. 12 for this manner of preparing papersheets.
18 E. L. Labarre, *Dictionary and encyclopaedia of paper and papermaking* (Amsterdam: Swets & Zeitlinger, 1952), p. 249, which describes four different sizes: *Imperiale* 74 × 50 cm, *Realle* 61.5 × 44.5 cm, *Meçane* 51.5 × 34.5 cm and *Reçute* 45 × 31.5 cm.,

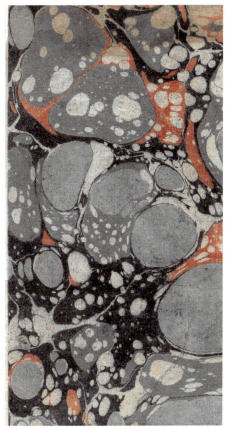

FIGURE 19   Three details of different marbled papers, dating from 1630 to 1750

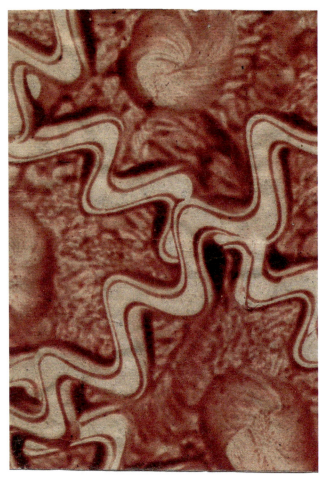

FIGURE 20 Detail of a so-called "Hernhutter" paper, decorated with starch paint, c.1750

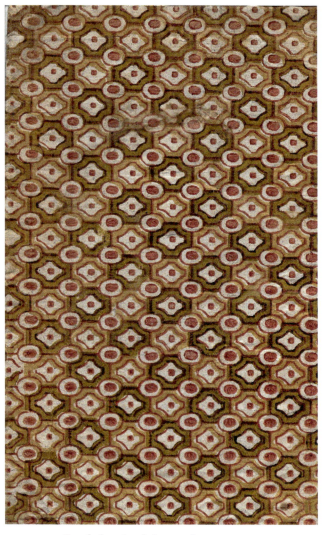

FIGURE 21 Detail of a printed, decorated paper, c.1770

gives an extensive overview of indications. For the seventeenth century, stock lists of plates from print publishers have been found, also based on paper format. Often, the format is also linked to the quality of the paper.

We encountered several watermarks in which the format was indicated, such as nos. 128, 381–384, 405, 409, 410, 494 and 567. The watermarks Elephant and Atlas can also be considered format indications. As an example, roughly speaking for a 17th-century publisher, the following division could be made:[19]

>   *Groote blatcaart*/Imperial/Elephant 55 × 60 cm.
>   *Groote kunstplaat*/ *Mediaen*/Royal 47 × 56 cm.
>   Single sheet/Writing/Double folio 30 × 40 cm.

The smaller formats, half sheet/half folio 20 × 30 cm., and *Quart blad* 20 × 15 cm., were based on the abovementioned double folio sheet. However, it will always remain difficult to establish standard sizes in paper.

Ream Wrappers

One group of objects that is very important to the research into the history of paper are the surviving packagings of papers. These so-called ream wrappers were made by using a wooden block, or occasionally a copper plate, to print an image of the watermark, sometimes also including the maker's name, factor, quality and place of production, onto a large, heavy piece of paper.[20] (Fig. 22) This was then wrapped around a "ream" of paper, consisting of 480 to 500 sheets. A number of reams (the exact number mostly depending on the format) was packed into a bale.

---

pp. 246–272, which describes an incredible amount of sizes and denominations. See also Laurentius, 'Clement de Jonghe', p. 117.
19   Ibid., pp. 109–116.
20   Th. & F. Laurentius, *Vijftig historische riemkappen* (Middelburg: Laurentius, 2015), pp. III–VII.

FIGURE 22 Depiction of a complete ream wrapper from the Honigh family, c.1820

FIGURE 23 Depiction of a classic ream wrapper for (L) paper with Arms of Amsterdam watermark, c.1700, and (R) a ream wrapper for paper in use during the Kingdom of Holland, 1806–1810

In almost all cases, the image is printed in red, probably because the reams originally used to be marked in red chalk.[21]

Since ream wrappers were packaging, intended to be thrown away, they were often printed badly and on inferior paper. This also makes them relatively rare. For some countries, such as Italy, not a single example is known. The earliest examples found date from about 1445, but then the next known example dates from after 1550.[22] Ream wrappers were intended for temporary use and as a result many wrappers are damaged, as they were used as packaging, in book bindings, or even to fill up tears in beams.

Despite all these issues, the remaining ream wrappers grant some unique insights into the production and trade in paper in Western Europe. (Fig. 23)

Wove Paper

As mention in the section on England, wove paper was invented in this country around 1756 by James Whatman. His innovation of the completely woven copper wire cover was revolutionary: from now on, it was possible to produce much smoother paper. Although the English paper makers tried to keep the manufacturing process a secret for some time, paper makers in continental Europe started to produce wove paper from about 1780. France was one of the first countries to adopt the new process, and wove paper produced by paper makers like I. Oser started to appear very early on in Basel as well. An important incentive for its use was the invention of lithography, a technique especially suited to printing on a smooth, even surface. In order to obtain a uniform surface that was as large as possible, the watermarks were moved to the borders of the sheet. This explains the scarcity of watermarks on this type of paper, since the borders were often cut off. However, we still did our best to collect a few good examples. During this work, we realised it was often difficult to take X-rays of this type of paper. Apparently, the more even paper structure affects the contrast of the image.[23]

Special Watermarks

Watermarks clearly show ongoing iconographic traditions. A classic example is how Wendelin Riehel's monogram was used as an indication of quality for over 250 years. Marks like the Foolscap and the Fleur de Lis were in use for many centuries. However, it is still possible to determine an evolution of images and derive a chronology.[24]

Apart from the common marks, sometimes commemorative designs appeared. An early example is the Postrider, designed to mark the Peace of Münster.[25] We also see watermarks designed for official papers intended for government use (with state crests, country and district names, portraits of heads of state and references to laws) or as a security measure against counterfeiting. Especially in the eighteenth century, this becomes a common usage. France was an early adopter, using notary paper indicating the department.[26]

Watermarks were also sometimes used for purely functional reasons, with watermarked lines as an example. Georg Quinat from Schwabach, active around 1750, was an early producer of such paper.[27] A closely related type are decorated stationary papers, which mostly date from the first half of the nineteenth century.

Watermarks Encountered

Anchor

The Anchor watermark is a classic mark, appearing from the 13th well into the nineteenth century.[28] The place of origin is usually given as Central Europe. On investigating eighteenth and nineteenth-century Italian papers, it was found that most were made in Marche, Umbria and Amalfi. Over the course of preparing this book, we mainly found Anchor watermarks in a sixteenth-century context.

---

21 In addition to the print, notes in red chalk are often found on the wrappers as well.
22 See Wolfgang Schlieder, *Riesaufdrucke* (München: K. G. Saur, 1989), pp. 16–17 for a very early example of a ream wrapper.
23 Laurentius, *Italian watermarks*. In our research for this catalogue, we encountered both laid and wove paper, and we noticed that obtaining good images is many times more difficult with the latter type.
24 See for example Laurentius, *Watermarks 1600–1650* and *Watermarks 1650–1700* for the evolution of the Foolscap. Using several different examples of a watermark, it is possible to date a specific mark when looking at the form and at specific elements, such as the number of bells on the cap.
25 Th. Laurentius, *Zeventiende-eeuwse postrijder watermerken* (Voorschoten: Laurentius, 1999), pp. 3–5. Another interesting example is Montgolfier's Balloon, which shows up as a watermark soon after the first balloon flight.
26 Laurentius, *Watermarks in paper*, pp. 6–7.
27 Laurentius, *Vijftig historische watermerken*, p. 29.
28 See Môsin, V., *Anchor watermarks* (Hilversum: Paper Publications Society, 1973) and Laurentius, *Italian watermarks*, pp. 5–6 and nos. 1–27.

Nos. 1 and 3–7 are classic examples of this mark; it sometimes appears with a separate star on top. A comparison between, for example, no. 4 from 1621 and no. 5 from 1554 shows very minimal development in this mark, which makes it difficult to date. No. 2, however, has a very distinctive linear design which often appears in graphic art published in Venice around 1600. Many of the examples examined are of Venetian origin, which means it is possible that other marks are also from this area.

Arrow

This mark appears to be of Italian origin. It shows up as early as the fifteenth century in paper in large formats.[29] Over the course of our research, we found one Italian example, no. 8, in a map published in Rome by Antonio Lafreri around 1558. The other marks all turned out to be varieties from the Troyes area in the Champagne region, probably copies of the Italian mark made by local paper makers. These papers were mainly used in Antwerp for the publication of maps in larger formats.

Atlas

This is a very distinctive watermark, only found in atlases produced by Joan Blaeu. Blaeu purchased this paper through the Dutch factor Pieter Haack of the Moulin Jouriaud in the town of St. Junien in the Limousin. It appears that other papers in this large format were also bought from this region through Haack.

Balloon

This watermark refers to the beginning of balloon flights at the end of the eighteenth century, a subject so popular that a watermark was dedicated to it.[30]

Basilisk

In the first half of the seventeenth century, the Northern Netherlands procured a lot of paper from Switzerland, specifically from Basel and Bern. Paper from Basel, with marks like Crozier and Basilisk, is quite common.[31] After 1648, import of this paper stopped almost entirely. Strangely enough, we found this mark in no. 23, a printed work that was supposed to have been published around 1662. After comparison, the paper was found to be from the early seventeenth century after all. The paper was most likely used only after being left on the shelf for a long time because of its irregular dimensions. This would make it the only example known to us of later use of older paper.

Bell

We found this mark only once, in an edition of a map by Lorenz Fries, printed in Lyon by the Trechsel brothers. The watermark's origin, the Beaujolais region, matches the place of origin for this variety described in the relevant literature.[32]

Bend

The Bend or Strasbourg Bend was a common watermark from the sixteenth century onwards. Nos. 27, 28 and 30 are examples from this period. Although the mark initially referred to the important staple town of Strasbourg, it soon became an indication of quality and size. Especially from about 1660, this mark became synonymous with paper in large formats. No. 29 is a typical example of this later use.

Bird

We recorded three marks with birds. Of these, the second variety, no. 32, is the most common. This is a typical Italian watermark, appearing frequently from the late 15th century until deep into the nineteenth century.[33] The rooster in no. 31 probably refers to the paper maker's name, Polleri. The peacock under no. 33 is an enigma, for apart from the date of the book in which the map in question appears, no other reference to this mark could be found.

Chaplet

This mark is regularly found in paper from mills in the Auvergne. It was used in heavy paper in large formats, and is often found with extensive countermarks showing the names of the paper makers, such as Thomas Dupuy in nos. 35–38. Products by Benôit Colombier and his widow, who worked in the same region, were found in no. 34. This maker will appear several more times in this book. The mark appears from the third quarter of the seventeenth century and was used throughout the eighteenth century.

---

29 See R. Peerlings, F. Laurentius, J. van den Bovenkamp, 'The watermarks in the Rome editions of Ptolemy's Cosmography and more', *Quaerendo*, 47 (2017), p. 318, nos. 25–29.

30 See Laurentius, *Vijftig historische watermerken*, p. 34.

31 See Laurentius, *Watermarks 1600–1650*, p. x, nos. 1–48.

32 Marius Audin, 'Vieux moulins à papier du Beaujolais', in *Contributions à l'histoire de la papeterie en France*, vol. IV (Grenoble: Editions de l'industrie papetière, 1936), p. 47 and 78–79.

33 See Laurentius, *Watermarks 1600–1650*, nos. 78–86 and Laurentius, *Italian watermarks*, nos. 31–108.

Circles

This watermark is common in Mediterranean papers and is found all through Western Europe.[34] It originates from Genoa and the surrounding area, but paper with this mark was also produced in Southern France.[35] Over the course of this research, we mainly found examples from the eighteenth century that were used in Portugal. Typical examples are nos. 43, 54, 58 and 64.

Coat of Arms

This subject is represented with no fewer than 83 examples. With six examples, the Amsterdam Coat of Arms shows a cross-section of the varieties within this category. The history of the origin of this mark is connected to the Dutch activities in the Angoumois-Limousin-Périgord triangle in France. From about 1648, these regions grew to be of crucial importance to the Dutch market.[36] No. 73 is a classic example of French paper intended for the Dutch market. Of course, due to the mark's popularity, it was copied in other places: no. 71 is a Norman example and no. 69 a German copy.

Typical for German paper is the liberal use of heraldic imagery. Nos. 75, 91–94, 96, 98, 100, 121–127, 130, 144, 147, 149 and 150 show an overview of some three centuries of paper production in an area reaching from Southern Germany to Bohemia. Some Coats of Arms are common, such as the Coat of Arms of Saxony, and easily placed. Others, such as no. 149, are impossible to identify, but can be classified as German due to their use. The late sixteenth century is amply represented with paper from Troyes and the Champagne region. Nos. 81 and 90 can be considered classic examples. We regularly encountered this paper in maps printed in Antwerp before about 1585. We also encountered a lot of paper from the Vosges and Alsace regions from this period, such as nos. 76 (Maulburg), 109 (Montbéliard), 123 (Docelles), 131 (Chénimenil) and 148 (Thann). Usage of these marks grew with the growing export of paper to the Netherlands from Southern Germany and Eastern France, with Strasbourg as the staple town, and with the decline of the Champagne as supplier. Other French material, such as nos. 85–87, is of Norman origin. This paper was mainly made for local French use, but part of the paper produced was exported to England.[37] In the late seventeenth century, paper makers even started producing special paper intended for the English market, as can be seen in no. 84.[38]

The important paper production centres in the Auvergne are well-represented. In centres of graphic print like Paris, large quantities of paper from Thiers and Riom was used. Therefore, it is not surprising that in the maps we researched that were published in Paris, we almost exclusively found paper from the Auvergne. Examples are nos. 78 and 103–105. Papers in large formats remarkably often have large and complicated marks, brandishing heraldry belonging to the French royal family, such as nos. 88 and 89. Also used in France were watermarks with the family crest of high-ranking persons, such as the cardinals Richelieu, Mazarin and Retz and Minister of Finance Le Tellier.[39] Nos. 95 and 152 show examples of such marks. Research into Portuguese documents also resulted in a group of marks with the Portugal Coat of Arms and a Coat of Arms with the word Libertas, among other finds.

Italy only plays a small part in this subject. Italian examples are no. 97 with a cardinal's Coat of Arms, and a Venetian paper with a Coat of Arms with three stars. The Netherlands is also represented with just one example, no. 141: the Coat of Arms of the city of Zwolle.

Crescent

We were able to record three varieties of this mark. A single crescent (no. 153) and a variety with three crescents (nos. 154–155). The single variety appears from the 15th century onwards. We found it in a map by Coronelli published around 1680. The 'Tre lune' variety was found in prints made in Venice between 1600 and 1778. One can therefore assume the origin of these watermarks lies in the Venice area.

---

34   Ibid., nos. 88–92 and Laurentius, *Watermarks 1650–1700*, nos. 4–39 for 17th-century examples.
35   See Laurentius, *Watermarks in paper*, nos. 32–39.
36   See Laurentius, *Watermarks 1650–1700*, pp. VI–VIII and Delâge 1990 for a detailed analysis of the Dutch trade involvement in these regions.
37   See Globe, *Peter Stent*, appendix C, pp. 191–192. Norman paper also appears in the Netherlands: see Laurentius, *Watermarks 1600–1650*, nos. 320–321 and 324–327; and Laurentius, *Watermarks 1650–1700*, nos. 385–387, 390 and 724–729. The designs of these marks are notably crude.
38   See Laurentius, *Vijftig historische riemkappen*, p. 13.
39   See G. Detersannes, *L'histoire de France en filigranes* (Paris: Publications du musée de l'affiche et du tract, 1981), pp. 101–115.

Cross

We recorded seven examples of this type of watermark. Two small crosses date from the sixteenth century. No. 156 is a fairly crude example; no. 157 is more structured. We assume the latter is Italian paper; the former is most likely from the Montbéliard region. Nos. 158–161 are examples of Mediterranean paper; no. 161 is certain to be a Genovese product.[40] This appears to be a smaller version of the Circle mark: there is a strong connection in design and place of origin. No. 162 is a very special paper: It was made by Jan Stuckx in the mill near Dendermonde. Since this mill was only operational for a short period of time, paper made there is rare.

Crossbow

We were able to record one example of this Italian mark. It appears in many different varieties: with a single circle, a double circle, and with an added star. Dates range from the fourteenth to the seventeenth century.[41] The example found dates from the mid-sixteenth century.[42]

Crown

We recorded several different varieties of this watermark. An example of an early variety is no. 164, a so-called High Crown. This is paper from the Vosges region, and the mark was used in this form from the early sixteenth century to about 1580. Nos. 165 and 166 are typical Italian marks, while nos. 167 and 168 are local French paper from the Auvergne and Normandy. Nos. 169–176 are all from Vannes, near Troyes, and were found in papers from the Champagne region, used in Antwerp in the second quarter of the sixteenth century. These later marks were found in paper in large formats used for maps.

Crozier

The Basel Crozier is a common watermark from the late sixteenth and early seventeenth century. Import of this paper was connected to changing political structures in the late 16th century, which caused the export of Swiss paper to expand rapidly. Nos. 177–179 and 181 are classic examples. No. 180 differs from other examples; it is possibly a copy, made in the Angoumois/Limousin in France, but with Dutch influences.[43] Also different is no. 188, a paper from the Augsburg area.

Date

Dated paper appeared more and more often in the eighteenth century. From 1742, French paper makers were required by the government to date their papers in the watermark.[44] In England as well, dating papers became customary. Many English paper makers, such as James Whatman, dated their papers by year. In wove paper, of which this is also an example, the dates are often found in the borders of the sheet. No. 272 has a very early date, 1633, which can be seen as a countermark with a Fleur de Lis.

Dovecot

We recorded two examples of this distinctive watermark. Both were found in paper from Riom in the Auvergne in France. This mark was used for paper in large formats.

Eagle

This mark occurs as early as the fourteenth century. In this catalogue, we mostly record examples from about 1570 to 1800. The earliest example is no. 200, in Italian paper. In this category of watermarks, the late sixteenth and early seventeenth centuries are dominated by paper from Southern Germany and Eastern France. Examples are nos. 191 and 195–198. An interesting element is a group of marks from the Holsiter Mühle in Burtscheid near Aachen. Somewhat superfluously, the word 'Ach[en]' is written inside the eagle's body.

A few later varieties of German origin show the evolution of the image after 1630. No. 199 and no. 205, a strange variety with a square frame, are good examples. No. 200 is typical paper of the Augsburg region; no. 193 is a local paper from Wendelstein. There is another interesting aspect to this latter example: It was found in a work published in Amsterdam in 1711. We occasionally noticed that a lot of local German paper appears in the Netherlands between about 1700 and 1715. This turns out to be connected to the War of the Spanish Succession, which must have severely impacted the importing of French paper, resulting in a need to find alternative sources. The old trade route to Southern Germany was reopened and for a short period of time, the import trade of German paper was revived. In France, the eagle appears from about 1660 as a large watermark on paper in large formats. Classic examples are nos. 202–204. These are mainly products of the Auvergne.

---

40   See Laurentius, *Watermarks 1600–1650*, nos. 236–242.
41   Ibid., nos. 259–262 for 17th-century varieties.
42   See Peerlings, *The watermarks*, type 5, fig. 41–42. These marks are closely related to the watermark discussed here.
43   See Laurentius, *Watermarks 1600–1650*, nos. 279, 280, 286 and 303. These marks show a close connection and display French initials.
44   See Detersannes, *L'histoire*, p. 148.

Elephant
This watermark is always associated with large formats, and in our research, we found no exceptions to this rule. On paper known for its sturdy, thick nature, the Elephant is a characteristic mark for maps. We were able to establish a workable chronology for the period between approximately 1655 and 1780. Nos. 208, 209 and 210 are typical examples for paper used in the Netherlands in the seventeenth century. They originate mostly from the Angoumois/Limousin region in France.[45] Nos. 206 and 207 are from Germany. These papers are from the Nuremberg region. A common eighteenth-century mark is no. 211, in paper made by Adriaan Rogge from Zaandam. No. 212 is an odd, late-eighteenth-century French example.

Figure
The earliest watermarks in this group that we found date from the mid-sixteenth century. These examples, nos. 213–215, depict a coat of arms with a kneeling saint. This mark is of Italian origin. Also Italian and dating from the sixteenth century is the pilgrim in a circle, no. 217. Clearly 17th-century, but impossible to identify further is the Marianne figure in no. 216. Based on the description by Heawood, we concluded that the paper must be Portuguese, but in our opinion it could also be French. No. 218 is paper made by paper maker Hans Koneberg, who worked in Kempten. The watermark is known as a Hildegard mark. The paper was often used in Augsburg. No. 219 depicts St. Michael, the Brussels civic crest. This paper was almost certainly produced by Petrus Joannus Bauwens' mill in Brussels.[46]

Fish
This mark we only found once, on paper from the Vosges region. It is possible that this paper was produced in Montfleury, near Grenoble, under the patronage of the Dauphin family.

Fleur de Lis
Together with Letters, the Fleur de Lis turned out to be one of the more expansive subjects of our research. The Fleur de Lis, or French Lily, is a mark that from the beginning of the Western European paper making industry until the 20th century has been used in all countries. We recorded examples from between 1513 and 1812, constituting a reasonably representative cross-section of the possibilities of this mark.

We divided the marks found typologically, starting with a completely free-standing lily. In this group, 25 examples have been recorded. The earliest variety, no. 224, dates from 1513 and was found on paper that is most likely Italian.[47] Following this first example, there is a series of Lilies from the Vosges region dating from the end of the sixteenth and the beginning of the seventeenth century: nos. 223, 225, 226 and 239. Two marks are from Normandy and Brittany: nos. 222 and 243. The paper in these cases was used in England. One set of marks was found in Portuguese documents. The earlier of these examples were papers from south-western France. Later examples, such as nos. 230, 231–234, 237, 238 and 240, were made in Portugal itself, although most likely by Italian paper makers working locally.

Of course, this variety is also found in France itself: nos. 235 and 241 are good examples. Especially notable is the detailed countermark with no. 245.

The next group is the Lily within a circle, a typical Italian version of this mark. It appears in many varieties from the late fourteenth until the eighteenth century. We recorded four typical examples from the seventeenth and eighteenth centuries. A very common variety is a coat of Arms with a French lily. We found seventeen examples in this group, all from the seventeenth and eighteenth centuries. Several large centres are represented, including the Auvergne with nos. 254, 258, 264 and 265; the Netherlands with nos. 262 and 267; and the Vosges region with nos. 252, 260 and 263. Typologically, a distinction can be made between varieties with a more ornamental coat of arms, such as no. 256, and those with a more austere look, such as no. 251. The latter type only appears in the seventeenth century.

The last group is a coat of arms with three lilies. Seven different varieties of this design have been recorded. The earliest marks date from the second half of the sixteenth century and originate once again from Troyes, from the mill of Siméon Nivelle. These marks were mainly found in early editions of maps by Abraham Ortelius. No. 272 is especially interesting. This mark has a detailed and dated countermark, which shows that the paper is from

---

45 We did also find a 'Dutch' elephant, dating from about 1680, in a mark by paper maker Pieter van der Ley from the Zaanstreek, but we were unable to secure an image of this example.

46 See Laurentius, *Vijftig historische riemkappen*, p. 14 for a ream wrapper from this mill.

47 The same lily is found within a circle in Italian incunables. For more information on this, see Peerlings, *The watermarks*, fig. 12–15.

FIGURE 24   A ream wrapper for Foolscap paper, probably from the Veluwe area, c.1660

Vitré in Brittany. Also, the abbreviation L XIII was added, most likely referring to Louis XIII, ruler of France at the time. The paper was made in 1633 by P. M. R. Le Jeune. No. 273 is a Norman paper, used in Brussels around 1695. This watermark seems quite archaic and is reminiscent of marks from the mid-seventeenth century. A late example is no. 274, which may even date from after 1815.

Flower

This mark is represented with three examples. Nos. 275 and 276 are typical Italian marks, in which a flower combined with a monogram is positioned in the lower corner of the sheet of paper. Given findings in earlier research, this paper must be from Northern Italy.[48] An odd variety is no. 277. This mark was found in a print published in London around 1670 and it is possible the paper is English.[49]

Foolscap, Five-Pointed

The Foolscap is one of the best-known watermarks – its name is still used to designate A4 paper. The mark appears from the late sixteenth century and is Swiss in origin.[50] No. 281 is a good example of an early Foolscap. In our research in the Zeeland archives in 2007 and 2008,

---

48   See Laurentius, *Watermarks 1600–1650*, nos. 402, 411 and 645.

49   Only Churchill gives a reference for this mark, but dated 1637. This print itself demonstrably contradicts such a date, which means it more likely should be dated to around 1670. Given England's dependence on Norman paper, it is possible this mark originates in Normandy.

50   Tschudin, *The ancient papermills*, p. 65, fig. 4.

we noticed that it was possible to map the change of the design of this mark over time. The five-pointed variety proved to be the precursor to the seven-pointed one. Apart from a few archaic Norman examples, this turns out to be an iron rule.[51] The mark disappears almost completely from about 1700. Its origins are mainly the Angoumois/Limousin/Périgord region, Normandy and the Veluwe, but it was also made in Germany. (Fig. 24) Nos. 280, 284 and 285 are typical five-pointers from the first half of the seventeenth century. Notable were nos. 279, 282 and 283, which we found in paper in large formats used for maps. Although the Foolscap is mainly associated with double folio paper, a French paper maker also once used it for a different paper format.

No. 286 is quite mysterious. The image appears to be related to a depiction of the god Bacchus seated on a lion, except in this case, the figure seems to be a fool riding what looks like a bear. Given the location the paper was found, it might originate in the Veluwe, in the East of the Netherlands. No. 278 is a German variety of the Foolscap, in which the monogram, normally present below, is missing. We have since seen other German Foolscap marks, in which the monogram is always absent.

Foolscap, Seven-Pointed

As mentioned above, the seven-pointed variety of the Foolscap appears later. The first examples, such as nos. 287 and 292, appear on the market from approximately 1651. No. 289 is a classic seven-pointer, dating from the third quarter of the seventeenth century. Nos. 288, 290 and 291 belong to the last generation, made at the end of this century.

Fortuna

This mark depicts Fortune as a woman on a globe, with a sail in her hands. The mark is typical for the eighteenth and nineteenth century. It appears mainly in the Netherlands, but German examples can be found as well.[52] The mark described here, no. 293, was produced by the Van der Ley brothers in Zaandijk in the Netherlands. The ream wrapper pictured in figure 13 was used as packaging with this type of watermark.

Grapes

Like Fleur de Lis, Grapes is a watermark that was made for a very long period of time in a large number of varieties. The mark is mainly of French origin and remained in production from the late Middle Ages until the nineteenth century. We recorded examples from between approximately 1535 and 1800. The 16th century is represented with eight examples. The earliest varieties are nos. 301 and 302, both maps by Lorenz Fries after a design by Martin Waldseemüller, in the edition printed in Lyon in 1535. These are very clear and detailed examples. The Beaujolais region is given as the place of origin of this paper.[53] Nos. 304, 309, 311 and 312 are marks from the second half of the sixteenth century, originating from Normandy, Brittany and central France. Nos. 310 and 324 are papers from Troyes and the surrounding area. These marks are all found on paper in large formats used for maps.

The seventeenth century is represented with seventeen examples. Nos. 294, 295 and 296 are simple, schematic examples. This type also appears combined with a countermark, as shown in nos. 315, 317 and 318. Nos. 297–300 are more detailed. Sometimes, the mark is combined with a monogram, as can be seen in nos. 304–308. An even more elaborate example can be seen in nos. 313 and 314, in which a separate French lily is added to the design. A striking variety is the circle with a name and a 'Grapes' in the centre, as seen in nos. 322 and 323. This paper was made by Benôit Colombier, one of the larger paper makers in Riom in the Auvergne. All seventeenth-century marks mentioned originate from Normandy, Brittany and the Auvergne, in central France. Simplification and schematisation of this mark continues in the eighteenth century, as can be seen clearly in nos. 316, 319, 320 and 321. These varieties are typical. An odd variety is no. 303, on Italian paper. It is completely different from the French marks.

Hand

The Hand watermark is one of the early marks from the fifteenth and sixteenth century, although we also recorded a few occasional later examples. The oldest example we encountered, no. 325, was found in a map from Berlinghieri's Geographia atlas, published in Florence around 1482. This paper is almost certainly Italian. Nos. 326, 333, 334, 335 and 337 are examples from the first half of the sixteenth century. The origin of these papers lies in France, including the area around Bordeaux and the Gascony region.

Nos. 327–332, 338 and 339 are from the second half of the sixteenth and the beginning of the seventeenth

---

51 Laurentius, *Watermarks 1650–1700*, p. VII.
52 Laurentius, *Vijftig historische watermerken*, p. 31, for a German example.
53 C. M. Briquet, *Les filigranes. Dictionnaire historique des marques du papier dès leur apparition vers 1282 jusqu'en 1600 avec 39 figures dans le texte et 16112 fac-similés de filigranes* (Amsterdam: Paper Publications Society, 1968), nos. 13065 en 13066.

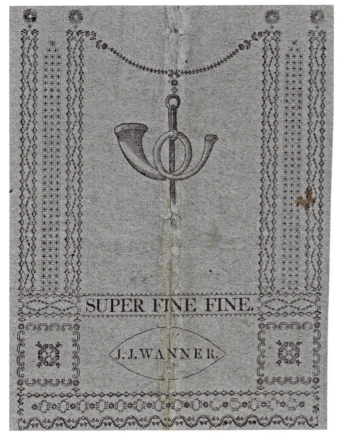

FIGURE 25 Depiction of two ream wrappers for paper with horn watermark (L) German paper, c.1820 and (R) paper made by Jean Villedary in France for the Dutch market, c.1680–1700

century. Apart from paper from the abovementioned French regions, Troyes in the Champagne is also represented. As mentioned, this mark occasionally still appears in the eighteenth century. We recorded two examples, nos. 330 and 338. No. 340 is a variety with two hands, again originating from the Champagne region.

Hat

We only recorded one example of this Italian watermark, originating in Lombardy in Italy.

Heart

Of this mark, we also photographed only one example. This is a mark from the second half of the sixteenth century, used in Venice. In the Letters section, a few more hearts combined with monograms can be seen.

Horn

Of this very common watermark, we recorded 23 different examples. The Horn appears as a watermark as early as the fourteenth century, and its use continues into the nineteenth century. (Fig. 25) As a result, it was almost impossible for us to compile something resembling a general overview, and for this reason we decided to focus mainly on the period between approximately 1550 and 1700. Most of the marks found are from the Vosges region, used for maps made in Antwerp, and date from about 1593 and later.[54] It is interesting to notice how from approximately 1590 (i.e., just after the fall of Antwerp) the source for paper imports, and specifically the paper used for maps, moves from Troyes and the Champagne region almost entirely to the Vosges region. In the Coat of Arms section, some varieties from these regions can be found with the Horn as a countermark, in paper made by Geninet.

Nos. 347 and 363, found in prints made in Augsburg and Nuremberg, are certainly German.

No. 364 is a French variety with a coat of arms combined with a post horn and a monogram, and no. 362 is possibly a Norman copy of a Swiss watermark. No. 365 is also from France, specifically from the Angoumois, and made by Leonard Laroche.

---

54 It is interesting to notice how from approximately 1590 (i.e., just after the fall of Antwerp) the source for paper imports, and specifically the paper used for maps, moves from Troyes and the Champagne region almost entirely to the Vosges region. In the Coat of Arms section, some varieties from these regions can be found with the Horn as a countermark, in paper made by Geninet.

Horse

Six watermarks with horses have been collected. Nos. 366–371 were all produced in Italy for the Portuguese market and are dated to approximately the last quarter of the eighteenth century. No. 371 is a mark from Hannover in Germany. Here, the horse is connected to the Lower Saxony state crest.

Horseman (Picador)

This mark, depicting a picador and a bull, was found in a Portuguese document. The paper is most likely Italian, intended for the Iberian market. It is dated to the late eighteenth century.

Imperial Orb

This mark was found in a map from an atlas by Matthäus Merian. The paper was produced in Samuel Koch's Mühle zu Thall in Worblaufen near Bern and is dated to after 1640.

Ladder

This watermark is Italian and appears from at least the fifteenth century. The mark sometimes appears in a circle, sometimes singly. Use of the mark continues into the second half of the sixteenth century. We found an example in a map published by Antonio Lafreri in Rome in 1558.

Letters

Of all subjects, this type is the best represented, with 95 examples dating from about 1556 to 1837. This very diverse group of marks can be subdivided into several types. Firstly, many letters appear as part of a monogram, which almost always refers to the paper's maker. In many cases, a figurative mark is combined with a monogram or a countermark. Examples are nos. 418, Hans Blum; 392, Claude de George, the famous paper maker from the Angoumois; 380, Arend van Rees; 421, Hendrik Dries van Emst; 426, Jochem Schut; 424, Leonard Laroche; 434, Lubbert van Gerrevink; and 450 Pieter van der Ley, the great innovator from the Zaan region.

Many paper makers marked their paper with their initials. Nos. 388–391, Nicolas Georgel, 399, Florentin Aubert, 407, Amé Geninet, 418, Hans Blum, 443, Nicolas Fuzelier and 455, Gregoire Vairel are typical examples of the papers produced in the Vosges region in the late 16th and early 17th centuries. They are very regularly found in paper used in the Netherlands. Nos. 385, Christian Blum, 396, Elias Kutter, 408 Georg Endter and 449, Josef Anton Unold are German marks of a later date. Especially no. 396 is typical for the eighteenth century and is often found in the Augsburg map production. Nos. 393 Simon Cornelisz. van Huysduynen, 401, Martin Orges and 420, Honigh represent Dutch makers from the Veluwe and the Zaan region.

In some cases, the monogram refers to the paper trader or *facteur* instead of the maker.[55] With nos. 381–384, 447–448 and 458, we found many traces of the Dutch factor Pieter Haeck among the marks in this catalogue. Haeck supplied large amounts of paper to Joan Blaeu, among others. Interesting varieties are nos. 381–384, in which Van Haeck's monogram appears combined with a large A. Another variety is no. 405, in which the letters GA are combined with facteur Gerard Verduyn's monogram. It is possible that A refers to Atlas and GA to Grande Atlas. In any case, both marks are found on paper in large formats, the type that was used for maps.

Much later, in the early nineteenth century, we again find format indications in German paper. Examples are nos. 409 and 410, with marks that read *Gr(oss) Med(ian)*. Further on, in the section Words, another complete format indication is listed.

Lastly, a group of marks was found with letters that have a more general meaning. Examples are nos. 424–426 with the letters IHS, the Christian symbol for Jesus. In nos. 444–446, we find the Gothic P mark, a general mark that disappears around 1600. Nos. 432–433 show the monogram of the French king, on paper produced on order from minister Le Tellier.

Lion

Two examples of this mark have been recorded in the course of this research. No. 471 is a mark of Italian origin, found in a Portuguese document. It most likely originates from the Veneto region in Northern Italy.[56] In no. 240, a Portuguese variety was found as a countermark. No. 472 is a paper produced in 1800 for the Batavian Republic. It depicts the Dutch lion with a flag. This paper was made by Jan Kool in Koog aan de Zaan.

Mace (Sceptre)

Described by Gaudrialt as Baton royal, this mark almost certainly depicts a sceptre.[57] The paper is French, but we have been unable to determine whether it is from Normandy or from the Auvergne.

---

55 See Laurentius, *Watermarks 1650–1700*, p. VIII for the extensive influence of the Dutch traders and French paper makers in the Angoumois. Monograms of these traders are found here regularly.

56 See Laurentius, *Italian watermarks*, nos. 187–189 for similar marks.

57 See Gaudriault, *Filigranes*, p. 100.

Moon

We were able to record two varieties of this mark. No. 474 is from a second edition of the Petrus Kaerius atlas, published in 1622. This reliably dates this watermark, although it does appear over a longer period.[58] Since Kaerius was involved in the *Compagnie der Duytse Papieren*, the origins of this watermark must lie in Southern Germany or Eastern France. The same is likely true for no. 475. Unfortunately, we were unable to find any references for this date, but given the time and place of use, it is a reasonable assumption.

Mountain

We photographed two different examples of this Italian mark. In no. 476, the image is placed in a double circle. Possibly there is a bird on top of the mountains, but we could not determine this conclusively.[59] No. 477 was used in Florence in 1661. The mark refers to Pope Alexander VII, a member of the Chigi family.

Names

From the sixteenth century, paper makers start to include their full name as a watermark. Early examples found in the course of our research included the paper makers in and around Troyes in the Champagne region, such as no. 480–482, Nicolas le Bé and no. 512, Claude Savois. In the seventeenth century, most full-name watermarks are found on French papers from the Auvergne, such as nos. 478, 506 and 514. Names continue to appear in France in the eighteenth and nineteenth centuries.[60] No. 496 is an interesting example: an early continental wove paper from the *Papeterie du Marais*.

The Netherlands are well-represented in the eighteenth and nineteenth centuries, with paper makers from the Veluwe region, such as no. 483 Berends, no. 507 Ledeboer and no. 518 Vos, and from the Zaanstreek, such as the Honig family with nos. 499–504 and Smidt van Gelder with no. 497. Of interest is the use of publishers' names as watermarks, such as nos. 492–494 for Georges Fricx and no. 487 for Covens & Mortier.

Official Watermarks

These watermarks only appear in France. Due to France being a centralised state, use of official watermarks was a normal occurrence in this country from the seventeenth century onwards. The four marks found are typical.[61] No. 522 is interesting due to the role the watermark plays in assigning value to the document.

Pascal Lamb

This is an Italian mark that appears from the late Middle Ages. Later on, varieties appeared, for example in France.[62] However, these were usually depicted inside a coat of arms; the Italian variety is almost always depicted in a circle. In this overview we have recorded two examples, both typically Italian: nos. 523 and 524.

Phoenix

A watermark that was only produced for a short period of time. It was used on French paper from the Limousin region that was exported to the Northern Netherlands around the mid-seventeenth century. (Fig. 26)

Pillars

We recorded two varieties of this mark. The earliest examples are nos. 528 and 529, again on paper from Troyes, from Edmond Denise's mill. Nos. 526 and 527 are later seventeenth-century marks on paper from Normandy.

Pot

This mark appears from the fifteenth to the seventeenth century. The four watermarks we recorded are from France, as are most instances of this mark. No. 533 is a classic example from the early seventeenth century. No. 530 is a distinctive model of Norman origin.[63]

Pro Patria

This mark was developed in France around 1690 for the Dutch market. It grew to be very popular in the eighteenth century, and was subsequently also used in the Netherlands and liberally copied throughout Europe. We recorded three classic models.

---

58 See Laurentius & Roos, *Met Schoone figueren*, pp. 27–28 and fig. 1. In this case, the mark was dated to 1643.

59 See Laurentius, *Italian watermarks*, nos. 31–108. It must have been a very common watermark in Italy.

60 See also the sections Eagle and Grapes, in which full names are regularly found as countermarks.

61 See Laurentius, *Watermarks in paper*, p. 6.

62 See Laurentius, *Watermarks 1600–1650*, nos. 648–660 and Laurentius, *Watermarks 1650–1700*, nos. 705–717.

63 This is a relatively late example of this mark. See Laurentius, 'Clement de Jonghe', pp. 107–108.

FIGURE 26 A ream wrapper for Phoenix paper, *c.*1655, Collection Zeeland Archives, Middelburg

Serpent

The Serpent is found as a watermark as early as the fourteenth century. We collected four examples from the seventeenth and eighteenth centuries. Nos. 537, 538 and 539 are from Germany and were made between 1590 and 1837. In these examples, the Serpent is of a heraldic character. The ream wrapper shown in figure 7 served as packaging for this type of paper. No. 540 is an interesting variety design. This paper was produced in the Angoumois/Périgord region, for the Dutch trader Van Ravesteyn. It's clearly derived from the Swiss *Heusler* watermark.[64]

Shell

This watermark is found in nineteenth-century fine writing paper and was produced throughout Western Europe.[65] This example was found on French paper.

Sphere

This watermark does not entirely fit the description; hearts and clubs are also used. However, because they still belong to a coherent group, they are classified under Sphere. The marks found all date from the early 17th century and are of French origin.

---

64 See Laurentius, *Watermarks 1600–1650*, nos. 690–691 for similar papers.

65 See Laurentius, *Italian watermarks*, nos. 283–289 for Italian examples.

FIGURE 27   A ream wrapper for Seven Provinces paper, c.1653, Collection Zeeland Archives, Middelburg

Star

Two examples of this mark have been recorded. An early example is no. 548, a mark from 1540 made in Basel. No. 549 is Genovese and from a much later date.

Sun

The Sun is found as a mark in several countries. No. 477 is an example of a Sun as a countermark in Italian paper. The marks in this catalogue are all French. Nos. 550 and 551 are examples from the mid-seventeenth century, on paper from Limousin, intended for the Dutch market.[66] No. 552 is found on a large-format paper from the Auvergne, produced in the mill run by Benôit Colombier's widow. It is very similar to the Grapes mark (no. 323) from the same mill. Also used for paper in large formats is no. 553, in which the monogram IHS is combined with a Sun mark. No. 554 is a local paper from the Bordeaux region. In no. 137, an Italian variety can be found as a countermark.

Sword

We found one example of this mark in late-seventeenth-century paper from the Nuremberg region.

Tower

This mark, found on paper produced near Ravensburg, depicts this city's civic crest. Although it was mainly used locally, it occasionally shows up in the Netherlands.[67]

Tree

This type, also known as *Fichtenpapier*, originates from the town of Roth, near Nuremberg.[68] Due to its popularity, it was later also produced by other mills, even as far away as Basel.

---

66   See Laurentius & Roos, *Met schoone figueren*, p. 30, fig. 11 for a very similar mark.

67   Nancy Ash & Shelley Fletcher, *Watermarks in Rembrandt's prints* (Washington, D.C.: National Gallery of art, 1998), no. 8.

68   Schlieder, *Riesaufdrucke*, p. 132.

Undetermined
One watermark proved impossible to identify. It appears to depict a coat of arms with a sword. Also worth noting is the geometric figure, which can also be seen as the countermark in no. 397. This figure was also impossible to identify further.

Unicorn
We recorded an eighteenth-century German example of this mark.

Vryheit (Freedom)
This mark, also known as Seven Provinces, occurs from around 1653. (Fig. 27) The oldest examples were made in France. In the eighteenth and nineteenth centuries, large quantities of this paper were produced in the Netherlands as well. The mark pictured is from the Zaanstreek, belonging to the Adriaan Rogge and Van der Ley mills.

Wheel
Three examples have been recorded. The oldest, dating from 1565, is a mark from the Venice region. Nos. 565 and 566 were both found in prints from the mid-seventeenth century. The paper is most likely from Mulhouse in the Alsace.

Words
This section is slightly problematic; it could also be incorporated in the Names or Letters sections. However, due to the length of this mark, we decided on including a separate description. The paper in question is wove paper from Germany. Like nos. 409 and 410, mentioned under Letters, this watermark indicates the paper's type and format, in this case: *super fein klein median*.

Index of Watermark Types

Anchor   30, 53 (Cat. Nos. 1–7)
Arrows   31–32, 53–54 (Cat. Nos. 8–20)
Atlas   28, 31, 38, 54 (Cat. No. 21)

Balloon   30n25, 31 54 (Cat. No. 22)
Basilisk   31, 54 (Cat. No. 23)
Bell   30n24, 31, 54 (Cat. No. 24)
Bend   31, 54–55 (Cat. Nos. 25–30)
Bird   31, 39, 55 (Cat. Nos. 31–33)

Chaplet   31, 55–56 (Cat. Nos. 34–42)
Circles   32, 33, 56 (Cat. Nos. 43–67)
Coat of arms   18, 32, 34, 37, 39, 42, 56–61 (Cat. Nos. 68–152)
Crescent   32, 61–62 (Cat. Nos. 153–155)
Cross   33, 62 (Cat. Nos. 156–162)
Crossbow   33, 62 (Cat. No. 163)
Crown   33, 62–63 (Cat. Nos. 164–176)
Crozier   31, 33, 63–64 (Cat. Nos. 177–182)

Date   1, 33, 34, 64 (Cat. No. 183)
Dovecot   33, 64 (Cat. Nos. 184–185)

Eagle   12, 33, 39n60, 64–65 (Cat. Nos. 186–205)
Elephant   28, 34, 65–66 (Cat. Nos. 206–212)

Figure   34, 36, 42, 66 (Cat. Nos. 213–219)
Fish   34, 66 (Cat. No. 220)
Fleur de Lis   30, 33, 34–35, 36, 66–70 (Cat. Nos. 221–274)
Flower   35, 70 (Cat. Nos. 275–277)
Foolscap   30, 30n24
    five-pointed   35–36, 70 (Cat. Nos. 278–286)
    seven-pointed   36, 70–71 (Cat. Nos. 287–292)
Fortuna   36, 71 (Cat. No. 293)

Grapes   36, 39n60, 41, 71–73 (Cat. Nos. 294–324)

Hand   36–37, 73–74 (Cat. Nos. 325–340)
Hat   37, 74 (Cat. No. 341)
Heart   37, 40, 74 (Cat. No. 342)
Horn   37, 37n54, 74–76 (Cat. Nos. 343–365)

Horse   38, 76 (Cat. Nos. 366–371)
Horseman   38, 76 (Cat. No. 372)

Imperial orb   38, 76 (Cat. No. 373)

Ladder   38, 76 (Cat. No. 374)
Letters   12, 34, 37, 38, 42, 76–83 (Cat. Nos. 375–470)
Lion   38, 83 (Cat. Nos. 471–472)

Mace   38, 83 (Cat. No. 473)
Moon   39, 83–84 (Cat. Nos. 474–475)
Mountains   39, 84 (Cat. Nos. 476–477)

Names   39, 39n60, 42, 84–86 (Cat. Nos. 478–518)

Official watermarks   39, 86 (Cat. Nos. 519–522)

Pascal lamb   39, 86 (Cat. Nos. 523–524)
Phoenix   39, 86 (Cat. No. 525)
Pillars   39, 87 (Cat. Nos. 526–529)
Pot   39, 87 (Cat. Nos. 530–533)
Pro Patria   39, 87 (Cat. Nos. 534–536)

Serpent   40, 87–88 (Cat. Nos. 537–540)
Shell   40, 88 (Cat. No. 541)
Sphere   40, 88 (Cat. Nos. 542–547)
Star   31, 32, 33, 41, 88 (Cat. Nos. 548–549)
Sun   41, 88–89 (Cat. Nos. 550–554)
Sword   41, 42, 89 (Cat. No. 555)

Tower   41, 89 (Cat. Nos. 556–559)
Tree   41, 89 (Cat. No. 560)

Undetermined   42, 89 (Cat. No. 561)
Unicorn   42, 89 (Cat. No. 562)

Vryheit   42, 89 (Cat. No. 563)

Wheel   42, 89 (Cat. Nos. 564–566)

Words   42, 89 (Cat. No. 567)

Index of Letters and Monograms

Note: The numbers in this Index of Letters and Monograms refer to the Catalogue-numbers of the watermarks. (For the Catalogue-numbers, see also the *Table of Watermarks* below.)

A   381, 382, 383, 385
AA   375, 376, 377
AB   332
AC   304
ACH   186, 187, 188, 189, 420
AE   378
AG   6, 161
AGC   3, 4, 5
AHB   315
AIR   317
AMA   112
AMC   114
AN   523
AO   337
AP   58, 134, 379
AR   43, 211
ARM   54
AS   146
AVR&C   380

B   385, 480, 481, 483
BA   342
BBL   27
BC   34, 89
BG   305
BSL   44, 45, 46
BV   386, 387
BGQC   372
BP   151
BRF   42
BSL   44, 45, 46
BV   386, 387

C
CC   53, 112, 390, 391, 392, 393
CCC   154, 155
CDG   392
CMT   139
CP   144, 145
CSH   393
CTS   394
CV   307, 308, 411, 412, 413, 444

D   23, 127, 287
DC   395
DD   306

DHS   555
DM   309
DO?   559

E   330, 403
EG   256
EK   397, 398, 399
EP   291
EPN   65

F   32
FA   399
FB   275, 276
FC   292, 400
FF   547
FG   310
FGGL   107
FGP   249
FL   40
FMO   401, 402
FP   102
FV   155

G   403
GA   120, 405, 406, 407
GAA   67
GAD   48
GAGM   55
GB   339
GBD   60
GBDI   59
GBP   56
GC   234
GCP   61, 62
GD   99
GDG   49
GDM   57
GE   408
GF   531
GG   103
GK   150
GM   138
GMC   233
GP   236
GPFF   108
GRMDE   409

INDEX OF LETTERS AND MONOGRAMS

GR. MED 410
GVD 405
GW 414
GWP 415
G8 404

H 416, 417
HB 76, 263, 418
HBL 235
HC 165, 166
HD 421
HG 135
HK 218
HML 244
HP 458
HS 182, 199
HT 201

I
IA 557
IB 419, 466
IC 422
ID 423
IDC 167
IDR? 530
IG 143
IH 424
IHL 538
IHS 103, 104, 105, 265, 267, 425, 426, 427, 515, 553
IM 318
IO 63, 64
IRM 66
IS 428
IV 525, 540
IYSVD 265

J
JHG 371

K 429
KC 285
KP 430

L 257, 272
LC 26, 285
LL 41, 431, 432, 433
LVG 267, 434

M 178, 419, 435, 436, 437
MAI 438
MAM 116, 117, 118
MB 258

MC 29, 439
MD 264
MG 440
MGIS, BULLE 441
MP 259
MS 347

N 123, 524
NA 50, 51, 52
NCHM 181
ND 191, 192, 260
NF 443
NG 388, 389, 390, 391

O
OAM 53

P 444, 445, 446
PC 76
PD 73
PG 94, 184
PH 21, 381, 382, 383, 384, 447, 448
PHV 98
PL 84
PM 74, 533, 544
PMD 526
PP 126
PR 543
PT 284
PV 100, 449, 545, 546
PVE 282, 283
PVL 450, 451, 452, 453, 454
PW 455

R 30, 200, 261, 456, 457, 458, 459, 512
RI 334
RM 312

S
SADP 238
SB 209, 210, 460
SE 560
SHD 461, 462
SM 463
SP 133

T
TAM 464
TB 313
TD 35
TMF 465

V 129
VDL 262, 293
VE 466
VG 73, 128

W 254
WM 468, 469, 470
WR 28, 30, 239, 265
WVH 467

Index of Names and Words

Note: The numbers in this Index of Names and Words refer to the Catalogue-numbers of the watermarks. (For the Catalogue-numbers, see also the *Table of Watermarks* below.)

ALMASSO   138, 513

Barge & Beal   479
Barthelemy   478
Berends & Zoon   483
Bouchet   485
Bru(n)   241
Budgen   484

Colle   108
Colombier   203, 322, 323, 486, 552
(De la Garde L'Ainé &) Compagnie   496
Covens & Mortier   487

Dangoumois   241
Degaroyjourné   340
Denise (Claude)   80
Denise (Edmond)   81, 82, 83, 169, 170, 171, 172, 174, 175, 176, 528, 529
Depot de la Marine   488
Dupuy (Thomas)   37, 38, 168, 185, 204, 489, 490

Fabrica Nova   242
Fichtner   491
Fricx   492, 493, 494

Gaggiero   495
Galiar   72
Geofroy   498
Gouault   90, 324, 327, 328, 329, 330
Greeven   536
Grosbon   493, 494

Hays   71
C. & I. Honig   499, 500
J. Honig   501
J. Honig & Zn.   502
J. Honig & Zoonen   504
Honi soit qui mal y pense   84

Imperial   128, 155

Jelin d'Alençon   505

Kiesling   266

Lebé (Nicolas)   480, 481, 482
Libertas   133, 134, 135, 136, 137, 138
Lejeune   243
Lebloys   506
Ledeboer & Zoonen   507

Malmenaide?   319
Mariane   216
Mauduit   87
Moyen Montgolfier Annonay   427

Nicard Limosin   508
Nivelle   268, 269, 270, 271
Nova   237
Nova Fabrica   119

Oorspronk   509
Oradour   173
Oser   510

Papeterie du (Marais)   496
Parodi a Genes   511
Passeport a l'Interieur   522
Peille   254
PMRLeie a Vitre   272
Polleri (Francesco)   31
Poyleve   314
Pro Patria   534, 535, 536

Quartino   120, 137

Rahm   560
Raiva Aranha   113
Ravensburg   559
Richard   514

Saint Francois   511
Sauvade Auvergne   515
Savois   512
(Fin de) Serve Chamaliere   245
Solernou   516
Staal-Anthoon   141
Super Fein Klein Median   567

Tamisier   321
Termonde   162
Timbre National   522
Toz do Ribeiro Silva   513

Van der Ley   293
Villedary   267
Vimal (Amable)   39

Vorno   136, 137, 139
Vos   518
Vryheyt   563

Wolfegg   517

Zwoll   141

Bibliography

Ash, Nancy & Fletcher, Shelley, *Watermarks in Rembrandt's prints* (Washington, D.C.: National Gallery of Art, 1998).

Ataide e Melo, A. F. de, *O papel como elemento de identificação* (Lisboa: Oficinas Graficas da Bibliotheca Nacional, 1926).

Audin, Marius, 'Vieux moulins à papier du Beaujolais', *Contributions à l'histoire de la papeterie en France*, vol. IV (Grenoble: Editions de l'industrie papetière, 1936).

Balmaceda, José Carlos, 'Las filigranas de los primeros impresos de Buenos Aires', *IPH Yearbook* 12 (1998), pp. 220 & 229.

Balston, J. N., *The elder James Whatman, Englands greatest papermaker (1702–1759)* (2 vols., West Farnleigh, Kent, J. N. Balston Publisher, 1992).

Bandeira, Ana Maria Leitâo, 'Paper manufacture in the district of Coimbra', *IPH Yearbook* 12 (1998), pp. 137–146.

Bartels, Klaus B., *Papierherstellung in Deutschland* (Berlin-Brandenburg: Be.Bra Wiss. Verlag GmbH, 2011).

Beck, Hans Ulrich, 'Jan van Goyen (1596–1656)', vol. I *Handzeichnungen* (Amsterdam: Van Gendt & Co, 1972), pp. 324–345.

Bower, Peter, *Turner's later papers* (London: Tate Gallery Publications, 1999).

Briquet, C. M. *Les filigranes. Dictionnaire historique des marques du papier dès leur apparition vers 1282 jusqu'en 1600 avec 39 figures dans le texte et 16112 fac-similés de filigranes* (Amsterdam: Paper Publications Society, 1968).

Buchmann, Gerhard, 'Geschichte der Papiermacher zur Oberweimar', '*Neue beiträge zur Geschichte der Stadt Weimar*, Band 1, Heft 3 (Weimar, 1936).

Churchill, W. A., *Watermarks in paper* (Amsterdam: Menno Hertzberger & Co., 1935/1967).

Cockx-Indestege, E., Greve, C., Porck, H., *Sierpapier & Marmering* (Den Haag / Brussel: Koninklijke Bibliotheek, 1994).

Coleman, D. C., *The British paper industry, 1495–1860* (Oxford: Clarendon Press, 1958).

Cottier, Elie, *L'Histoire d'un vieux métier* (Clermont Ferrand: Editions Mont-Louis, 1938).

Decker, Viliam, *Djiny rucnei Nyrobi papiera na Slovensku* (Matica Slovenská, 1982).

Delâge, Gabriel, *L'Angoumois au temps des marchands Flamands* (Paris: Libraire Bruno Sepulchre, 1990).

Delâge, Gabriel, *Moulins à papier d'Angoumois, Périgod et Limousin* (Paris: Libraire Bruno Sepulchre, 1991).

Detersannes, G., *L'histoire de France en filigranes* (Paris: Publications du Musée de l'affiche et du tract, 1981).

Doss, Dora & Schlieder, Wolfgang, 'Besitzer und Papiermacher auf Papiermühlen in Sachsen und angrenzenden Gebieten', *IPH Sonderband* (Marburg, IPH, 1993).

Duval, Jacques, *Moulins à papier de Bretagne d XVIe au XIXe siècle* (Paris: L'Harmattan, 2005).

Eineder, G., *The ancient papermills of the former Austro-Hungarian empire and their watermarks* (Hilversum; The Paper Publication Society, 1960).

Fiskaa, H. M., 'Das eindringen des Papiers in die Nordeuropäischen Länder im Mittelalter', *Papiergeschichte*, heft 3–4 (1967), pp. 28–29.

Fiskaa, H. M. & Nordstrand, O. K., *Paper and watermarks in Norway and Denmark* (Amsterdam: The Paper Publication Society, 1978).

Gaudriault, Raymond, *Filigranes et autres caracteristiques des papiers en France au XVII et XVIII siècles* (Paris: CNRS editions, 1995).

Gelas, Jos de, 'The making of paper in Brabant', *IPH Yearbook* 8 (1990), pp. 46–49.

Globe, Alexander, *Peter Stent, London printseller 1642–1665* (Vancouver: University of British Columbia, 1985), Appendix C.

Grosse-Stoltenberg, R., 'Die Grünberger Papiermühle', *IPH Yearbook* 3 (1982), p. 199.

Haemmerle, Albert, *Buntpapier* (München: Verlag Georg D. W. Callwey, 1961).

Heawood, E., 'The use of watermarks in dating old maps and documents', *Royal Geographical Journal* (London, 1924), pp. 391–412.

Heawood, E., 'Further notes on paper used in England after 1600', *The Library*, vol. II, (Oxford: Oxford University Press, 1948).

Heawood, E., *Watermarks* (Hilversum: Paper Publications Society, 1950).

Heitz, Paul, *Les filigranes avec la Crosse de Bâle* (Strasbourg: Heitz & Mündel, 1904).

Heijbroek, J. F. & Greven, T. C., *Sierpapier, marmer-, brocaat- en sitspapier in Nederland* (Amsterdam: Uitgeverij De buitenkant, 1994).

Hills, Richard L., *Papermaking in Britain 1488–1988* (London: Athlone Press, 1988).

Hinterding, E., *Rembrandt as an etcher* (Ouderkerk aan de IJssel: Sound & Vision Publishers, 2006).

Hössle, Friedrich von, *Geschichte der alten Papiermühlen im ehemaligen Stift Kempten und in der Reichstadt Kempten* (Augsburg: Verlag der Jos. Rösselschen Buchhandlung, 1900).

Hössle, Friedrich von, *Die alten Papiermühlen der freien Reichstadt Augsburg* (Augsburg: Verlag der Math. Riegerschen Buchhandlung, 1907).

Hunter, Dard, *Papermaking, the history and technique of an ancient craft* (New York: Dover Publications Inc., 1978).

Jongh, Jane de, *Van Gelder Zonen 1784–1934* (Haarlem: De Erven F. Bohn NV, 1934).

Jaffé, A., 'Zur Geschichte des Papiers und seiner Wasserzeichen', *Pfälzisches Museum-Pfälzische Heimatkunde*, heft 3–4 (1930), pp. 71–84.

Jambe, Georges, 'Les papetiers du Pays de Montbéliard', *Bulletin et memoires de Soc. D'emulation de Montbéliard*, vol. LXXII, 99 (1976).

Janot, Jean-Marie, *Les moulins à papier de la région Vosgiennes* (2 vols., Nancy: Imprimerie Berger-Levrault, 1952).

Jaspers, Nina Linde, *Schoon en werkelijk aangenaam, Italiaanse importkeramiek uit de 16ᵉ en 17ᵉ eeuw in Nederlandse bodem*, MA thesis (Amsterdam: Universiteit van Amsterdam, 2007).

Labarre, E. J., *Dictionary and encyclopaedia of paper and papermaking* (Amsterdam: Swets & Zeitlinger, 1952).

Laurentius, F., 'Clement de Jonghe (ca. 1624–1677), kunstverkoper in de Gouden Eeuw', *Bibliotheca Bibliographica Neerlandica*, vol XL (Houten: Hes & De Graaf, 2010).

Laurentius, F. & Roos, M. J., *Met veele schoone Figueren verciert* (Middelburg/IJmuiden: Roos & Laurentius, 2012), pp. 26–30.

Laurentius, Th. & Laurentius, F., 'Het geheim van Brokaatpapier' in Maas, Nop (ed.), *Waardevol oud papier, feestbundel bij het tienjarig bestaan van Bubb Kuyper* (Haarlem: Bubb Kuyper, 1996), pp. 188–191.

Laurentius, Th. & Laurentius, F., *Watermarks 1600–1650, found in the Zeeland Archives* (Houten: Hes & De Graaf publishers BV, 2007).

Laurentius, Th. & Laurentius, F., *Watermarks 1650–1700, found in the Zeeland Archives* (Houten: Hes & De Graaf publishers BV, 2008).

Laurentius, Th. & Laurentius, F., *Vijftig historische watermerken* (Middelburg: Laurentius, 2013).

Laurentius, Th. & Laurentius, F., *Vijftig historische riemkappen* (Middelburg: Laurentius, 2015).

Laurentius, Th. & Laurentius, F., *Italian watermarks 1750–1860* (Leiden: Brill, 2016).

Laurentius, Th. & Laurentius, F., *Watermarks in paper from the South-west of France, 1560–1860* (Leiden: Brill, 2018).

Laurentius, Theo, *Zeventiende-eeuwse postrijder watermerken* (Voorschoten: Laurentius, 1999).

Le Clert, Louis., *Le papier, rechers et notes pour servir à l'histoire du papier, principalement à Troyes et aux environs depuis le quatorzième siècle* (Paris: A l'Enseigne de Pegase, 1926).

León, Rafael, 'La ostentacion de San Hilario', *IPH Yearbook* 12 (1998), pp. 30–34.

Likachev, N. P., *Lickachev's watermarks* (Amsterdam: The Paper Publications Society, 1994).

Lindt, J., *The paper-mills of Berne and their watermarks* (Hilversum: The Paper Publications Society, 1964).

Marabini, Edmund, 'Die Papiermühlen im Gebiete der Weiland freien Reichstadt Nürnberg', *Bayerische Papiergeschichte*, vol. 1 (1894).

Marabini, Edmund, 'Die Papiermühlen im ehemaliger Burggrafenthum Nürnberg', *Bayerische Papiergeschichte*, vol. 2 (1896).

Marmol, F. del, *Dictionnaire des filigranes* (Paris & Namur: Marchal et Billard & Jacques Godenne, 1900).

Meder, Joseph, *Dürer catalog* (Vienna: Verlag gilhofer & Ranschburg, 1932).

Môsin, V., *Anchor watermarks* (Hilversum: The Paper Publications Society, 1973).

Nijssen, Jaak, 'Die Papiermühlen im Maastricht-Aachener Raum (ca. 1570–1640), insbesondere in Schoppen ('s-Gravenvoeren)', *IPH Yearbook* 8 (1990), pp. 96–119.

Peerlings, R., Laurentius, F., Bovenkamp, J. van den, 'The watermarks in the Rome editions of Ptolemy's Cosmography and more', *Quaerendo*, 47 (2017), pp. 307–327.

Peerlings, R., Laurentius, F., Bovenkamp, J. van den, 'New findings and discoveries in the 1507/8 Rome edition of Ptolemy's Cosmography', *Quaerendo*, 48 (2018), pp. 139–162.

Piccard, G., *Die Wasserzeichenkartei Piccard*, vol. I–XVII (Stuttgart: Verlag W. Kohlhammer, 1961–1997).

Preaud, Maxim., Cassel, P., Grivel, M., Bitouzé, C. le, *Dictionnaire des editeurs d'estampes à Paris sous l'Ancien Régime* (Paris: Promodis, Editions du Cercle de la librairie, 1987).

Preger, Max, 'Ravensburger Wasserzeichen', *Schwabischer Heimat*, heft 1 (1982), pp. 91–98.

Preger, Max, 'Barocke Wasserzeichen aus Ravensburg', *Schriften des Vereins für Geschichte des Bodensees und seiner Umgebung*, Heft 101 (1983), pp. 91–98.

Ravenshill, William, 'A curious "Saint" watermark on a Saxton atlas of c. 1590', *IPH yearbook* 10 (1994), p. 5.

Reynard, Pierre-Claude, *Histoires de papier, la papeterie Auvergnate et ses historiens* (Auvergne: Presses universitaires Blaise-Pascal, 2001).

Ribeiro, Alegre, 'La fabrication du papier au Portugal', *IPH Yearbook* 10 (1994).

Robinson, M. S., *Van de Velde drawings in the National Maritime Museum* (Cambridge: University Press, 1958).

Schlieder, Wolfgang, *Riesaufdrucke* (München: K. G. Saur, 1989).

Schmidt, Friedrich, 'Papierherstellung in Augsburg bis zum Frühindustrialisierung' in Gier, Helmut & Janota, Johannes (eds) *'Augsburger Buchdruck und Verlagswesen'* (Wiesbaden: Harrassowitz Verlag, 1997).

Stoppelaar, J. H. de, *Het papier in de Nederlanden, gedurende de Middeleeuwen, inzonderheid in Zeeland* (Middelburg: J. C. & W. Altorfer, 1869).

Talbierska, Jolanta, *Stefano della Bella* (Warsow: Neriton, 2001).

Tschudin, W. Fr., *The ancient papermills of Basle and their marks* (Hilversum: Paper Publications Society, 1958).

Tschudin, P. F., *Schweizer Papiergeschichte* (Basel: Basler Papiermühle, 1991).

Van Aken, J., 'An improvement in Grenz radiography of paper to record watermarks, chain and laid lines', *Studies in conservation*, vol. 48, 2 (2003), pp. 103–110.

Van der Coelen, P., Laurentius, Th., Pelletier, S. W., Rassieur, T., Slatkes, L. J., *Everyday life in Holland's Golden Age* (Amsterdam: Museum Het Rembrandthuis, 1998), Appendix B.

Van der Heijden, H. A. M., *Oude kaarten van Nederland*, vol. I (Alphen aan de Rijn: Canaletto, 1998), pp. 154–155.

Van Eeghen, I. H., *De Amsterdamse boekhandel 1680–1725* (Amsterdam: Scheltema & Holkema, 1978).

Van Wegens, Inge, 'The Duchy of Brabant claims its place in the European paper history', *IPH Congressbook* 11 (1996).

Valls i Subira, Oriol, *Paper and watermarks in Catalonia* (Amsterdam: Paper Publications Society, 1970).

Valls i Subira, Oriol, *La historia del papel en España* (3 vols., Madrid: Empresa nacional de celulosas SA, 1978).

Veron de la Combe, Louis de, *Contribution à l'histoire de la papeterie en France*, vol. XI (Grenoble, L'edition de l'industrie papetière, 1950).

Villeroy, Marie-Jeanne, 'Papiers et papetiers dans le Bocage sous l'Ancien Régime, première partie', *Le Pays Bas-Normand, revue trimestrielle*, nos. 1–2 (2003).

Villeroy, Marie-Jeanne, 'Papiers et papetiers dans le Bocage sous l'Ancien Régime, seconde partie', *Le Pays Bas-Normand, revue trimestrielle*, 1 (2004).

Voorn, Henk, *Rondom J. Chr. Schäfer* (Amsterdam: De Papierwereld, 1950).

Voorn, Henk, *The papermills of Denmark & Norway and their watermarks* (Hilversum: Paper Publication Society, 1959).

Voorn, Henk, *De papiermolens in de provincie Noord Holland* (Haarlem: Stichting voor het onderzoek van de geschiedenis van de Nederlandse papierindustrie, 1960).

Voorn, Henk, 'Early papermaking in Portugal', *The Papermaker*, 30 (1961).

Voorn, Henk, 'De papiermolen van Louis de Geer', *De papierwereld*, XVII, (1962).

Voorn, Henk, 'Uit de oudste geschiedenis van de Amsterdamse papierhandel', *Proost Prikkels*, 303 (1967).

Voorn, Henk, *Old Ream Wrappers* (North Hills, Pa: Bird & Bull Press, 1969).

Voorn, Henk, *De papiermolens in de provincie Zuid-Holland* (Wormerveer: Stichting voor het onderzoek van de geschiedenis van de Nederlandse papierindustrie, 1973).

Voorn, Henk, *De papiermolens in de provincie Gelderland* (Haarlem: Stichting voor het onderzoek van de geschiedenis van de Nederlandse papierindustrie, 1985).

Weiss, Wisso, 'Papier und Wasserzeichen zu Heine-Autographen', *Heine Jahrbuch* (1972).

Woodward, David, *Catalogue of watermarks in Italian printed maps, c. 1540–1600* (Chicago: University of Chicago press, 1996).

Table of Watermarks

No./Type	Date	Found in	Place of production	Papermaker	References
Anchor					
1	c.1572–1580	Map of Flandriae by Antonio Lafreri, Duchetti edition.	Italy, Venice area		Woodward 157, Tooley 553, Mosin 346–434
2	c.1600–1620	Etching by Isaac Maior (ca. 1576–1630).	Italy, Venice area		Woodward 177, Mosin 1983 Type IV
3	c.1550–1560	Map from the "Isolario Atlas" by Benedetto Bordone, Aldine edition.	Italy, Venice area		Woodward 168
4	1621	Etching by Giuseppe de Ribeira, Bartsch 5, first state.	Italy, Fabriano?		Mosin 1262
5	c.1554	Map of "Terra Tavola" by Tramonta.	Italy, Venice area		Woodward 165, Tooley KN 002-RN-6
6	c.1535	Map of Asia from "Geographia" by Francesco Berlinghieri, second edition by Giunti.	Italy, Venice area		Mosin 642–827
7	c.1570	Engraving by Mario Cartaro (c.1540–1620), first state of II.	Italy, Venice area		Mosin 899–900
Arrow					
8	c.1558	Map of "Frisia" by Antonio Lafreri.	Central or North Italy		Woodward 188. Heawood 1929–10, Tooley 299
9	1593–1598	Map of Zeeland from "Theatrum Orbis terrarum" by Abraham Ortelius, 8th state, 1st text.	France, Troyes area		
10	1588	Map of Zeeland from "Theatrum Orbis terrarum" by Abraham Ortelius, Spanish edition.	France, Troyes area		
11	1578	Map of Germania Interior from "Speculum orbis Terrarum" by Gerard de Jode.	France, Vannes/Troyes	Jehan Gouault	Gaudriault p. 128, Briquet 6283
12	1578	Map of Holland from "Speculum orbis Terrarum" by Gerard de Jode.	France, Vannes/Troyes	Jehan Gouault	Gaudriault p. 128, Briquet 6283
13	1579	Map of Zeeland from "Theatrum Orbis terrarum" by Abraham Ortelius, 6th state, 3rd text, 4th lettering.	France, Vannes/Troyes	Jehan Gouault	Gaudriault p. 128, Briquet 6283
14	1579	Map of Zeeland from "Theatrum Orbis terrarum" by Abraham Ortelius, before the atlas edition.	France, Vannes/Troyes	Jehan Gouault?	Gaudriault p. 128, Briquet 6283

No./Type	Date	Found in	Place of production	Papermaker	References
15	1593	Map of Zeeland from "Theatrum Orbis terrarum" by Abraham Ortelius, 7th state, 4th text, first lettering.	France, Vannes/Troyes	Jehan Gouault	Gaudriault p. 128, Briquet 6283
16	c.1593–1603	Map of Zeeland from "Theatrum Orbis terrarum" by Abraham Ortelius, 8th state, 4th text.	France, Vannes/Troyes	Jehan Gouault?	Gaudriault p. 128, Briquet 6283
17	1574	Map of Zeeland from "Theatrum Orbis terrarum" by Abraham Ortelius, 5th state, 3rd text.	France, Vannes/Troyes	Jehan Gouault?	Gaudriault 600, Briquet 6283
18	1574	Map of Zeeland from "Theatrum Orbis terrarum" by Abraham Ortelius, 5th state, 3rd text.	France, Vannes/Troyes	Jehan Gouault?	Gaudriault 600, Briquet 6283
19	1573	Map of Zeeland from "Theatrum Orbis terrarum" by Abraham Ortelius, 4th state.	France, Vannes/Troyes	Jehan Gouault?	Gaudriault 600, Briquet 6283
20	1571	Map of Zeeland from "Theatrum Orbis terrarum" by Abraham Ortelius, 2nd state, first text.	France, Vannes/Troyes	Jehan Gouault?	Gaudriault 600, Briquet 6283

Atlas

No./Type	Date	Found in	Place of production	Papermaker	References
21	1662	Map of the Seven Provinces from the "Atlas Maior" by Joan Blaeu.	France, Limousin, Moulin Jouriaud, St. Junien	Leonard Teillet for the facteur Pieter Haeck.	Heawood 1362–1363.

Balloon

No./Type	Date	Found in	Place of production	Papermaker	References
22	1795–1820	Letter.	Germany, Baden, Niefern	Jacob Friedrich Hornbacher	

Basilisk

No./Type	Date	Found in	Place of production	Papermaker	References
23	ca. 1610	Engraving by Joannes de Jongh (ca. 1640–1684), Hollstein 3.	Switzerland, Basel	Düring	Tschudin 1958 no. 311, Laurentius 2007 no. 30, Heitz no. 175

Bell

No./Type	Date	Found in	Place of production	Papermaker	References
24	c.1535–1540	Map of China from "Geographia" by Cladius Ptolemy published by Lorenz Fries, edition by Trechsel.	France, Beaujolais area		Audin 1936, pp. 47, 78–79

Bend

No./Type	Date	Found in	Place of production	Papermaker	References
25	1651	Map of Sas van Gent from "Frederick Hendrick van Nassau" by Isaac Commelin.	The Netherlands, Veluwe area		Heawood 128, Gaudriault 205

TABLE OF WATERMARKS

No./Type	Date	Found in	Place of production	Papermaker	References
26	1654	Map of Doesburg from "XIV boeken der Gelderssse geschiedenissen" by Arend van Slichtenhorst.	The Netherlands, Veluwe area	LC	Heawood 128, Gaudriault 205
27	1611	Map of Amsterdam from "Rerum et urbis Amstelodamensium historia" by Johannes Pontanus.	Germany, Lörrach	Bartlin Blum	Tschudin 1958 p. 31, Laurentius 2007 no. 69
28	c.1600–1620	Map of Le Mans from "Le theatre Francoys" by Maurice Bougereau, Le Clerc edition.	France, Strasbourg area?		Laurentius 2007 no. 74
29	1705–1739	Map of the world from the "Atlas Historique" by Henry Abraham Chatelain.	France, Angoumois, La Couronne, Moulin de la Courade?	Michel Carroy?	
30	1635	Map "Obsidio et expugnatio Sylvae Ducis" by E. van Meteren.	The Netherlands, Veluwe area?	R	
Bird					
31	1782	Document from Portugal.	Italy	Francesco Polleri	Heawood nos. 3476 & 827
32	c.1800	Document from Portugal.	Italy, Marche/Umbria region		Heawood nos. 167 & 168, Laurentius 2016 no. 57
33	1612	Map of Utrecht from "Beschryvinghe van alle de Nederlanden" by Lodovico Guiccardini, edition published by Janssonius.			
Chaplet					
34	1689	Map of the Indian Ocean from "Voyages" by Jean de Thevenot.	France, Auvergne, Barot (Ambert), La Vigue, La Frédrière	Jeanne Dupuy, widow of Benoit Colombier	Heawood nos. 226–227
35	1687	Map of "Royaume de Siam" by Vincenzo Coronelli & J. B. Nolin.	France, Auvergne, Riom, Grande Rive	Thomas Dupuy I	Heawood nos. 234, 238–241, Gaudriault 4319
36	1681–1712	Map of "Pays-Bas" from "Atlas Nouveau" by Alexis Hubert Jaillot.	France, Auvergne, Riom, Grande Rive	Thomas Dupuy I	Gaudriault p. 129
37	1743	Map of Gand, Bruges and Flanders published by Etienne Louis Crépy.	France, Auvergne, Riom, Grande Rive	Thomas Dupuy II	Heawood no. 241, Gaudriault p. 203
38	1747	Map of "La Zelande" from "Atlas général … Europe" by George Louis le Rouge.	France, Auverge, Riom, Grande Rive	Thomas Dupuy II	Heawood no. 238, Gaudriault no. 300
39	1787	Map of "Luxembourg" by Nolin, edition by Mondhare & Jean.	France, Auvergne, Riom	Amable Vimal	Gaudriault p. 278

No./Type	Date	Found in	Place of production	Papermaker	References
40	1705	Map of "L'Europe" by Nicolas de Fer.	France, Limoges?	F. L. (Laroche?)	Gaudriault pp. 230–231
41	1705	Map of "Comte de Flandre" by Nicolas de Fer.	France, Limoges/Angoumois	Leonard Laroche	Heawood nos. 1699 & 2958, Gaudriault no. 4201, p. 231
42	1780	Map of "Turquie" by Jean Claude Dezauché.			
Circles					
43	1703	Document from Portugal.	Italy, Genua area		Nicolai II pl. CXXXIII, no. 3
44	c.1670–1710	Document from Portugal.	Italy, Genua area		
45	c.1670–1710	Document from Portugal.	Italy, Genua area		De Ataide de Melo 1926 no. 141, Laurentius 2008 nos. 32–36
46	c.1660–1680	Document from Portugal.	Italy, Genua area		Heawood no. 735, Laurentius 2008 nos. 32, 33, 36
47	1695	Document from Portugal.	Italy, Genua area		Heawood nos. 724–731?
48	Before 1693	Document from Portugal.	Italy, Genua area		Laurentius 2008 nos. 33–36
49	c.1660–1675	Document from Portugal.	Italy, Genua area		Laurentius 2008 nos. 33–36
50	c.1660–1700	Document from Portugal.	Italy, Genua area		Nicolai II pl. CXXXIII, no. 3, Laurentius 2008 no. 35
51	c.1660–1665	Document from Portugal.	Italy, Genua area		Laurentius 2008 no. 35
52	c.1660–1665	Document from Portugal.	Italy, Genua area		Laurentius 2008 no. 35
53	c.1650–1700	Document from Portugal.	Italy, Genua area		Nicolai II pl. CXXXIII, no. 3
54	c.1650–1670	Document from Portugal.	Italy, Genua area		De Ataide de Melo 1926 no. 129, Laurentius 2008 nos. 27–31
55	1667	Document from Portugal.	Italy, Genua area		Laurentius 2007 no. 91
56	c.1650–1670	Document from Portugal.	Italy, Genua area		De Ataide de Melo 1926 no. 129, Laurentius 2008 nos. 28–31
57	1668	Document from Portugal.	Italy, Genua area	G. D. M.	Heawood nos. 261–262
58	c.1650–1690	Document from Portugal.	Italy, Genua area	A. P.	Heawood nos. 265, 266, 268
59	c.1720–1725	Document from Portugal.	Italy, Genua area	G. B. D.	Heawood no. 280
60	1652	Document from Portugal.	Italy, Genua area	G. B. D.	
61	c.1660–1675	Document from Portugal.	Italy, Genua area	G. C.	Laurentius 2008 nos. 5–9
62	c.1660–1675	Document from Portugal.	Italy, Genua area	G. C.	Heawood no. 300
63	c.1670	Document from Portugal.	Italy, Genua area		Heawood no. 267
64	c.1670	Document from Portugal.	Italy, Genua area		Del Marmol p. 92, Heawood no. 267
65	1668	Document from Portugal.	Italy, Genua area	E. P.	De Ataide de Melo 1926 no. 135, Heawood nos. 818, 821, 822, Laurentius 2008 no. 38
66	1695	Album dated 1695.			
67	c.1600	Map of "Belgii Inferioris" published by Matteo Florimi.	Italy, northern part	G. A.	Woodward nos. 301, 307
Coat of Arms					
68	1716	Printed document from Groningen.	France, Angoumois?		Laurentius 2008 no. 165
69	c.1690–1700	Anonymous engraving from Augsburg.	Germany?		

TABLE OF WATERMARKS

No./Type	Date	Found in	Place of production	Papermaker	References
70	1683–1709	Map of France, published by Daniel de Feuille.	The Netherlands, Zaan area	Cornelis Simonsz. Huysduynen	Laurentius 2008 nos. 150, 152, 153
71	c.1685–1696	Blank sheet.	France, Normandy	P. Hays	Heawood nos. 380 & 647
72	c.1750	Blank sheet.	France, Limousin/Angoumois	R. Galiard	Gaudriault p. 211
73	1678	Map of Delfland by Floris Balthasar van Berckenrode, fourth edition.	France, Limousin/Angoumois, Moulin Pisseloube	Pierre Dexmier?	Laurentius 2008 no. 181
74	1722–1730	Handvesten van Amsterdam, published by Johannes van Septeren.	France, Angoumois	P. M.	
75	1730–1745	Optica print, published by Balthasar Probst in Augsburg.	Germany, Augsburg area		Heawood nos. 569–547
76	1625	Map of Amsterdam from "Beschryvinghe van alle de Nederlanden" by Lodovico Guiccardini, edition published by Janssonius.	Germany, Maulburg	Hans Blum?	Delâge p. 229, no. 2, Heawood no. 568, Laurentius 2007 no. 121, Voorn 1960 no. 16
77	1599–1638	Map of Holland, published by Willem Jansz. Blaeu.	France, Alsace, Montbéliard area		
78	c.1670–1675	Etching by Abraham Bosse, published in Paris.	France, Auvergne, Thiers area		Gaudriault no. 1035
79	c.1645–1650	Etching by Jean Morin, published in Paris.	France, Auvergne, Thiers area		Gaudriault no. 84, Mazel 2004 pp. 357–359
80	c.1584	Map of "Germania Inferior" from "Theatrum Orbis terrarum" by Abraham Ortelius, 6th state.	France, Troyes, Foudry	Claude Denise III	Le Clert p. 304, vol. II pl. XXX
81	1584	Map from the Additamentum III atlas by Abraham Ortelius.	France, Troyes, Foudry	Edmond & Claude Denise	Le Clert, vol. II pl. XXX
82	1584	Map of Zeeland from "Theatrum Orbis terrarum" by Abraham Ortelius, 6th state, 3rd text.	France, Troyes, Foudry	Edmond & Claude Denise	Le Clert, vol. II pl. XXX
83	1584	Map of Zeeland from "Theatrum Orbis terrarum" by Abraham Ortelius, 6th state.	France, Troyes, Foudry	Edmond & Claude Denise	Le Clert, vol. II pl. XXX
84	c.1695–1700	Blank sheet.	France, Normandy, Sourdeval	P. L.	Del Marmol nos. 39–40, Laurentius 2013, p. 13
85	c.1645–1655	Etching by Herman van Swanevelt, first state.	France, Normandy		Detersannes pp. 106–107
86	c.1630–1655	Map of Touraine, published by Jacques Honervogt I in Paris.	France, Auvergne or Normandy		Heawood no. 651
87	1677	Illustration to "A genealogical History" by Richard Gaywood, published in London.	France, Normandy	P. Mauduit	Heawood nos. 667, 668, 680

No./Type	Date	Found in	Place of production	Papermaker	References
88	After 1644	Map of France by Melchior Tavernier, edition by Pierre Mariette?	France, Auvergne, Riom	Benoit Colombier	Gaudriault no. 4028, Heawood no. 673
89	1655–1691	Map of the Betuwe-Veluwe, published by Pierre Mariette II in Paris.	France, Auvergne, Ambert area	Benoit Colombier	Gaudriault no. 4028, Heawood no. 673
90	1578	Map of Zeeland from "Speculum orbis Terrarum" by Gerard de Jode, published in Antwerp.	France, Troyes, Vannes	Jean Gouault	Le Clert p. 330, no. 131
91	c.1559	Blank sheet.	Germany, Kaufbeuren		Heawood no. 509, Meder no. 217
92	1550–1570	Map of North America by Caspar Vopelius, published in Cologne.	Germany, Kaufbeuren		Briquet no. 914 & 915
93	1550–1570	Map of the world, halfcircular, published in Augsburg.	Germany, Kaufbeuren		Briquet no. 914 & 915
94	1769	Etching by C. G. Ehrlich.	Germany, Saxony, Wittenberg	P. G. (Vernau family)	Doss & Schlieder p. 156, Tafel VI, no. 23
95	c.1750	Map of Vera Cruz, published by Isaac Tirion in Amsterdam.	France, Auvergne	Thomas Dupuy?	Heawood no. 720
96	1595	Titlepage to the atlas by Abraham Ortelius.	Belgium/Germany, 's-Gravenvoeren, Schoppener Mühle	Jacob von Lintzenich	Nijssen p. 96
97	1603	Map of "Frisia" by Claudio Duchetti, Orlandi edition.	Italy		Woodward no. 45
98	c.1780	Map of "Pomeraniae", published by the heirs of J. B. Homann in Nurnberg.	Germany, Wolfeg, Altorf-Karbach, Hegau	Josef Anton Unold	Heawood 3134
99	1678	Map of the Lower Rhine, published by Bouttats in Antwerp.	Belgium, Diegem or France, Franche Comté	G. D.	Laurentius 2008 no. 701
100	c.1780	Map of Italy, published by the heirs of J. B. Homann in Nurnberg.	Germany, Wolfeg, Altorf-Karbach, Hegau	Josef Anton Unold	Heawood 3134
101	c.1660–1695	Document from France.	France		
102	1773	Document from Portugal.	The Netherlands, Veluwe area	F. P. ordered by the papermerchants Sebille & Wend	Churchill no. 201, Nicolai vol. II, pl. XXII, Voorn 1985 p. 162
103	1681	Map of "Hollande" By Alexis Hubert Jaillot in Paris.	France, Auvergne, Riom or Thiers	G. C.	Heawood nos. 684–686
104	1689	Map of China from "Voyages" by Jean de Thevenot.	France, Auvergne, Riom or Thiers	Philippe Cusson?	Gaudriault p. 92, no. 165, Heawood nos. 684–686
105	1679	Map of "Indes orientales" from the "Cartes de geographie ... fideles" published by Pierre Duval in Paris.	France, Auvergne	Philippe Cusson?	Gaudriault p. 92, no. 165, Heawood nos. 684–686

No./Type	Date	Found in	Place of production	Papermaker	References
106	c.1780–1820	Blank sheet.	France, eastern part		Gaudriault no. 512, Janot no. 356
107	1795	Document from Portugal.	Italy	Giusti	See no. 3 of this catalogue
108	1773	Document from Portugal.	Italy, Tuscany, Colle		Heawood no. 3289
109	1580	Map of "Germania" from "Tabulae Geographicae" by Gerard Mercator.	France, Montbéliard area		Heawood no. 598
110	1580	Map of Zeeland from "Theatrum Orbis terrarum" by Abraham Ortelius, 5th state, German text.	France, Montbéliard area		Heawood no. 598, Briquet 2103
111	c.1760	Blank sheet	Italy or Portugal?		
112	1775	Document from Portugal.	Portugal	A. M. A.	De Ataide de Melo no. 154
113	c.1800	Document from Portugal.	Portugal	Raiva Aragna	
114	1785	Document from Portugal.	Portugal	A. M. C.	Heawood 3742
115	1755	Document from Portugal.	Portugal		De Ataide de Melo nos.?, Churchill no. 260, Voorn 1961 no. ?
116	c.1750	Blank sheet.	Portugal, Coïmbra	M. A. M.	De Ataide de Melo nos. 161 & 173, Bandera 1998 p. 137, no. 12
117	c.1750	Blank sheet.	Portugal, Coïmbra?	Italian papermaker?	De Ataide de Melo nos. 173 & 179
118	c.1750	Blank sheet.	Portugal, Coïmbra?	Italian papermaker?	De Ataide de Melo nos. 173 & 179
119	c.1745	Blank sheet.	Italy, Genua-Bologna area		Valls i Subira vol. II, p. 48, nos. 14 & 15
120	c.1750	Document from Portugal.	Portugal, Louzâ	C. A.	Del Marmol p. 65, Heawood no. 1872
121	1623–1627	Map "Generale Pascaert Schipvaert" from "Zeespiegel van de Westersche schipvaert", published by Willem Jansz, Blaeu in Amsterdam.	France, Vosges		Heawood nos. 531–536, Janot no. 197
122	1623–1627	Map "Pascaert van de Noordzee" from "Zeespiegel van de Westersche schipvaert", published by Willem Jansz, Blaeu in Amsterdam.	France, Vosges		Heawood nos. 531–536, Janot no. 197
123	1612	Map of "Belgica" from "Beschryvinghe van alle de Nederlanden" by Lodovico Guiccardini, edition published by Janssonius.	France, Vosges, Docelles		Heawood no. 528, Janot no. 197

No./Type	Date	Found in	Place of production	Papermaker	References
124	1612	Map of "Bommel" from "Beschryvinghe van alle de Nederlanden" by Lodovico Guiccardini, edition published by Janssonius.	France, Vosges, Docelles		Heawood no. 528, Janot no. 197
125	1601	Map to "Von Gelegenheit ... Neue Welt" by Jan Huigen van Linschoten, published by Theodor de Bry.	France, Haute Saône		Briquet no. 5012, Heawood nos. 524 & 528
126	1613	Map of the XVII Provinces from "Beschryvinghe van alle de Nederlanden" by Lodovico Guiccardini.	France, Haute Saône, Moulinde Magny-les-Lure	Pierre Pinette	Gaudriault no. 781
127	c.1609	Map of Lier from "Beschryvinghe van alle de Nederlanden" by Lodovico Guiccardini.	France, Vosges, Epinal area	Düring?	Janot nos. 72 & 197
128	1784	Map of "L. Empire de Chine" from "Atlas Universel" by Pietro Santini, published in Venice.	Italy, Pordenone	Valentino Galvani	Heawood nos. 687, 819, 823, 824
129	c.1581	Map of Zeeland from "Theatrum Orbis terrarum" by Abraham Ortelius, 5th state, French text.	Italy?		
130	c.1615	Engraving by Theodor Holtmann, published in Cologne.	Germany, NordRhein Westphalen, Witten/Strünkede		Witten no. 32
131	c.1609	Map of Salzburg by Abraham Ortelius.	France, Vosges, Chenimenil, Moulin de l'Isle	Demange Aubert	Janot no. 138
132	1609–1612	Map of Zeeland by Abraham Ortelius, 9th state, Spanish text.	France, Vosges, Chenimenil, Moulin de l'Isle	Demange Aubert	Janot no. 138
133	1750	Document from Portugal.	Italy, Tuscany, Vorno	S. P.	De Ataide e Melo no. 174, Heawood no. 826
134	c.1750	Document from Portugal.	Italy, Tuscany, Vorno	A. P. (Antonio Polleri?)	De Ataide e Melo no. 174, Heawood no. 826
135	1755	Document from Portugal.	Italy, Tuscany, Vorno?	H. G.	Heawood nos. 825 & 826
136	c.1750	Document from Portugal.	Italy, Tuscany, Vorno		De Ataide e Melo no. 174, Heawood no. 826
137	c.1750	Document from Portugal.	Italy, Tuscany, Vorno		De Ataide e Melo no. 174, Heawood no. 826
138	1792	Document from Portugal.	Italy, Tuscany	Giorgio Magnani	Eineder no. 1752
139	1747	Document from Portugal.	Italy, Tuscany, Vorno	C. M. T. (Thomate family?)	Bandeira no.?

TABLE OF WATERMARKS

No./Type	Date	Found in	Place of production	Papermaker	References
140	c.1610	Map of Utrecht from "Civitates Orbis Terrarum" by Georg Braun and Frans Hogenberg.	Germany, Würzburg area		Heawood no. 546, Laurentius 2007 nos. 223 & 224
141	c.1815	Drawing by Baron Isendoorn à Blois.	The Netherlands, Oldebroek, Molecaten	Willem Antoon & A. E. Staal	Voorn 1985 p. 577
142	1639	Map of "Tetrarchia Ducatus Gelriae Neomagensis" from "Historicae Gelricae" by Johannes Pontanus.			
143	1635	Map of the Netherlands from "Historie de Neder-landscher ... geschiedenissen" by Emanuel van Meteren.	France, Troyes area	Gouault family?	Heawood nos. 580–586
144	1673	Map of the XVII Provinces from "Teatro del Belgico" by Galeazzo Gualdo Priorato, published in Frankfurt am Main.	Bohemia, Komotau (Chomotow)	K. C. P.	Piccard vol. Turm, p. 322, Schlieder pp. 96 & 97
145	1673	Map of Amsterdam from "Teatro del Belgico" by Galeazzo Gualdo Priorato, published in Frankfurt am Main.	Bohemia, Komotau (Chomotow)	K. C. P.	Piccard vol. Turm, p. 322, Schlieder pp. 96 & 97
146	1693	Map of Amsterdam from "Beschrijvinge van Amsterdam" by Casparus Commelin.	Switzerland, Jura, Bascourt	A. S.	Heitz no. 111, Tschudin 1991 p. 184
147	1624–1665	Etching by Johann Wilhelm Baur, published in Augsburg.	Germany, Hirschbach near Nurnberg	Mattheus Schleger	Marabini 1894 p. 133, Heawood no. 1086
148	1598–1626	Blank sheet.	France, Alsace, Vieux Thann	Hans Strehlin?	Gaudriault no. 209
149	c.1520–1540	Engraving by an anonymous artist.	Germany, Nurnberg, probably Tullnau papermill		Marabini 1894 p. 43
150	1720	Map from "Force d'Europe" by Gabriel Bodenehr, published in Augsburg.	Germany, Augsburg area	G. K.	Heawood no. 1497
151	1789	Map of "Allemagne" published by I. W. A. Jaeger in Frankfurt.	Germany, Hessen, Grunberg		Grosse-Stoltenberg 1982 p. 199
152	1638	Engraving by Sebastien Vouillemont.	France, Auvergne, Thiers	Claude Cluzel	Gaudriault pp. 119–120, Heawood no. 799
Crescent					
153	c.1687	Map of the canal between Haarlem and Amsterdam by Vincenzo Coronelli.	Italy, Venice area.		Heawood no. 847
154	c.1595–1620	Engraving, published by Giacomo Franco in Venice.	Italy, Venice area.		Heawood no. 865

No./Type	Date	Found in	Place of production	Papermaker	References
155	1778	Map of "Archipel des Indes Orientalis" by Robert, published by Pietro Santini in Venice.	Italy, Lombardia	F. V.	Eineder no. 723
Cross					
156	1567	Map of "Belgica" from "Beschryvinghe van alle de Nederlanden" by Lodovico Guiccardini, first edition.	France, Montbéliard area		Briquet no. 5458
157	1551–1562	Engraving by Antonio Salamanca, published in Rome.	Italy		
158	c.1620	Blank sheet.	France, south-west part.		De Ataide e Melo no. 122, Heawood nos. 951–961, Valls i Subira p. 61, no. 17
159	c.1610–1620	Blank sheet.	France, south-west part.		Heawood nos. 970–972
160	c.1610–1620	Document from Portugal.	Spain		Heawood nos. 951–983
161	1608	Document from Portugal.	Italy, Genua?	A. G.	Heawood no. 962, Laurentius 2007 nos. 239–241
162	1777	Map of the Kempen and Eindhoven, part of the map of the Austrian Netherlands by Joseph de Ferraris.	Belgium, Dendermonde	Jan Stuckx & Co.	Van Lil 1985 p. 44
Crossbow					
163	1550–1560	Map of "Nova Asiae Tabula" by Buckinck, published by Antonio Lafreri in Rome.	Italy, northern part		
Crown					
164	1569	Map of Gand from "Beschryvinghe van alle de Nederlanden" by Lodovico Guiccardini, Sylvius edition.	France, Vosges, Epinal area		Briquet nos. 4973 & 4974, Janot nos. 4, 107, 108, 165, 168, 189, Piccard vol. I, no. 12
165	1565–1606	Map of "Africa" from "Navigationi et Viaggi" by Giovanni Battista Ramusio, published in Venice.	Italy, Venice area	H. C.	Heawood nos. 999 & 1000
166	1565–1606	Map of "Sumatra" from "Navigationi et Viaggi" by Giovanni Battista Ramusio, published in Venice.	Italy, Venice area	H. C.	Heawood nos. 999 & 1000
167	1635	Map of "Guinea" from "Atlas sive Cosmographicae" by Gerardus Mercator, Hondius-Spark edition, published in London.	France, Normandy	I. D. C.	Heawood no. 1017

TABLE OF WATERMARKS

No./Type	Date	Found in	Place of production	Papermaker	References
168	1672	Etching by Paulus van Somer, published in Paris.	France, Auvergne, Grande-Rive	Thomas Dupuy I	
169	1578–1600	Map of Zeeland from "Speculum orbis Terrarum" by Gerard de Jode, published in Antwerp.	France, Troyes	Edmond Denise	Detersannes p. 91, Le Clert vol. II, p. 318, no. 110
170	1578–1600	Map of Zeeland from "Speculum orbis Terrarum" by Gerard de Jode, published in Antwerp.	France, Troyes	Edmond Denise	Gaudriault no. 413
171	1578–1600	Map of "Germaniae Pars" from "Speculum orbis Terrarum" by Gerard de Jode, published in Antwerp.	France, Troyes	Edmond Denise	Gaudriault no. 413
172	1593	Map of "Holland" by Cornelis de Jode.	France, Troyes, Vannes	Edmond Denise II	Gaudriault no. 413, Le Clert no. 113
173	c.1615–1625	Map of "Germaniae Pars" by Nicolaes van Geelkercken.	France, Troyes area	Denise family?	Briquet nos. 5097 & 5098, Laurentius 2007 no. 264, Le Clert 121
174	1593	Map of Zeeland by Petrus de Jode.	France, Troyes, Vannes	Edmond Denise II	Gaudriault no. 413, Le Clert nos. 110–113
175	1593	Map of "Geldria" from "Speculum orbis Terrarum" by Gerard de Jode, published by his son in Antwerp.	France, Troyes, Vannes	Edmond Denise II	Gaudriault no. 413, Le Clert nos. 110–113
176	1596–1597	Title page to "Typus totius Orbis terrarum" by Jodocus Hondius Sr.	France, Troyes, Vannes	Edmond Denise II	Gaudriault no. 413, Le Clert nos. 110–113
Crozier					
177	1544	Map of Transsylvania from "Cosmographia" by Sebastian Münster.	Switzerland, Basel, Albanstal	Wittwe Gernley	Briquet no. 1276, Heitz nos. 2–10, Tschudin 1991 p. 177
178	c.1585	Map of "Bolonia Guines Comitatus" from "Tabulae Geographicae" by Gerardus Mercator.	Germany, Hochberg	Heusler	Briquet no. 1292, Tschudin no. 128
179	1572–1617	Map of "Blitti" from "Civitates Orbis Terrarum" by Georg Braun and Frans Hogenberg, Latin edition.	Switzerland, Basel		
180	1623–1627	Map "Pascaert van de Vliestroom" from "Zeespiegel van de Westersche schipvaert", published by Willem Jansz, Blaeu in Amsterdam.	France, Vosges, Strasbourg area		

No./Type	Date	Found in	Place of production	Papermaker	References
181	1630	Map of America from "Beschrijvinghe van West-Indien" by Johannes de Laet.	Switzerland, Basel	Heusler	Heawood no. 1201, Tschudin 220
182	1656	Map of "Polonia" by Gaspar Bouttats.	Germany, Rothenbach near Nurnberg	Hans Conrad Stainitz?	Heawood no. 1090 & 3781, Marabini 1894 pp. 51 & 120
Date					
183	1808	Map of Zeeland, published by John Stockdale in London.	England		
Dovecot					
184	1693	Map of "Le Comté de Zeelande" from "Atlas Nouveau" by Alexis Hubert Jaillot.	France, Auvergne, Riom	Pierre Gourbeyre?	Gaudriault nos. 4262–4262, Heawood nos. 223 & 1227
185	1757	Map of "Pays-Bas" from "Atlas Universel" by Robert de Vaugondy, published in Paris.	France, Auvergne, Riom, Grand-Rive	Thomas Dupuy II	Heawood nos. 2404 & 2952
Eagle					
186	1582	Map of Rouen from "Civitates Orbis Terrarum" by Georg Braun and Frans Hogenberg, French edition.	Germany, Aachen, Burtscheid, Holsiter Mühle	Dietrich von Haeren?	Briquet no. 200, Heawood no. 560, Nijssen p. 96
187	1579	Map of "Namurcum" from the Additamentum I atlas by Abraham Ortelius.	Germany, Aachen, Burtscheid, Holsiter Mühle	Dietrich von Haeren?	Briquet no. 200, Heawood no. 560, Nijssen p. 96
188	1585	Map of "Westfaliae" from "Tabulae Geographicae" by Gerardus Mercator.	Germany, Aachen, Burtscheid, Holsiter Mühle	Dietrich von Haeren?	Briquet no. 200, Heawood no. 560, Nijssen p. 96
189	1579	Map of Zeeland from "Theatrum Orbis terrarum" by Abraham Ortelius, 5th state.	Germany, Aachen, Burtscheid, Holsiter Mühle	Dietrich von Haeren?	Briquet no. 200, Heawood no. 560, Nijssen p. 96
190	1635	Map of "Coevorden" from "Historie de Neder-landscher … geschiedenissen" by Emanuel van Meteren.	France, Strasbourg area	Nicolas Dürckheim	Laurentius 2007 no. 363
191	1612	Title page to "Beschryvinghe van alle de Nederlanden" by Lodovico Guiccardini.	France, Vosges, Cernay (Thann), Moulin de Bas	Nicolas Dürckheim	Gaudriault p. 273, Laurentius 2007 nos. 365 & 366
192	1612	Engraving by Pieter Bast, from "Beschryvinghe van alle de Nederlanden" by Lodovico Guiccardini.	France, Vosges, Cernay (Thann), Moulin de Bas	Nicolas Dürckheim	Gaudriault p. 273, Laurentius 2007 nos. 365 & 366
193	1711	Illustration to "Reizen naar Moscovius" by Cornelis de Bruyn, published in Amsterdam.	Germany, Nurnberg area, Wendelstein an der Schwarzach	Sixtus Meier	Marabini 1894 p. 43

No./Type	Date	Found in	Place of production	Papermaker	References
194	1572	Map of "Holland" from "L'isole piu famose del mondo" by Tomaso Porcacchi.	Italy		Briquet no. 209, Woodward nos. 54–58
195	1617	Map of "Holland" from "Germania Inferior id est XVII provincuarum" by Petrus Kaerius.			Heawood no. 1283
196	1596	Map of China from "Itinerario" by Jan Huygen van Linschoten.	France, Vosges		
197	1585	Map of "Frisia occ." from "Tabulae Geographicae" by Gerardus Mercator.	France, Vosges, Epinal area		Briquet no. 304
198	1583	Map of France from "Civitates Orbis Terrarum" by Georg Braun and Frans Hogenberg.	France, Vosges, Epinal area		Briquet nos. 252–254
199	c.1630	Map of Gelderland by Pieter Goos, published in Amsterdam.	Germany, southern part	H. S.	
200	c.1700–1725	Etching by Elias Baeck, published in Augsburg.	Germany, Augsburg area		
201	c.1630	Map of Brabant by Pieter Goos, published in Amsterdam.	Germany, Southern part	H. T.	
202	1693 a+b	Map of the Meuse and Scheldt rivers by Claude Auguste Berey, published in Paris.	France, Auverge, Lyon, Riom or Saches.	Benôit Colombier	Gaudriault no. 29, Heawood no. 1323
203	1693	Map of the Meuse and Scheldt rivers by from "Neptune Francois" published by Pieter Mortier in Amsterdam.	France, Auverge, Riom, Moulins La Vigne, La Fredière or Barot.	Jeanne Dupuy, widow of Benoit Colombier.	Gaudriault no. 29, Heawood no. 1323
204	1794	Map of "Scheldeloop" by Charles Francois Beautemps Baupré.	France, Auvergne, Riom, Grand-Rive	The heirs of Thomas Dupuy.	Heawood no. 1317
205	c.1666	Map of Louvain from "Beschryvinghe van alle de Nederlanden" by Lodovico Guiccardini.	Germany, Nurnberg area, Amthof, Bayreuth	Johann Gipfer	Heawood no. 1292

Elephant

No./Type	Date	Found in	Place of production	Papermaker	References
206	c.1660	Map of "Europiae" by Jacob Sandrart, published in Nurnberg.	Germany, Neurenberg area		
207	c.1695	Map of "Regidania", published by David Funck in Nurnberg.	Germany, Neurenberg area		
208	1655–1660	Map of "Comitatus Hollandia" published by Frederik de Wit in Amsterdam.			

No./Type	Date	Found in	Place of production	Papermaker	References
209	1662	Map of "Zuid Beveland & Schouwen" published by Willem Jansz. Blaeu in his Maior atlas.	France, Limousin, Limoges, Moulin de Marchais	Jean Bardet	Churchill no. 186, Gaudriault no. 562, Heawood no. 1331
210	1662	Map of "America", published by Willem Jansz. Blaeu in his Maior atlas.	France, Limousin, Limoges, Moulin de Marchais		Churchill no. 186, Gaudriault no. 562, Heawood no. 1331
211	1784–1793	Map of "Novae Persiae" published by Reinier Ottens in Amsterdam.	The Netherlands, West-Zaandam, Mill De Walvis (Whale)	Adriaan Rogge	Heawood no. 1333, Voorn 1960 no. 192
212	c.1780	Map of "Holland", anonymously published in France.			
Figure					
213	1558	Map of "Geldriae Cliviae" by Jacob Bos, published by Michele Tramezzino in Venice.	Italy		Woodward no. 24, Tooley no. 232
214	c.1550	Engraving by anonymous engraver.	Italy, Fabriano?		Briquet no. 7628, Heawood no. 1352
215	1609	Engraving by Marco Sadeler, published in Venice.	Italy, Fabriano?		Briquet no. 7628, Heawood no. 1348, Leon pp. 30–34, Woodward no. 25.
216	1662	Flyleaf to "De Vyerighe colom", published by Arnold Colom in Amsterdam.	Portugal?		Heawood no. 1343
217	1568	Map of "La vera descrittione della Gallia Belgica" by Paolo Forlani in Venice.	Italy		Woodward no. 6
218	1663–1692	Etching by Bernhard Zaech from Augsburg.	Germany, Kempten, Au	"Hildegard"	Van Hössle p. 22
219	c.1720–1740	Blank sheet.	Belgium, Brussels?	Bauwens?	Del Marmol p. 114
Fish					
220	1597	Map of "Asian Regnum" from "Descriptiones Ptolemaicae Augmentum" by Cornelis van Wytvliet, published in Louvain.	France		
Fleur de Lis					
221	c.1659	Etching by Wenceslaus Hollar, published in London.	France, Brittany		Globe p. 191, no. 3
222	c.1690–1730	Map of Amsterdam from "Topographia", published by the Merian family.	Switzerland, Bassecourt		Lindt nos. 769 & 770
223	1598	Map of "Persia" from "Itinerarium Orbis Christiani" by Johannes Metellus.	France, Alsace/Vosges, Strasbourg?		Briquet nos. 7093–7096

TABLE OF WATERMARKS

No./Type	Date	Found in	Place of production	Papermaker	References
224	1513	Map of Northern Africa from "Geographia opus novissima ... pressum" by Martin Waldseemuller, published in Strasbourg.	Italy?		Piccard vol. XII, nos. 96–98
225	1617	Map of Cambrai from "Beschryvinghe van alle de Nederlanden" by Lodovico Guiccardini.	France		Heawood nos. 1405 & 1406
226	1613	Map of Zuid Holland from "Tabularum Geographicarum" by Petrus Bertius, edition of 1613.	France, Alsace/Vosges, Strasbourg?	Nicolas Dürkheim	Laurentius 2007 nos. 74 & 75, Piccard XII, nos. 865–870
227	1608	Document from Portugal.	France, south western part		Nicolaï CXLVI, no. 9
228	1601	Document from Portugal.	France, Gironde		Heawood no. 3826, Nicolaï CXXIII, no. ?
229	1588	Document from Portugal.	France, Gascogne		Briquet no. 7182
230	c.1750	Document from Portugal.	Italy?		De Ataide e Melo no. 173
231	c.1750	Document from Portugal.	Portugal, Louza?	Italian maker in Portugal?	De Ataide e Melo no. 155, Heawood no. 1872
232	c.1750	Blank sheet.	Italy, Tuscany?		De Ataide e Melo no. 173
233	1755	Document from Portugal.	Portugal	Italian maker in Portugal?	De Ataide e Melo no. 173, Heawood nos. 1878–1881
234	c.1750	Blank sheet.	Portugal	Italian maker in Portugal?	De Ataide e Melo no. 173, Heawood nos. 1878–1881
235	1675	Map of "Comté de Flandre" by Pierre Du Val, published in Paris.	France, Auvergne		
236	1728	Etching by Jacopo Vezzani.	Italy, Amalfi?	G. Prota?	
237	c.1750	Document from Portugal.	Portugal, Alenquer Mill?	Italian maker in Portugal?	De Ataide e Melo nos. 172, 174, 177, Voorn 1961 no. 2
238	1745–1755	Document from Portugal.	Portugal, Coïmbra, Louza	Italian maker in Portugal?	De Ataide e Melo no. 155, Heawood no. 1872
239	1639	Map of "Arnhemensis Ducatis Gelriae" from "Historicae Gelricae" by Johannes Pontanus.	France, Alsace/Vosges, Strasbourg-area		
240	1770	Document from Portugal.	Italy, Tuscany?		De Ataide e Melo nos. 164, 173, Heawood 3169
241	1783	Map of "Het Westelijk Ye", published in Amsterdam.	France, Angoumois	B. Brun	Churchill no. 542, Gaudriault p. 181, Heawood no. 3169

No./Type	Date	Found in	Place of production	Papermaker	References
242	c.1745	Blank sheet.	Italy, Genua-Bologna area		Valls i Subira vol. III, p. 48, nos. 14 & 15
243	1676	Map of "The kingdom of China" from "Prospect of … world" by John Speed, second edition.	France, Brittany, Vannes	Michel le Jeune	Gaudriault p. 234, Heawood nos. 1506, 1514, 1682
244	c.1630	Map of "Flandria" by David Custos (Custodis), published in Augsburg.	Germany, Southern part, Upper Rhine area		Piccard vol. ?, no. 239
245	1785 a + b	Drawing by an anonymous master.	France, Auvergne, Riom, St. Victor, Chamelières	Blaise Serve	Gaudriault p. 268
246	c.1550–1570	Blank sheet.	Italy, Amalfi	G. C.	Heawood nos. 1566–1570, Piccard nos. 890–913.
247	c.1600–1620	Engraving by an anonymous engraver from Italy.	Italy, Northern part		Heawood no. 1608
248	c.1750	Blank sheet.	Italy, central part		Heawood nos. 1593–1603
249	c.1750	Blank sheet.	Italy, Marche/Umbria area?		Heawood nos. 1596, 1598–1603
250	1652	Etching by Adriaen van Ostade, early state.	France, South western part		Godefroy no. 10, Laurentius 2008 nos. 309–319, Vander Coelen pp. 73 & 83
251	1652	Etching by Adriaen van Ostade, final state.	France, South western part		Godefroy no. 10, Laurentius 2008 nos. 309–319, Vander Coelen pp. 73 & 83
252	1658	Map of Zeeland from the "Atlas Maior" by Johannes Janssonius.	France, Alsace/Vosges, Strasbourg area		Heawood no. 1728
253	c.1730	Blank sheet.	France		Churchill no. 388, Heawood no. 1654
254	1726	Map of Amsterdam "Beschrijvinge van Amsterdam" by Casparus Commelin.	France, Angoumois	Peille?	
255	1648	Title page to "Afbeeldsels der voornaemste gebouwen" by Philip Vingboons, published by Blaeu in Amsterdam.	France, Limousin		Heawood no. 1746
256	1658	Engraving by Robert Nanteuil, first state of two.	France, Auvergne	E. G.	Heawood no. 1726, 1791, 1800
257	1654	Map of "Ducatus Geldriae et comitatus … descriptio" from "XIV boeken der Gelderssse geschiedenissen" by Arend van Slichtenhorst.	The Netherlands, Veluwe?		Heawood no. 1778

TABLE OF WATERMARKS

No./Type	Date	Found in	Place of production	Papermaker	References
258	c.1650	Blank sheet.	France, Angoumoumois/Limousin/Périgord		Laurentius 2008 no. 356
259	c.1675	Blank sheet.	France, Agoumois/Limousin/Périgord		Laurentius 2008 no. 340
260	1613	Map of "Germania Inferior" from "Tabularum Geographicarum" by Petrus Bertius, edition of 1613.	France, Alsace, Cernay (Thann)	Nicolas Dürkheim	Gaudriault pp. 147 & 319, Heawood no. 3767, Heitz no. 306
261	1643	Engraving by Crispyn de Passe.	France, Limousin?	R	Heawood no. 1777
262	c.1755	Map of Noord- en Zuid Beveland", published by Isaac Tirion in Amsterdam.	The Netherlands, Zaandijk, De Bonsem/De Wever/Het Fortuin mills		Heawood nos. 1833 & 1838
263	1625	Map of "XVII Provinciën" from "Beschryvinghe van alle de Nederlanden" by Lodovico Guiccardini, Janssonius edition.	France, Strasbourg area		
264	c.1650	Map of the Holy Land by Herman van Borculo, later 17th century edition.	France, Angoumois		Gaudriault no. 659. Heawood no. 1717, Laurentius 2008 no. 321
265	1684	Etching by Willem de Ryck.	France, Angoumois, Angoulème	Daniel Juilhard for the merchants Ysbrand & Levinus Vincent	Gaudriault p. 226, Laurentius 2008 nos. 755 & 756
266	1812	Map of Australia, published in Germany.	Germany, Ober Langenau	Anton Kiesling	Papiergeschichte VII, p. 12
267	c.1740	Map of the Saldanha Bay, manuscript V.O.C. map.	The Netherlands, Koog aan de Zaan	Lubbert van Gerrevink	Heawood no. 1829
268	1570	Map of Zeeland from "Theatrum Orbis Terrarum" by Abraham Ortelius, first edition.	France, Troyes, Moulin de Pétal	Simeon Nivelle	Briquet no. 1836, Le Clert no. 238
269	1570	Map of the World from "Theatrum orbis terrarum" by Abraham Ortelius.	France, Troyes, Moulin de Pétal	Simeon Nivelle	Le Clert II, p. 406, no. 241
270	1570	Map of Zeeland from "Theatrum Orbis Terrarum" by Abraham Ortelius, first edition.	France, Troyes, Moulin de Pétal	Simeon Nivelle	Briquet no. 1836, Le Clert no. 238
271	1573	Map of Zeeland from "Theatrum Orbis Terrarum" by Abraham Ortelius, 3rd state, 1st text.	France, Troyes, Moulin de Pétal	Simeon Nivelle	Briquet no. 1836, Le Clert no. 238

No./Type	Date	Found in	Place of production	Papermaker	References
272	1636	Map of "Guinea Nova descriptio" from "Atlas sive Cosmographicae" by Gerardus Mercator, Janssonius edition.	France, Brittany, Vitré near Rennes	P. M. R. Leje (= Le Jeune)	Churchill no. 386, Deval p. 220, Gaudriault p. 191, Heawood no. 638
273	1695	Engraving by Gaspar Bouttats, published in Antwerp.	France, Normandy, Sourdeval	Jean Conard	Gaudriault p. 191, Heawood no. 638, Villeroy no. 30
274	c.1800	Blank sheet.	France, Normandy?		
Flower					
275	c.1685–1700	Blank sheet.	Italy, Northern part		Heawood no. 2598
276	c.1685–1700	Blank sheet.	Italy, Northern part		Heawood nos. 2596–2598
277	c.1637	Engraving published by Samuel Speed in London.	England		Churchill no. 521
Foolscap, five-pointed					
278	c.1640	Blank sheet.	Switzerland, Mümliswil	M. Bürgi?	Laurentius 2007 nos. 504, 506, 507
279	c.1640–1645	Map of Valenciennes published by Willem Jansz. Blaeu in his Maior atlas.	France, Angoumois/ Limousin		Heawood no. 1934, Laurentius 2007 nos. 486, 489, 552
280	c.1640	Monotype by Anthonis Sallaert.	France, Angoumois		Laurentius 2007 no. 542
281	1589	Document from the Netherlands.	Switzerland, Basel	Düring	Gaudriault p. 156, Laurentius 2007 no. 510
282	1644	Map of "Flandriae Teutoniae" published by Willem Jansz. Blaeu in his Maior atlas.	France, Angoumois/ Limousin		Heawood no. 1934, Laurentius 2007 nos. 486, 489, 552
283	1644	Map of Zeeland published by Willem Jansz. Blaeu in his Maior atlas.			Heawood no. 1934, Laurentius 2007 nos. 486, 489, 552
284	1654	Illustration to "xiv boeken der Gelderssse geschiedenissen" by Arend van Slichtenhorst.	The Netherlands, Veluwe?		
285	1654	Map of Roermond from "xiv boeken der Gelderssse geschiedenissen" by Arend van Slichtenhorst.	France, Périgord	Leonard Clauzure	Churchill no. 344, Delâge 1991 p. 254, Laurentius 2007 nos. 524–527, Laurentius 2008 no. 406
286	1654	Map of "Velouwe" from "xiv boeken der Gelderssse geschiedenissen" by Arend van Slichtenhorst.	The Netherlands, Veluwe?		
Foolscap, seven-pointed					
287	c.1680	Etching by Adriaen van Ostade.	The Netherlands, Veluwe?		Heawood no. 2026
288	c.1685	Etching by Adriaen van Ostade.	The Netherlands, Veluwe?		Van der Coelen p. 75, Laurentius 2008 no. 475
289	c.1670	Etching, published by Clement de Jonghe in Amsterdam.	The Netherlands, Veluwe?		Laurentius 2010 p. 103, Type 7e, Laurentius 2008 no. 428
290	c.1690	Blank sheet.	The Netherlands, Veluwe?		Laurentius 2008 no. 509

No./Type	Date	Found in	Place of production	Papermaker	References
291	1709–1727	Map of Utrecht from "De Vyerighe colom", published by Arnold Colom in Amsterdam, edition by Paul de la Feuille.	France, Angoumois/Périgord	E. P.	Laurentius 2008 no. 522
292	1650–1670	Map of Gelderland from "La Genealogie des ... Nassau" by J. J. Orlers, later edition.	France, Angoumois	Francois Chatonnet?	Laurentius 2008 nos. 414, 434, 436
Fortuna					
293	1817	Map of Zeeland and Zeeuws Vlaanderen by Charles Francois Beautemps Baupré.	The Netherlands, Zaandijk	Jan claas and Aris van der Ley.	Churchill no. 193, Voorn 1960 p. 27, plate 193
Grapes					
294	Before 1644	Map of the XVII Provinces by Melchior Tavernier, published in Paris.	France, Brittany		
295	c.1624–1666	Map of "Gallia" by Jean Jolivet, published by Jacques Honervogt I in Paris.	France, Brittany/Auvergne		
296	c.1760	Etching by Cornelis Dusart, later impression.	France, Auvergne/Limousin		Heawood no. 2328
297	1639	Map of "Orbis Terrae novissima descriptio" by Jodocus Hondius from "Theatre Geographique de France" published by Jean Leclerc V in Paris.	France, Normandy		
298	c.1684	Map of "Médoc" from "Le Theatre Geographique de France" by Jean Leclerc IV, later edition.	France		Heawood no. 2120
299	c.1684	Map of "Anjou" from "Le Theatre Geographique de France" by Jean Leclerc IV, later edition.	France		Heawood nos. 2293, 2295
300	c.1684	Map of "Isle de France" from "Le Theatre Geographique de France" by Jean Leclerc IV, later edition.	France		Heawood no. 2095
301	c.1525	Map of "China" from "Geographia" by Claudius Ptolemy, published by Lorenz Fries in Strasbourg.	France, Beaujolais area		Briquet nos. 13065 & 13066
302	c.1525	Leaf from "Geographia" by Claudius Ptolemy, published by Lorenz Fries in Strasbourg.	France, Beaujolais area		Briquet nos. 13065 & 13066

No./Type	Date	Found in	Place of production	Papermaker	References
303	1784	Engraving from "Vita de Pittori", published in Naples.	Italy		Heawood no. 2420
304	1584	Map of "Holland" from "Spieghel der Zeevaert" by Lucas Janz. Waghenaer.	France	A. C.	Briquet no. 13163
305	1588	Map of Zeeland from "The Mariners mirrour" by Jodocus Hondius.	France, Normandy	B. G.	
306	Before 1657	Map of "Catalonia", published by Pierre Mariette I in Paris.	France, Troyes	Gilles Gouget	Le Clert no. 146
307	c.1654	Map of "El Dorado" by Pierre Du Val, published in Paris.	France, Normandy?	C. V.	Heawood no. 2192
308	c.1650	Map of "Nova Universi orbis descriptio" by Jodocus Hondius from "Theatre Geographique de France" published by Jean Leclerc V in Paris.	France	C. V.	Heawood no. 2192
309	1572–1574	Map of Zeeland from "Theatrum Orbis terrarum" by Abraham Ortelius, 2nd state, French text.	France, Normandy/Brittany	M. D. or D. M.	Briquet nos. 13163–13156, Heawood nos. 2163 & 2164
310	Before 1595	Engraving by Hieronymus Wierix, published by Gerard de Jode in Antwerp, 1st state.	France, Troyes area	Jean Gouault	Gaudriault no. 949
311	1572–1574	Map of Zeeland from "Theatrum Orbis terrarum" by Abraham Ortelius, 2nd state, French text.	France, Normandy/Brittany	M. D. or D. M.	Briquet nos. 13163–13156, Heawood nos. 2163 & 2164
312	1575	Map of France from "La Cosmographie universelle ... monde" by Francois de Belle Forest, published in Paris.	France, central /south-western part		Briquet no. 13160
313	1631	Map of "Picardie" from "Le Theatre Francoys" by Maurice Bougereau, edition by Jean Leclerc IV in Paris.	France, Western part?	T. B.	Heawood 2332
314	c.1633–1644	Map of "Holland" from "Cartes generales ... Allemagne" by Christophe Tassin.	France, Limousin, Limoges	Jean Poylève	Churchill no. 386, Gaudriault p. 258, Haewood no. 628, Laurentius 2012 pl. 3
315	c.1633–1644	Map of "Pays-Bas" from "Cartes generales ... Allemagne" by Christophe Tassin.	France, Normandy?	A. H. B.	
316	c.1750–1800	Blank sheet.	France, Rennes-Poitiers	A. Bureau	Gaudriault p. 182

No./Type	Date	Found in	Place of production	Papermaker	References
317	c.1639	Map of "Touraine" from "Le Theatre Francoys" by Maurice Bougereau, edition by Jean Leclerc IV in Paris.	France	A. I. R.	Heawood nos. 2224, 226, 2227, 2229
318	1658–1665	Map published by Nicolas Berey I in Paris.	France, Auvergne	I. M.	Laurentius 2008 nos. 610–612
319	1740–1760	Map of the world, anonymous, published in France.	France, Auvergne, Riom	Malmenaide family	Gaudriault p. 239
320	1756	Map of the Netherlands in ancient times, anonymous engraver and publisher.	France, Auvergne, Ambert	Damien Tamizier	Gaudriault no. 962, Heawood no. 2372
321	1755	Map of "Quievrain de Hons" from "Histoire militaire de Flandre ... Inclusivement" by Jean de Beaurain.	France, Auvergne, Riom	Damien Tamizier	Gaudriault pp. 139 & 270, no. 974, Heawood no. 2388
322	c.1660	Etching y Louis Meunier, published by Jacques van Merlen in Paris.	France, Auvergne, Riom	Benoît Colombier	Gaudriault p. 190, nos. 126 & 958, Heawood nos. 2426–2432
323	c.1655	Engraving by an anonymous engraver, published in France.	France, Auvergne, Riom	Benoît Colombier	Heawood nos. 2427–2429
324	1578	Map of Zeeland from "Speculum orbis Terrarum" by Gerard de Jode, published in Antwerp.	France, Troyes, Vannes.	Jean Gouault I	Briquet no. 13215, Le Clert II p. 328, plate XXXVII, no. 131.

Hand

No./Type	Date	Found in	Place of production	Papermaker	References
325	c.1535	Map of "Nona d Asia" from the "Geographia" by Francesco Berlinghieri, second edition by Giunti.	Italy		
326	1520–1550	Leaf from a book.	France, Northern part		Briquet nos. 11406 & 11406
327	1578	Map of the Rhine from "Speculum orbis Terrarum" by Gerard de Jode, published in Antwerp.	France, Troyes, Vannes	Jehan Gouault	Briquet no. 11458, Heawood no. 2557, Le Clert p. 336, pl. XXXVII, no. 130
328	1572–1617	Map of "Goa" from "Civitates Orbis Terrarum" by Georg Braun and Frans Hogenberg.	France, Troyes, Vannes		Briquet no. 11458, Heawood no. 2557, Le Clert p. 336, pl. XXXVII, no. 130
329	1572–1617	Map of "Middelburg" from "Civitates Orbis Terrarum" by Georg Braun and Frans Hogenberg.	France, Troyes, Vannes		Briquet no. 11458, Heawood no. 2557, Le Clert p. 336, pl. XXXVII, no. 130
330	c.1760–1785	Engraving published by André Basset in Paris.	France, Auvergne, Riom	Artaud or Marcheval	Gaudriault p. 144, no. 833
331	1585	Document from Portugal.	France, southwest part		Briquet no. 10924
332	c.1575–1580	Document from Portugal.	France, southwest part		Briquet no. 11055
333	c.1585	Document from Portugal.	France, southwest part		Briquet no. 11029

No./Type	Date	Found in	Place of production	Papermaker	References
334	c.1550	Blank sheet.	France, Bordeaux area		Gaudriault no. 818, Nicolaï II, pl. XCIV, nos. 1–23
335	c.1550	Document from Portugal.	France, Gascogne/Guienne area		De Ataide e Melo no. 69, Gaudriault p. 143, Nicolaï II, pl. XCVI
336	1555	Document from Portugal.	France, Gascogne/Guienne area		De Ataide e Melo no. 69, Gaudriault p. 143, Nicolaï II, pl. XCVI
337	1500–1530	Document from Portugal.	France, southwest part		Briquet no. 10750, Heawood nos. 2452–2462
338	c.1560	Document from Portugal.	France, southwest part		Briquet no. 10859, Heawood nos. 2470 & 2471, Nicolaï II, pl. XCVII, no. 5
339	1730	Document from Portugal.	France, Bordeaux area	G. B.	Laurentius 2018 no. 74, Nicolaï II, pl. LXXXVIII, nos. 13 & 15
340	1586	Map of Zeeland from "Theatrum Orbis terrarum" by Abraham Ortelius, 6th state.	France, Troyes, Les Moulins de Fouchy	Innocent de Garoys & Guillaume Journeé	Briquet no. 11617, De Stoppelaar pl. XVI, no. 11, Le Clert p. 301, nos. 71 & 73
Hat					
341	c.1685–1695	Blank sheet.	Italy, Lombardia		Heawood nos. 2596–2598
Heart					
342	1561	Map of "Anatolia" from "Geographia di Tolomeo" by Girolamo Ruscelli, published in Venice.	Switzerland, Geneva area		Briquet p. 259, nos. 4238–4280
Horn					
343	1617	Map of The Hague from "Civitates Orbis Terrarum" by Georg Braun and Frans Hogenberg.	France, Vosges, Brouvellieures		Briquet no. 7840, Gaudriault no. 383, Heawood nos. 2620, 2623, Janot no. 150
344	1617	Map of Dordrecht from "Civitates Orbis Terrarum" by Georg Braun and Frans Hogenberg.	France, Vosges, Brouvellieures		Briquet no. 7840, Gaudriault no 383, Heawood nos. 2620, 2623, Janot no. 150
345	1609	Map of Roermond from "Delle guerre di Fiandra" by Pompeo Giustiniani, published in Antwerp.	France, Vosges, Brouvellieures		Briquet no. 7840
346	1605	Map of the XVII Provinces published by Johannes Baptista Vrints I in Antwerp.	France, Vosges, Brouvellieures		Gaudriault no. 383, Heawood nos. 2624 & 2627

No./Type	Date	Found in	Place of production	Papermaker	References
347	c.1670	Etching by Roelant Roghman, published by Melchior Küsell in Augsburg.	Germany, Kottern	Marcus Schachenmayer?	Von Hössle p. 50
348	c.1593	Map of the Netherlands by Cornelis de Hooghe?, published in Antwerp.	France, Vosges, Epinal area		Briquet no. 7862, De Stoppelaar pl. II, no. 5, Gaudriault no. 384, Heawood no. 2640,
349	c.1598–1606	Map of Vlissingen from "Civitates Orbis Terrarum" by Georg Braun and Frans Hogenberg.	France, Vosges, Epinal, Docelles	Claudon Vincent?	Briquet no. 7862, De Stoppelaar pl. II, no. 5, Gaudriault no. 384, Heawood no. 2640,
350	1598	Map of Zeeland from "Theatrum Orbis terrarum" by Abraham Ortelius, 8th state.	France, Vosges, Epinal, Docelles	Aubert or Claudon Vincent	Briquet no. 7862, De Stoppelaar pl. II, no. 5, Gaudriault no. 384, Heawood no. 2640,
351	c.1598–1606	Map of Vlissingen from "Civitates Orbis Terrarum" by Georg Braun and Frans Hogenberg, Latin text.	France, Vosges, Epinal, Docelles	Claudon Vincent?	Briquet no. 7862, De Stoppelaar pl. II, no. 5, Gaudriault no. 384, Heawood no. 2640,
352	c.1603–1606	Map of Zeeland from "Theatrum Orbis terrarum" by Abraham Ortelius, 8th state, without text.	France, Vosges, Docelles, Chenimenil, Moulin de L'Isle	Demange Aubert	Gaudriault p. 111, no. 384, Heawood no. 2646
353	c.1603–1606	Map of "Terra Sancta" from "Theatrum Orbis terrarum" by Abraham Ortelius.	France, Vosges, Docelles, Chenimenil, Moulin de L'Isle	Demange Aubert	Gaudriault p. 111, no. 384, Heawood no. 2646
354	1595–1599	Map of the Canary Islands from "Caertboeck vande Midlandse Zee" by Willem Barentsz., published in Amsterdam.	France, Vosges, Docelles, Chenimenil, Moulin de L'Isle	Demange Aubert	Heawood no. 2639
355	c.1606–1609	Map of Bourgogne from "Theatrum Orbis terrarum" by Abraham Ortelius, Spanish text.	France, Vosges, Docelles, Chenimenil, Moulin de L'Isle	Demange Aubert	Gaudriault no. 384, Heawood nos. 2640–2647
356	c.1606–1609	Map of Zeeland from "Theatrum Orbis terrarum" by Abraham Ortelius, 8th state.	France, Vosges, Docelles, Chenimenil, Moulin de L'Isle	Demange Aubert	Gaudriault no. 384, Heawood nos. 2640–2647
357	c.1608–1609	Map of Zeeland from "Theatrum Orbis terrarum" by Abraham Ortelius, 9th state.	France, Vosges, Docelles, Chenimenil, Moulin de L'Isle	Florentin & Demange Aubert	Gaudriault no. 384, Heawood nos. 2640–2647
358	c.1606–1612	Map of Bourgogne from "Theatrum Orbis terrarum" by Abraham Ortelius, Spanish text.	France, Vosges, Docelles, Chenimenil, Moulin de L'Isle	Aubert family	Gaudriault no. 384, Heawood nos. 2640–2647

No./Type	Date	Found in	Place of production	Papermaker	References
359	1601	Titlepage to the Ortelius atlas, published by Moretus in Antwerp.	France, Vosges, Chenimenil area	Aubert?	Heawood no. 2636
360	c.1602–1606	Map of Bourgogne from "Theatrum Orbis terrarum" by Abraham Ortelius, Spanish text.	France, Vosges, Chenimenil area	Aubert?	Heawood no. 2636
361	1606–1612	Map of Zeeland from "Theatrum Orbis terrarum" by Abraham Ortelius, 9th state.	France, Vosges, Chenimenil area	Aubert?	Heawood no. 2636
362	1662	Titlepage to "De Vyerighe colom", published by Arnold Colom in Amsterdam.	France, Normandy		Heawood no. 1215, Villeroy II, nos. 19 & 31
363	1683	Engraving by Johann Boener, published in Nurnberg.	Tirol?		Eineder 247–251
364	1633	Etching by Jacques Callot.			Gaudriault no. 395
365	1654	Map of Zutphen from "XIV boeken der Gelderssse geschiedenissen" by Arend van Slichtenhorst.	France, angoumois, La Couronne, moulin Girac	Leonard Laroche	Nicolaï II pl. CXLVII
Horse					
366	1783	Document from Portugal.	Italy	Giusti	Gaudriault 304, Balmaceda pp. 220 & 229, no. 58
367	1795	Document from Portugal.	Italy	Giusti	Gaudriault 304, Balmaceda pp. 220 & 229, no. 58
368	1795	Document from Portugal.	Italy	Giusti	Gaudriault 304, Balmaceda pp. 220 & 229, no. 58, no. 113
369	1782	Document from Portugal.	Italy	Giusti	Gaudriault 304, Balmaceda pp. 220 & 229, no. 58
370	c.1795	Document from Portugal.	Italy	Giusti	Gaudriault 304, Balmaceda p. 220 & 229, no. 58
371	1840	Document from Hannover.	Germany, Hannover area	J. H. G.	Weiss 1972, p. 189
Horseman					
372	c.1780–1790	Blank sheet.	Italy, Genua	Giacomo Gambino?	Churchill no. 571
Imperial Orb					
373	1654–1659	Map of "Belgica" from "Topographiae Germaniae" by the Merian family.	Switzerland, Bern, Worblaufen, Muhle Zu Thall	Samuel Koch	Tschudin 1991 p. 179
Ladder					
374	1558	Map of The Netherlands published by Antonio Lafreri in Rome.	Italy, Fabriano?		Briquet no. 5924, Woodward nos. 238–241
Letters					
375	c.1688	Map from "T'Vergulde licht der Zeevaart" by Hendrik Donker, published in Amsterdam.	The Netherlands, Veluwe, Ugchelen	Jochem Schut?	

TABLE OF WATERMARKS

No./Type	Date	Found in	Place of production	Papermaker	References
376	c.1688	Map of "Pascaert van de zeekusten van Rusland" from "T'Vergulde licht der Zeevaart" by Hendrik Donker, published in Amsterdam.	The Netherlands, Veluwe, Ugchelen	Jochem Schut?	
377	c.1688	Map from "T'Vergulde licht der Zeevaart" by Hendrik Donker, published in Amsterdam.	The Netherlands, Veluwe, Ugchelen	Jochem Schut?	
378	c.1740–1760	Map of the XVII Provinces published by Giambattista Albrizzi in Venice, 1st state.	Italy, Venice area		Gaudriault no. 2012, Heawood no. 2864
379	?	Blank sheet.	Portugal?		
380	1843–1850	Blank sheet.	The Netherlands, Apeldoorn, Ordermark, Hennemansmolen	Arend Rees & Co.	Voorn 1985 pp. 369–370
381	c.1637	Map of "Brabantiae" published by Hendrick Hondius.	France, Limousin	Traded by Pieter Haeck	Heawood no. 2850
382	c.1637	Map of Malines by Johannes Janssonius.	France, Limousin	Traded by Pieter Haeck	Heawood no. 2850
383	c.1637	Map of "Comitatus Hollandiae" published by Hendrick Hondius.	France, Limousin	Traded by Pieter Haeck	Heawood no. 2850
384	c.1637	Map of "Episcop. Ultratraiectinus" published by Hendrick Hondius.	France, Limousin	Traded by Pieter Haeck	Heawood no. 2850
385	c.1671–1675	Map of the XVII Provinces from "Topographiae Germaniae" by the Merian family.	Germany, Lörrach	Christian Blum	
386	c.1630	Engraving by Isaac Maior.	Italy, Bergamo		Briquet no. 9313, Eineder nos. 1137–1145
387	c.1690–1696	Map of "Parte occidentale della China" from "Atlante Veneto" by Vincenzo Coronelli, published in Venice.	Italy, Venice area		
388	1629	Map of "Ducatus Geldriae" by Hendrick Hondius.	France, Vosges, Docelles, Moulin Grand Meix	Nicolas Georgel	Gaudriault no. 538, Heawood no. 2890, Janot no. 126, Laurentius 2007 no. 255
389	1628	Map of "America sive India nova" from "Tabulae Geographicae" by Gerardus Mercator, Hondius/Janssonius edition.	France, Vosges, Docelles, Moulin Grand Meix	Nicolas Georgel	Gaudriault no. 538, Heawood no. 2890, Janot nos. 121 & 126, Laurentius 2007 no. 255

No./Type	Date	Found in	Place of production	Papermaker	References
390	c.1629	Map of "Belgii sive Germaniae" by Hendrick Hondius.	France, Vosges, Docelles, Moulin Grand Meix	Nicolas Georgel	Gaudriault no. 538, Heawood no. 2890, Janot nos. 121 & 126, Laurentius 2007 no. 255
391	1628	Map of "Frisia" by Claes Jansz. Visscher.	France, Vosges, Docelles, Moulin Grand Meix	Nicolas Georgel	Gaudriault no. 538, Heawood no. 2890, Janot nos. 121 & 126, Laurentius 2007 no. 255
392	c.1679	Etching by Adriaen van Ostade.	France, Angoumois	Claude de George	Laurentius 2008 no. 513
393	1685–1693	Map of Middelburg from "Teatro Belgico" by Gregorio Leti.	The Netherlands, West-Zaandam	Cornelis Simonsz. Huysduynen	Laurentius 2008 no. 513, Voorn 1960 p. 117, no. 143
394	c.1760–1770	Map of "Ost-Flandern" published in Austria.	Germany, Kottern, Heggen Mühle	A. Steynhauser	Eineder no. 347, Von Hössle p. 41
395	c.1578	Map of "Tribus Zabulon terra Sancta" from "Theatrum Orbis terrarum" by Abraham Ortelius.	France, Troyes	Claude Denise	Briquet no. 9335
396	c.1741–1756	Map of "Zeelandia" from "Atlas Minor" by Tobias Conrad Lotter from Augsburg.	Germany, Ravensburg, ölschwang, Oberen Papiermühle	Elias Kutter	Preger 1983 p. 95
397	c.1741–1756	Map of "Belgium foederatum" by Johann Baptist Homann from Nurnberg.	Germany, Ravensburg, ölschwang, Oberen Papiermühle	Elias Kutter	Preger 1983 p. 95
398	1741–1756	Map of "Comitatis Hollandiae" published by the heirs of J. B. Homann in Nurnberg.	Germany, Ravensburg, ölschwang, Oberen Papiermühle	Elias Kutter	Preger 1983 p. 95
399	c.1585	Map of "Lotharingia Comitatus" from "Tabulae Geographicae" by Gerardus Mercator.	France, Vosges, Chénimenil	Florentin Aubert	Gaudriault nos. 529–530, Janot no. 106
400	?	Etching by Adriaen van Ostade.	France?		
401	1609	Map of "Holland" from "Theatrum Orbis terrarum" by Abraham Ortelius.	The Netherlands, Veluwe, Apeldoorn, Beekbergen	Marten Orges	Heawood nos. 3195–3198
402	1611	Map of Zeeland from "Tabulae Geographicae" by Gerardus Mercator, edition by Hendrick Hondius.	The Netherlands, Veluwe, Apeldoorn, Beekbergen	Marten Orges	Heawood nos. 3195–3198
403	1804–1810	Map of the Brabantse Kempen published by the Geographischen Institut in Weimar.	Germany, Weimar		Buchmann no. 1936

TABLE OF WATERMARKS

No./Type	Date	Found in	Place of production	Papermaker	References
404	1556	Map of West Africa from "Navigationi et Viaggi" by Giovanni Battista Ramusio, published in Venice.	Italy		
405	After 1651	Map of "Hollandiae" published by willem Jansz. Blaeu.	France, Limousin	Traded by Gerard Verduyn	Delâge 1990 p. 118, Heawood no. 2851
406	1597–1611	Map of "Holland" from "Tabulae Geographicae" by Gerardus Mercator, edition by Hendrick Hondius.	France, Vosges, Epinal	Amé Géninet	Briquet no. 9821, Janot no. 83, Laurentius 2007 no. 630
407	1590–1611	Map of "Asiae III Tab." from "Tabulae Geographicae" by Gerardus Mercator, edition by Hendrick Hondius.	France, Vosges, Epinal	Amé Géninet	Gaudriault no. 1015, Janot no. 83
408	1643	Map of Colmar from "Topographiae Germaniae" by the Merian family.	Germany, Nurnberg area, Wendelsteiner Papiermühle	Georg Endter	Marabini 1894 p. 68, Piccard Horn nos. 561 & 562
409	1810	Engraving by Konrad Westermayer, published in Hanau.	Germany		
410	c.1820	Engraving by Moritz Steinla.	Germany		
411	c.1572–1594	Map of "Amstelredamum" from "Civitates Orbis Terrarum" by Georg Braun and Frans Hogenberg.	France, Vosges, Docelles, Papeterie de Grennevo	Claudon Vincent	Gaudriault no. 1015, Heawood no. 3180, Janot no. 83, Laurentius 2007 no. 630
412	c.1572–1594	Views of Arnhem, Venlo, Gelre, Roermond from "Civitates Orbis Terrarum" by Georg Braun and Frans Hogenberg.	France, Vosges, Docelles, Papeterie de Grennevo	Claudon Vincent	Gaudriault no. 1015, Heawood no. 3180, Janot no. 83, Laurentius 2007 no. 630
413	c.1582–1603	Map of Kampen from "Civitates Orbis Terrarum" by Georg Braun and Frans Hogenberg.	France, Vosges, Docelles, Papeterie de Grennevo	Claudon Vincent	Gaudriault no. 1015, Heawood no. 3192, Janot pp. 9 & 329
414	c.1604	Map of Tournai from "Civitates Orbis Terrarum" by Georg Braun and Frans Hogenberg.	France, Vosges, Docelles, Vraichamp	Grégoire Vairal	Janot p. 311, no. 143
415	1791–1815	Map of the Channel from "De lichtende Zeefakkel" published by the Van Keulen family.	The Netherlands, Vaasen, The Geelmolen I	Hendrik Mentink	Voorn 1985 p. 183
416	c.1698	Map of Amsterdam by Willem Jansz. Blaeu, published by Frederik de Wit.	The Netherlands, Veluwe area?		
417	c.1628	Map of Zeeland from "Theatrum Orbis terrarum" by Abraham Ortelius, 9th state.	France, Southwestern part		Nicolaï II pl. XLI, nos. 8–13

No./Type	Date	Found in	Place of production	Papermaker	References
418	c.1600	Map of Zeeland from "Theatrum Orbis terrarum" by Abraham Ortelius.	Germany, Lörrach/Maulburg	Hans Blum	Laurentius 2007 no. 631
419	c.1627	Map of Santvliet by Michael Florent van Langren.	France, Vosges, Epinal area		Briquet no. 5750
420	c.1679	Map of "Germany Inferieure" by Nicolas Sanson, edition by Mariette.	The Netherlands, Zaandijk	Jacob & Adriaen Cornelisz. Honig	Gaudriault no. 4005, Laurentius 2008 no. 148b, Voorn 1960 p. 38
421	1690–1700	Map from "De lichtende Zeefakkel" published by the Van Keulen family.	The Netherlands, Glederland, Heerde, The Hoornse Veen	Hendrik Dries van Emst	Churchill no. 28, Gaudriault p. 293, no. 4116, Laurentius 2008 nos. 115, 155, 157, Voorn 1985 p. 550
422	1705	Map of China by Nicolas de Fer.	France, Auvergne, Riom	I. Chabrier?	Gaudriault nos. 731 & 4136
423	c.1690	Map of Zeeland from "De lichtende Zeefakkel" published by the Van Keulen family.	France, Normandy?	Durand	Heawood no. 3108
424	c.1684	Map of Northern Italy by Pierre Duval, edition by Besson.	France, Angoumois, La Courade	Leonard Laroche	Gaudriault p. 231, Heawood no. 2958
425	1812	Map of "Partie septentrionale d'Empire Francais" from "Atlas complet ... Universelle" by C. Malte-Brun.	France, Auvergne		
426	1638	Engraving by Antony van der Does.	France, Angoumois?		
427	c.1770–1780	Map of Vienna by George Louis la Rouge.	France, Ardèche, Vidalon/Annonay	Montgolfier	Gaudriault nos. 736 & 737
428	c.1669	Map of "Soute eylanden ofte Ilhas de Cabo Verde" from "T'Vergulde licht der Zeevaart" by Hendrik Donker, published in Amsterdam.	The Netherlands, Ugchelen, "In het Voorslop" mill	Jochem or Jan Schut	Gaudriault no. 788, Laurentius 2008 nos. 549, 792, 793, Voorn 1985 pp. 416–418
429	c.1673	Map of the XVII Provinces from "Topographiae Germaniae" by the Merian family.	Germany, Lörrach?		
430	c.1662	Map of Rijnland from "De Vyerighe colom", published by Arnold Colom in Amsterdam.	The Netherlands, Veluwe area	K. P.	
431	c.1684	Map of Northern Italy by Pierre Duval, edition by Besson.	France, Angoumois, La Courade	Leonard Laroche	Gaudriault p. 231, Heawood no. 2958

No./Type	Date	Found in	Place of production	Papermaker	References
432	c.1672	Map of "Terres dites Antartiques" from the "Cartes de geographie … fideles" published by Pierre Duval in Paris.	France, Auvergne, Riom	"Le Tellier" paper by Bénoit Colombier?	Talbierska nos. 1.42 & 1.43
433	c.1660	Etching by Stefano della Bella.	France, Auvergne, Riom	"Le Tellier" paper by Bénoit Colombier?	Talbierska nos. 1.42 & 1.43
434	1748–1787	Map of "Diocesis Leodiensis" from "De Vyerighe colom", published by Arnold Colom in Amsterdam, edition by D. Weege.	The Netherlands, Egmond aan den Hoef	Lubbert van Gerrevink	Voorn 1960 p. 97
435	1652	Etching by Pieter Quast.		M.	Heawood nos. 3030 & 3031, Laurentius 2010 p. 100, Type 6
436	1623	Map of "De gaten van Brouwershaven" from "Zeespieghel" by Willem Jansz. Blaeu.		M.	
437	1577–1585	Map of "Flandriae" by Antonio Lafreri, edition by Claudio Duchetti.	Italy, Venice area	M.	Heawood no. 3026, Woodward no. 328
438	c.1730–1745	Blank sheet.	Germany, Southern part	M. A. I.	Heawood nos. 574, 1378, 3107
439	c.1775–1784	Map of "Belgium Foederatum" by Joseph Marianus from Augsburg.	Germany, Augsburg/Nurnberg area	M. G.	Heawood no. 3224
440	1784	Map of "Walcheren" by Mathias Albrecht Lotter from Augsburg.	Germany, Augsburg/Nurnberg area	M. G.	Heawood no. 3224
441	1743–1770	Blank sheet.	France, central part, Manufacture de Montargis?	G. I.	Gaudriault p. 302
442	1613	Map of the "Brittenburg" from "Beschryvinghe van alle de Nederlanden" by Lodovico Guiccardini.		M. P.	Churchill no. 381, Delâge 1991 p. 245, Nicolaï no. 177
443	c.1614	Map of Zeeland from "Theatrum Orbis terrarum" by Abraham Ortelius, 10th state, without text.	France, Vosges, Epinal area, Dinozé	Nicolas Fuzelier	Gaudriault p. 211, Janot p. 188, no. 12
444	1609	Map of Lochem from "Delle guerre di Fiandra" by Pompeo Giustiniani, published in Antwerp.	France, Vosges, Epinal		Janot nos. 70 & 82
445	1598	Map of the West coast from "De natura nova orbis" by José de Acosta, published in Cologne.	France, Vosges?		Laurentius 2007 no. 633

No./Type	Date	Found in	Place of production	Papermaker	References
446	1596	Map of Zeeland from "Europae totius … descriptio" by Matthias Quad, published in Cologne by Bussemacher.	France, Vosges, Epinal area, Docelles	Guerin?	Gaudriault no. 754, Janot nos. 61 & 80
447	1662	Map of the VII Provinces from the Atlas Maior by Joan Blaeu.	France, Limousin	Traded by Pieter Haeck	Gaudriault no. 256
448	1649	Map of Tiel from "Stedeboek" by Joan Blaeu.	France, Limousin	Traded by Pieter Haeck	Heawood no. 1362
449	c.1780	Map of the moon, published by the heirs of J. B. Homann in Nurnberg.	Germany, Wolfeg, Altorf-Karbach, Hegau	Josef Anton Unold	Eineder no. 291, Heawood nos. 1377 & 1378
450	After 1675	Map of "Pascaert Guinea-Goudkust" from "De lichtende Zeefakkel" published by the Van Keulen family.	The Netherlands, Koog aan de Zaan, "De Wever" & "De Bonsem" mills	Pieter van der Ley	Heawood no. 3020, Voorn 1960 pp. 320–330
451	1682	Map of Delfland/Schieland from "The English Atlas" by Moses Pitt & Steven Swart.	The Netherlands, Koog aan de Zaan, "De Wever" & "De Bonsem" mills	Pieter van der Ley	Heawood no. 3020, Voorn 1960 pp. 320–330
452	1737	Map of Castricum published by Covens & Mortier.	The Netherlands, Koog aan de Zaan, "De Wever" & "De Bonsem" mills	Pieter van der Ley	Heawood no. 3020, Voorn 1960 pp. 320–330
453	After 1690	Map of "Carte des Entrées d'Escaut" by Pieter Mortier.	The Netherlands, Koog aan de Zaan, "De Wever" & "De Bonsem" mills	Pieter van der Ley	Heawood no. 3020, Voorn 1960 pp. 320–330
454	After 1690	Map of Scandinavia by Frederik de Wit.	The Netherlands, Koog aan de Zaan, "De Wever" & "De Bonsem" mills	Pieter van der Ley	Heawood no. 3020, Voorn 1960 pp. 320–330
455	c.1617–1623	Map of "Lips" from "Civitates Orbis Terrarum" by Georg Braun and Frans Hogenberg.	France, Vosges, Fraichamps	Gregoire Vaizel	Gaudriault p. 274
456	c.1617–1623	Engraving from "Civitates Orbis Terrarum" by Georg Braun and Frans Hogenberg.	France, Vosges, Fraichamps	Gregoire Vaizel	Gaudriault p. 274
457	c.1617–1623	Engraving from "Civitates Orbis Terrarum" by Georg Braun and Frans Hogenberg.	France, Vosges, Fraichamps	Gregoire Vaizel	Gaudriault p. 274
458	c.1645	Map of "Leodiensis Dioceses Typus" by J. B. van Doetecum, edition by Blaeu.	France, Limousin	Traded by Pieter Haeck	Laurentius 2010 p. 28, type 8a
459	c.1620	Engraving by Lucas Kilian from Augsburg.	Germany	R	Briquet no. 8975

No./Type	Date	Found in	Place of production	Papermaker	References
460	1649	Map of "Provinciadi Flandria" from "Chorographica descriptio ..." by Johannes Montecalerio, published in Milan.	Italy, Venice area		Churchill nos. 506 & 507
461	1735	Map of Europe, published by the heirs of J. B. Homann in Nurnberg.	Germany, Nurnberg, Burgthann	Sebastian Heerdegen	Heawood no. 3231, Marabini 1896 p. 58
462	1735	Map of "Asiae", published by the heirs of J. B. Homann in Nurnberg.	Germany, Nurnberg, Burgthann	Sebastian Heerdegen	Heawood no. 3231, Marabini 1896 p. 58
463	1587	Map of Zeeland from "Civitates Orbis Terrarum" by Georg Braun and Frans Hogenberg.			
464	1585	Map of the land of the Scythians from "Tabulae Geographicae" by Gerard Mercator, without text.			
465	1837	Document from France.	France, Provence?		
466	1662	Map of "territorium Bergense" from Atlas Major by Joan Blaeu.	France, Limousin?		
467	1673	Map of the XVII Provinces by Jacob von Sandrart, published in Nurnberg.	Germany, Nurnberg area		
468	c.1800	Map of Bruges, Oostende and Damme by E. H. Fricx, edition By Covens, Mortier and Son.			
469	c.1800	Map of Zeeland by Frederik de Wit, later edition.			
470	After 1751	Map of "Oostzeeland" published by Covens & Mortier.			
Lion					
471	c.1782	Document from Portugal.	Italy, Tuscany?	A. G.	Heawood 3168 & 3169
472	1800	Map of "Bataafsche Republiek", published by J. Allart in Amsterdam.	The Netherlands, Koog aan de Zaan, "De Bonsem" mill	Jan Kool	Churchill no. 197, Voorn 1960 p. 516
Mace					
473	c.1660–1690	Blank sheet.	France, Auvergne or Normandy		Gaudriault p. 100, Heawood nos. 3171–3176
Moon					
474	1622	Map from "Germania Inferior ..." by Petrus Kaerius.	France, Alsace, Strasbourg area		Laurentius/Roos 2012 p. 26, type 1

No./Type	Date	Found in	Place of production	Papermaker	References
475	c.1580	Map of Douai from "Civitates Orbis Terrarum" by Georg Braun and Frans Hogenberg.	France, Vosges?		
Mountains					
476	c.1600	Map of the XVII Provinces by Matteo Florimi, published in Sienna.	Italy		
477	1661 a+b	Map of "Carta particolare d'una parte … Pakas" from "Dell'arcano del Mare" by Robert Dudley, published in Florence.	Italy, Tuscany?		Heawood nos. 786, 1127, 1353, 1624, 2607, 3130, 3131, 3896
Names					
478	Before 1666	Engraving by Nicolas de Son, published by Jean Leblond I in Paris.	France, Auvergne	R. Barthelemy	Gaudriault p. 171
479	1788	Engraving by Auguste Sandoz.	France, Auvergne, Riom	V. Beal & Barge	Gaudriault pp. 124 & 170
480	1577–1589	Map of Zeeland from "Theatrum Orbis terrarum" by Abraham Ortelius, 4th state, German text.	France, Troyes	Nicolas le Bé	Le Clert pp. 352–379, pl. XLVI, no. 189
481	1575–1588	Map of the world from "La cosmographie universelle" by André Thevet.	France, Troyes	Nicolas le Bé	Heawood nos. 2877 & 2878, Le Clert vol. II, nos. 189–191
482	1582	Map of Malines from "Beschryvinghe van alle de Nederlanden" by Lodovico Guiccardini, edition published by Plantin.	France, Troyes	Nicolas le Bé	Heawood no. 2877, Le Clert vol. II, no. 189
483	1780–1815	Blank sheet.	The Netherlands, Ugchelen, "De kleine Bazemolens"	J. Berens & Zoon	Voorn 1985 pp. 430–431
484	1813	Document from England.	England, Kent, Dartford Mill	J. Budgen	Bower 1999 p. 134
485	c.1820	Anonymous print, published in France.	France, Auvergne, Riom	J. Bouchet	Gaudriault p. 178, Heawood no. 3798
486	1693	Map of "L'Escaut et Meuse" by Claude Auguste Berey, published in Paris.	France, Auvergne, Riom	Bénoit Colombier	Gaudriault no. 126, Heawood no. 1323
487	After 1723	Map of the eastern part of Flanders by Covens & Mortier.	The Netherlands, Zaan area	C. & I. Honig	
488	1826	Map of "Côte de Bresil" published by the Depot de la Marine.	France, Auvergne	Pierre Francois Dupuy?	

TABLE OF WATERMARKS 85

No./Type	Date	Found in	Place of production	Papermaker	References
489	1747	Map of "Middelburg en Zelande" from "Atlas général ... Europe" by George Louis le Rouge.	France, Auvergne, Riom	Thomas Dupuy II	Gaudriault p. 203, Heawood no. 241
490	1807	Map of "Mer du nord", published by the Depot de la Marine.	France, Auvergne, Riom, Grand-Rive	Pierre Francois Dupuy	Gaudriault p. 203
491	1867	Document from Germany.	Germany	G. Fichtner	
492	1709	Map of "Boulenois et Picardie" by Jacobus Harrewijn, published by Fricx in Brussels.	Belgium, Brussels area	Georges Fricx	Claessens 1958 p. 291
493	1745	Map of "Carte particuliere des environs de Bruges" published by Fricx in Brussels.	Belgium, Brussels area	Georges Fricx	Claessens 1958 p. 291
494	1744	Map of "Carte particuliere des environs d'Anvers ..." published by Fricx in Brussels.	Belgium, Brussels area	Georges Fricx	Claessens 1958 p. 291
495	c.1800–1840	Blank sheet.	Italy	Gaggiero	Heawood no. 3740
496	c.1790–1800	Engraving published in The Netherlands.	France, Le Marais, Coulommiers	De la garde l'Aîné et compagnie Papeterie du Marais.	Gaudriault p. 197, Heawood no. 3384
497	After 1816	Map of Zeeland from the map by Cornelis Krayenhoff.	The Netherlands, Zaan area, Wormer, "Eendragt" mill	Pieter Smidt van Gelder.	De Jongh p. 73, Voorn 1960 p. 433
498	1813	Document from France.	France, Grenoble, Malaucêne	Family Geoffroy	Gaudriault p. 213
499	c.1800	Map of Vienna, published by Artaria in Vienna.	The Netherlands, Zaandijk, "Veenboer" or "Vergulde Bijkorff" mills	C. & I. Honig	Voorn 1960 pp. 388–392
500	Before 1738	Map of "L'isle de Walcheren" by Covens & Mortier.	The Netherlands, Zaandijk, "Veenboer" or "Vergulde Bijkorff" mills	C. & I. Honig	Heawood nos. 3346–3348, Voorn 1960 p. 126
501	After 1830	Map of Antwerp during the Revolt published by Broese in Breda.	The Netherlands, Zaandijk	J. Honig & Zoon/Zoonen	Voorn 1960 p. 125
502	After 1830	Map of Antwerp during the Revolt published by L. Springer.	The Netherlands, Zaandijk	J. Honig & Zoon/Zoonen	Voorn 1960 p. 125
503	1748–1787	Map of "Machliniae" from "De Vyerighe colom", published by Arnold Colom in Amsterdam, edition by D. Weege.	The Netherlands, Zaandijk, "Veenboer" mill	J. Honig & Zoon	Voorn 1960 p. 299, no. 133
504	1823	Map of "Holland" published by F. J. Weygand in The Hague.	The Netherlands, Zaandijk, "Vergulde Bijkorff" mill	J. Honig & Zonen	Heawood nos. 3344–3345, Voorn 1960 p. 344

No./Type	Date	Found in	Place of production	Papermaker	References
505	c.1780	Blank sheet.	France, Normandy, Alencon	N. Jelin	Gaudriault p. 224, no. 132
506	c.1690	Map of Portugal by an anonymous publisher.	France, Limousin	I. Le Bloys	Gaudriault p. 232
507	c.1780–1832	Blank sheet.	The Netherlands, Brummen, "Haar" mill	J. H. Ledeboer	Voorn 1960 pp. 307–308
508	c.1750–1765	Etching by Andries Pauli, later edition.	France, Limousin, Saint Leonard, Moulin La Roche	Leonard Nicard	
509	c.1820	Map of "Ijslandt pascaert" from "De lichtende Zeefakkel" published by the Van Keulen family.	The Netherlands, Gelderland, Loenen	Evert van Oorspronk	Voorn 1960 pp. 182 & 342
510	1819	Etching by J. C. Erhard.	Germany or Austria		
511	1805–1815	Blank sheet.	Italy, Liguria, Genua	Parodi	
512	1585	Map of Kampen from "Civitates Orbis Terrarum" by Georg Braun and Frans Hogenberg.	France, Troyes	Claude Savois	Briquet nos. 8998 & 8999, Le Clert no. 312
513	c.1800	Blank sheet.	Portugal		
514	c.1690–1700	Blank sheet.	France, Auvergne, Riom/Ambert	Bénoit Richard	Gaudriault p. 261, no. 137
515	c.1745	Map of "Mixique & La Floride" by Guillaume Delisle.	France, Auvergne, Riom	J. Sauvade	Gaudriault p. 267, Heawood no. 239
516	1755	Document from Spain.	Spain, Catalonia, Odena	Caspar Solernou	Heawood no. 1708, Oriol Valls p. 270, no. 13
517	c.1785	Map of "Ost- und Westscheld" published by the heirs of Christoph Weigel.	Germany, Wolfeg, Altorf-Karbach, Hegau	Josef Anton Unold	Heawood 1378 & 1379, Eineder nos. 291–318
518	c.1730–1740	Blank sheet.	The Netherlands, Gelderland, Loenen "Horstenkamp" mill or Ugchelen, "Bazemolen"	Anthonie Vos	Voorn 1985 p. 424
Official marks					
519	1763	Document from France.	France		
520	c.1730	Document from France.	France, Normandy		Laurentius 2018 p. 6, no. 4
521	1760	Document from France.	France, Normandy		
522	1848	Document from France.			
Pascal Lamb					
523	1672	Map of "Provincie unite de Paesi Bassi" by an anonymous Italian publisher.	Italy		Heawood no. 2838
524	c.1650–1660	Engraving by Dominico Santi.	Italy, Venice		Gaudriault no. 2
Phoenix					
525	c.1651	Etching by Adriaen van Ostade.	France, Limousin	Michel Gros?	Gaudriault p. 146, no. 850, Churchill no. 489

No./Type	Date	Found in	Place of production	Papermaker	References
Pillars					
526	1635	Map of Utrecht from "Atlas sive Cosmographicae" by Gerardus Mercator, Hondius-Spark edition, published in London.	France, Normandy	Jean Vaulegard	Churchill nos. 525, 527–529, Gaudriault no. 866, Heawood no. 3534, Laurentius 2007 nos. 670 & 671, Villeroy II p. 190, no. 27
527	c.1690–1695	Document from France.	France, Normandy, Brouains	P. Mauduit?	Churchill no. 306, Gaudriault no. 866, Heawood no. 3492, Villeroy II p. 147, no. 20
528	c.1570–1571	Map of Zeeland from "Theatrum Orbis terrarum" by Abraham Ortelius, 2nd state.	France, Troyes	Edmond Denise	Le Clert pp. 305–306, pl. XXXIII, no. 107
529	1570	Map of Zeeland from "Theatrum Orbis terrarum" by Abraham Ortelius, 1st state.	France, Troyes	Edmond Denise	Le Clert pp. 305–306, pl. XXXIII, no. 107
Pot					
530	1667	Map of Asia from "Tresor des cartes geograpiques … " published by a member of the Jollain family in Paris.	France, Normandy	Julien Durand?	Gaudriault p. 204, Heawood no. 3677, Villeroy I pp. 183–184
531	1618	Map of the Hemispheres from "Journael of beschrijvinghe …" by Willem Schouten.	France?		
532	1611	Map from "Rerum et urbis Amstelodamensium historia" by Johannes Pontanus.	France, Normandy		Villeroy II nos. 11–13 & 28
533	1601	Document from Portugal.	France, Normandy	P. M.	De Ataide e Melo no. 86, Gaudriault no. 269
Pro Patria					
534	1748–1787	Map of "Partie de la Flandre occidentale" from "De Vyerighe colom", published by Arnold Colom in Amsterdam, edition by D. Weege.	The Netherlands, Zaan area	J. Honig & Zoon	Voorn 1960 no. 133
535	1748–1787	Map of "Comitatus Namurci" from "De Vyerighe colom", published by Arnold Colom in Amsterdam, edition by D. Weege.	The Netherlands, Zaan area	J. Honig & Zoon	Voorn 1960 no. 133
536	c.1700–1710	Blank sheet.	The Netherlands, Gelderland, Apeldoor area, "Dijksgraaf" or "Order" mill	Wilhelm Greeve	Voorn 1960 pp. 320 & 374
Serpent					
537	1750–1800	Blank sheet.	Germany, southwestern part or Austria		Eineder nos. 1618–1623, Decker nos. 475–477

No./Type	Date	Found in	Place of production	Papermaker	References
538	1826–1837	Print published by G. N. Renner in Nurnberg.	Germany, Kaufbeuren?	I. H. L.	Briquet 13839
539	1596	Map of "Franciae" from "Europae totius … descriptio" by Matthias Quad, published in Cologne by Bussemacher.	Germany, Memmingen		Briquet nos. 5512–5519, Heawood no. 3772
540	1635	Map of "Galliae Belgicae" from "Beschryvinghe van alle de Nederlanden" by Lodovico Guiccardini, edition published by Blaeu.	France, Angoumois/ Périgord	Elie Vaslet? For the trader J. van Ravestein	Gaudriault nos. 837–840
Shell					
541	1829	Document from France.	France, Auvergne, Velay?		Gaudriault p. 110, Laurentius 2016 nos. 283–287, Veron de la Combe p. 93
Sphere					
542	1607	Document from Portugal.	France, southwestern part?		Heawood nos. 3827–3846, Nicolaï II pl. CXXIV, no. 19
543	c.1600–1630	Document from Portugal.	France, southwestern part?		Nicolaï II pl. CXXIII, no. 8
544	1602	Document from Portugal.	France, Angoumois		Nicolaï II pl. CXXII, no. 18, pl. CXXIII, no. 1
545	1608	Document from Portugal.	France, Normandy, Sourdeval	Pierre Vaulegard	Gaudriault nos. 1007 & 1010, Nicolaï II pl. CXXIII, no. 8, Pl. CXXV, no. 9
546	1608	Document from Portugal.	France, Angoumois, La Couronne, Moulin de Cottier	Pierre Varlet	Delâge 1991 p. 123, Gaudriault p. 307, no. 1005
547	1601	Document from Portugal.	France, Angoumois, Moulin de Clauzure	Foucaud Lamy	De Ataide e Melo no. 114, Delâge 1991 p. 246, Gaudriault no. 1006, Heawood no. 3806, Nicolaï pl. CXXII, no. 7
Star					
548	1734	Map of the Philippines.	Italy, Genua? Or Portugal?	C. M. T. (Tomate family?)	Heawood no. 3863
549	1540	Map of Africa from "Cosmographia" by sebastian Münster, published in Basle.	Switzerland, Basle	Dürr	Heawood nos. 1174, 1175, 1178
Sun					
550	1649	Map of Holland from the "Stedeboek" by Joan Blaeu.	France, Limousin		Heawood no. 3894, Laurentius & Roos p. 30, no. 11
551	1640–1660	Blank sheet.	France, Limousin		Gaudriault p. 155, nos. 996–999, Heawood no. 3894

TABLE OF WATERMARKS 89

No./Type	Date	Found in	Place of production	Papermaker	References
552	c.1673	Map of "Le comte de Zeelande" by Nicolas Sanson, edition by Mariette.	France, Auvergne	Jeanne Dupuy, widow of Bénoit Colombier	Gaudriault p. 190
553	c.1716–1719	Map of Northern Italy from the "Cartes de geographie ... fideles" published by Pierre Duval, edition by Besson in Paris.	France, Angoumois, La Courade	Leonard Laroche	Gaudriault p. 231
554	1636	Document from Portugal.	France, Bordeaux area	R. M.	Gaudriault no. 995, Nicolaï II pl. CXXI
Sword					
555	c.1700–1720	Print by Christoph Weigel.	Germany, Augsburg area	H. S.	Heawood no. 3928
Tower					
556	c.1695–1700	Etching by Felix Meyer.	Germany, Ravensburg, Schonreute, Middle mill	Joachim Aicham	Heawood no. 3940, Piccard vol. III, p. 271, nos. 161–166
557	1614	Engraving by Egidius Sadeler.	Germany, Ravensburg		Preger 1982 p. 27
558	1676	Print by Michael Fennitzer, published in Nurnberg.	Germany, Ravensburg		Heawood no. 3940
559	c.1685	Engraving, published by Johann Leonhardt Bugel.	Austria, Eberstein, Waldkirche	Sebastian Edel	Piccard vol. III, p. 293, no. 41
Tree					
560	c.1690–1700	Blank sheet.	Austria, Tirol?	I. G. Rahm	Eineder no. 1683
Undetermined					
561	c.1610	Document from France.	France		
Unicorn					
562	1750–1800	Blank sheet.	Germany, Fischlaken an der Ruhr, Scheppener Mill?	Herman Langenbach?	Del Marmol p. 83, Laurentius 2015 no. 25
Vryheit					
563	1740–1750	Map of "Diemermeer/Watergraafsmeer" by an anonymous publisher.	The Netherlands, Zaan area	Adriaan Rogge or Van der Ley	Churchill no. 95, Heawood no. 3149, Voorn 1960 no. 110
Wheel					
564	1556	Map of Venice from "Navigationi et Viaggi" by Giovanni Battista Ramusio & Ferrando Bertelli, published in Venice.	Italy, Venice area		Briquet no. 13234, Woodward no. 186
565	c.1647	Etching by Ferdinand Bol.	France, Alsace, Mulhouse		Ash & Fletcher Wheel type A.a
566	c.1646–1647	Etching by an anonymous Rembrandt pupil.	France, Alsace, Mulhouse		Ash & Fletcher Wheel type A.a
Words					
567	c.1820	Engraving by G. G. Vogel.	Germany	Super fein klein median	

Catalogue

∴

1 1572-1580

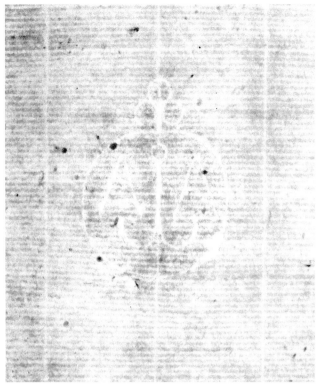

2 1600-1620

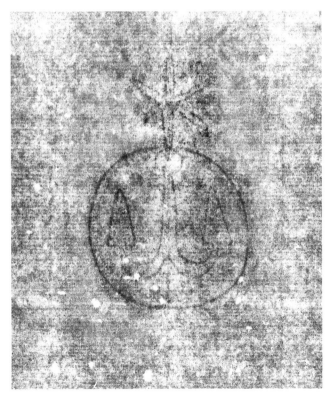

3 1550-1560

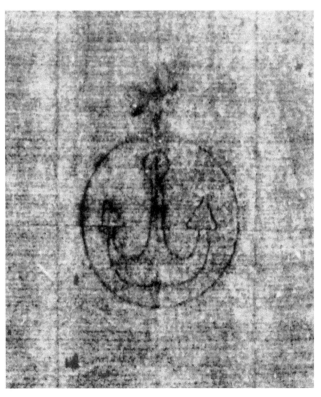

4 1621

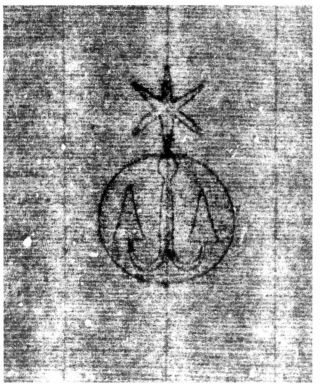

5   1554

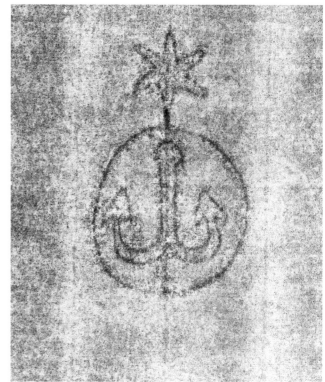

6   1535

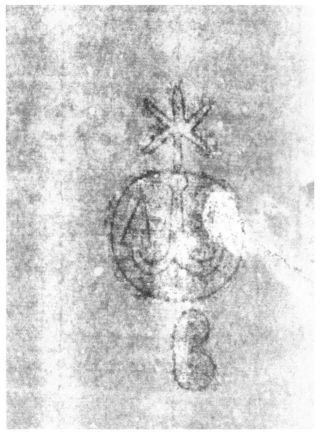

7   1570

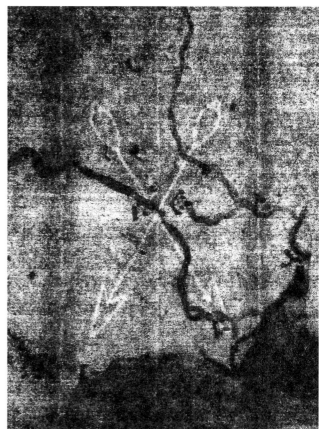

8   1558

ARROW

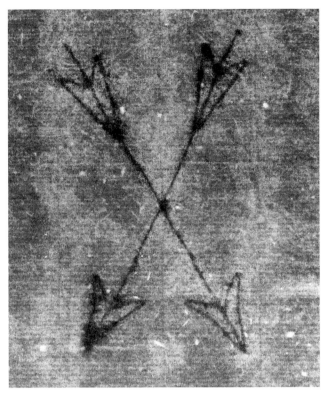

9   1593-1598

10   1588

11   1578

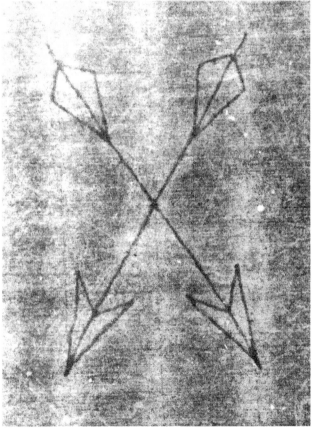

12   1578

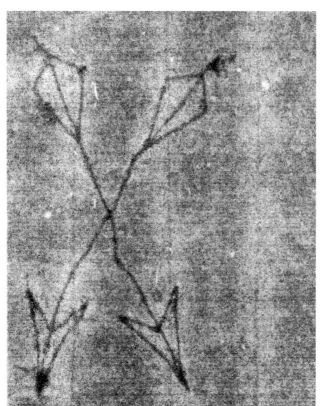

13   1579

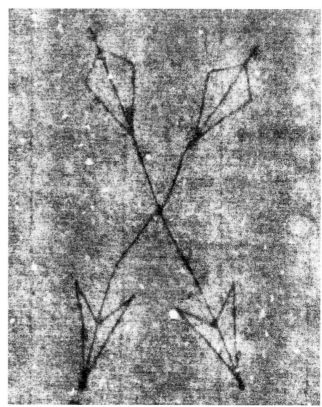

14   1579

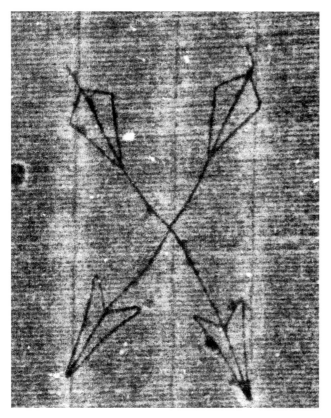

15   1593

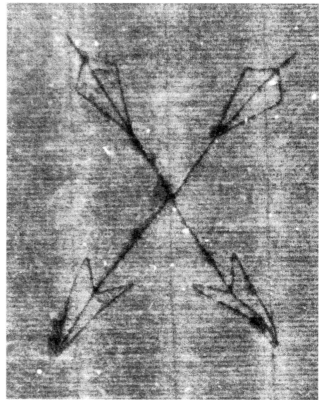

16   1593-1603

ARROW

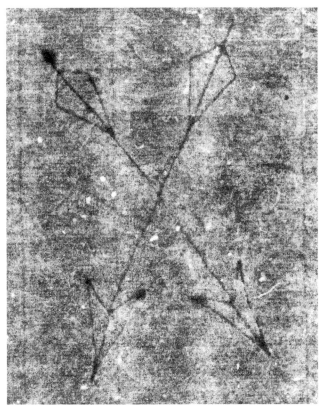

17　　　　　　　　　　　　　1574

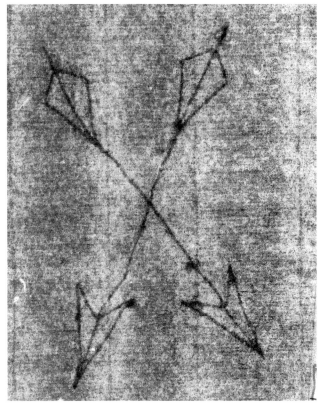

18　　　　　　　　　　　　　1574

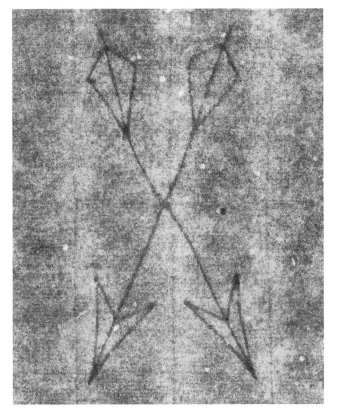

19　　　　　　　　　　　　　1573

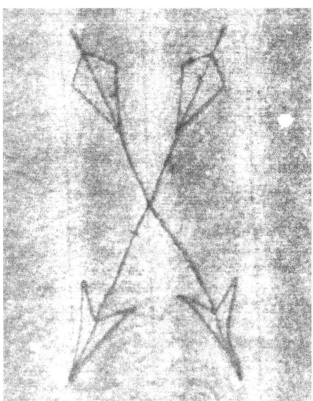

20　　　　　　　　　　　　　1571

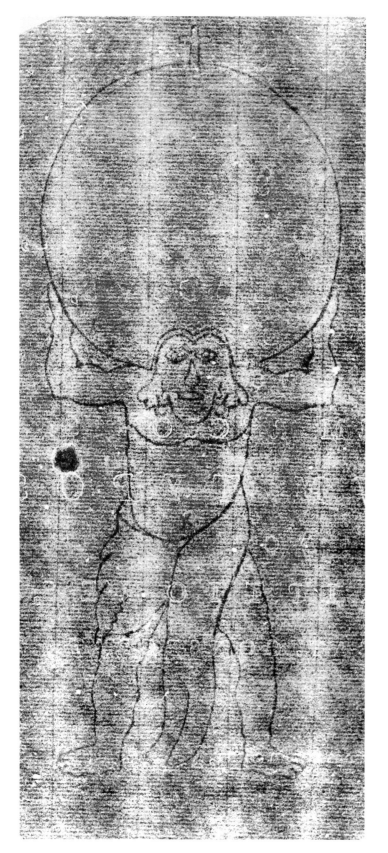
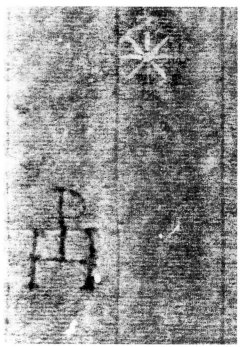

21a   1662   21b

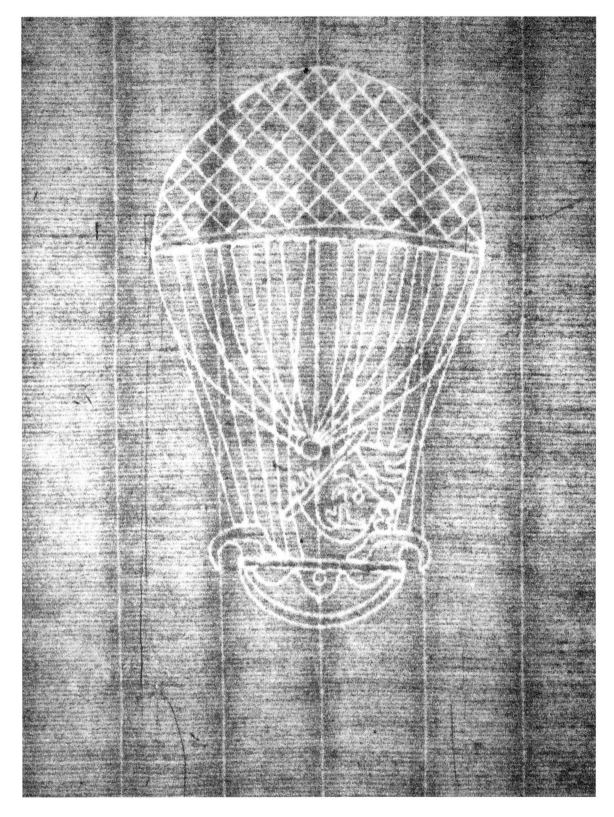

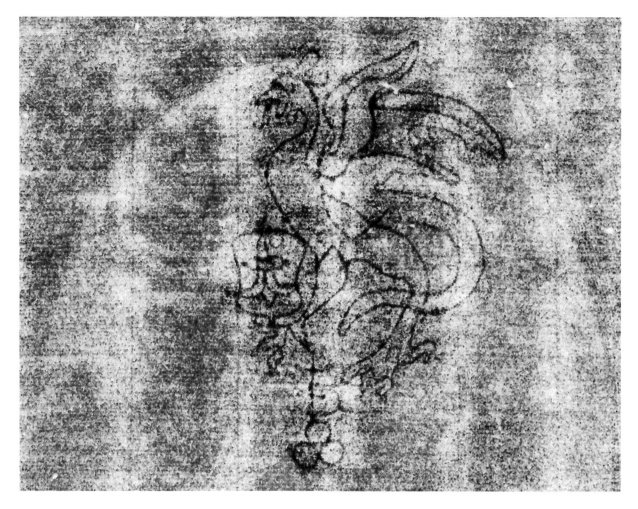

23　　　　　　　　　　　　　　　　　　　　　　　　　　　　1610

24　　　　　1535-1540

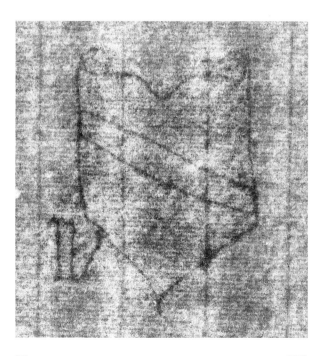

25　　　　　1651

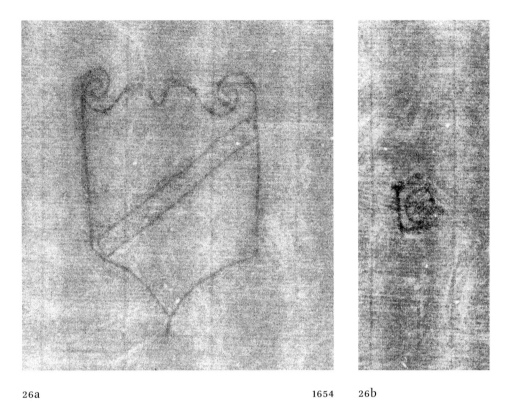

26a   1654   26b

27   1611

BEND

28   1600-1620

29a   1705-1739

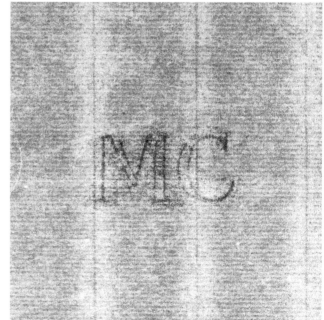

29b

30a 1635

30b

31a 1782

31b

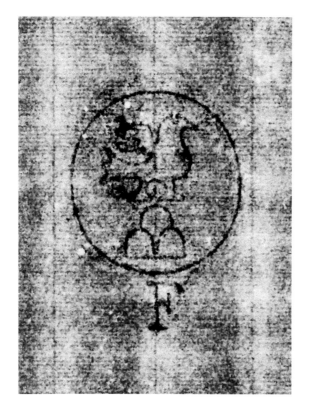

32   1800

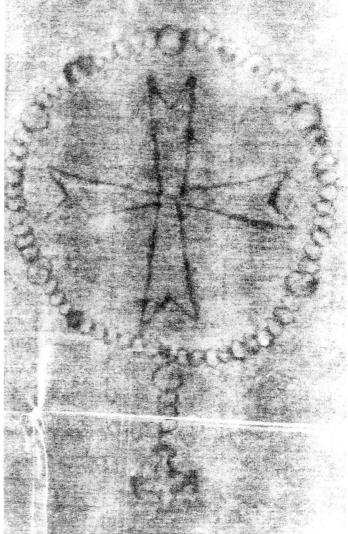

34a   1689

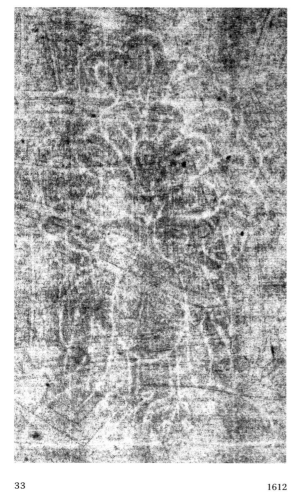

33   1612

34b

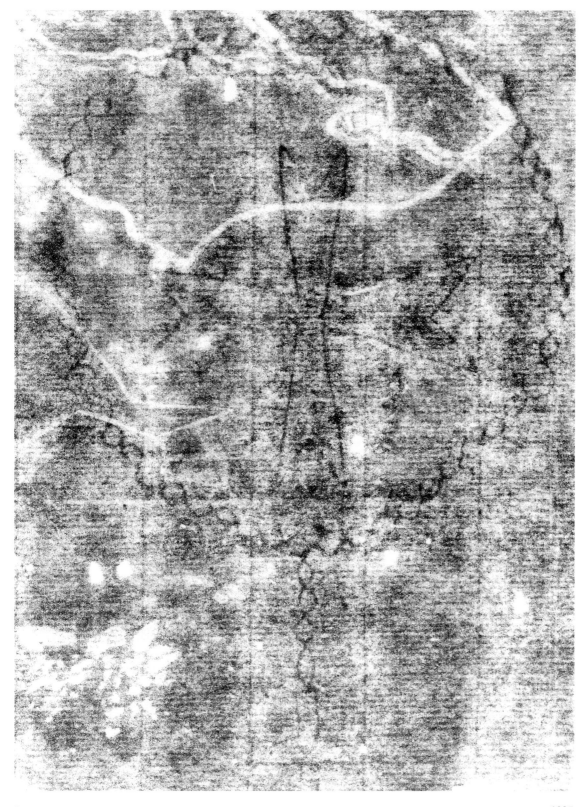

35a

1687

35b

36a

1681-1712

36b

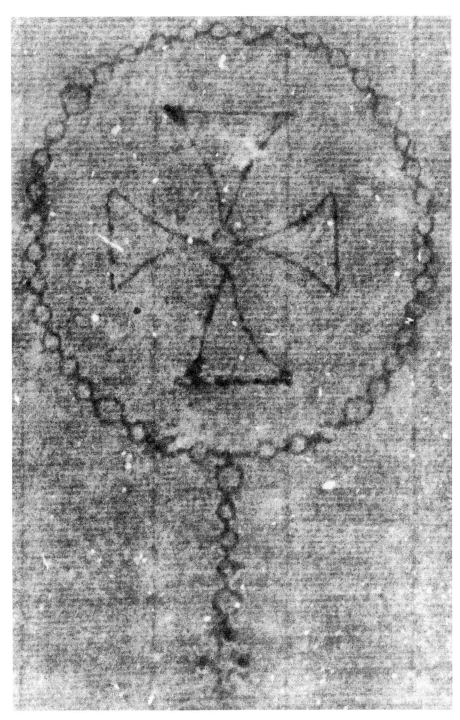

37a 1743

37b

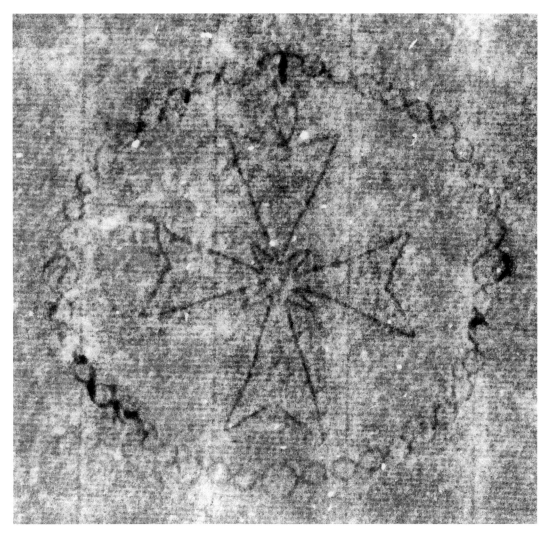

38a   1747

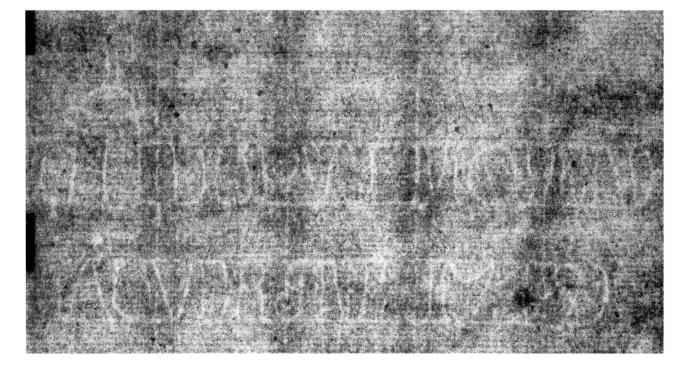

38b

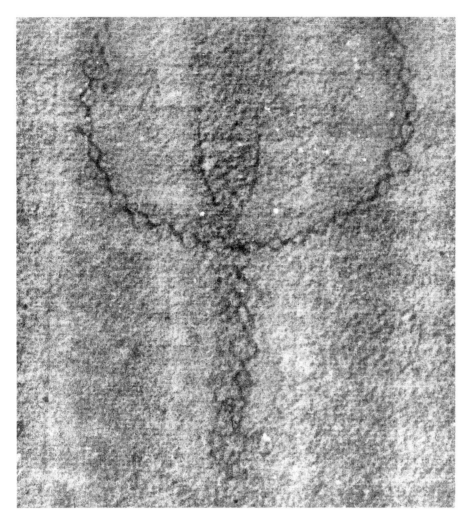

39a 1787

39b

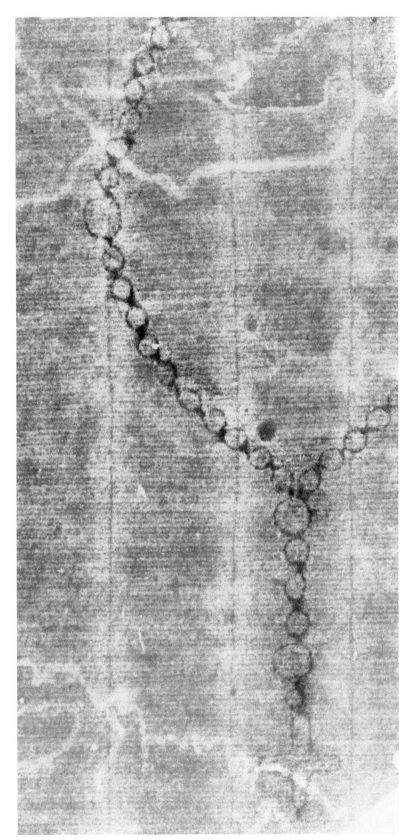

40a 1705 40b

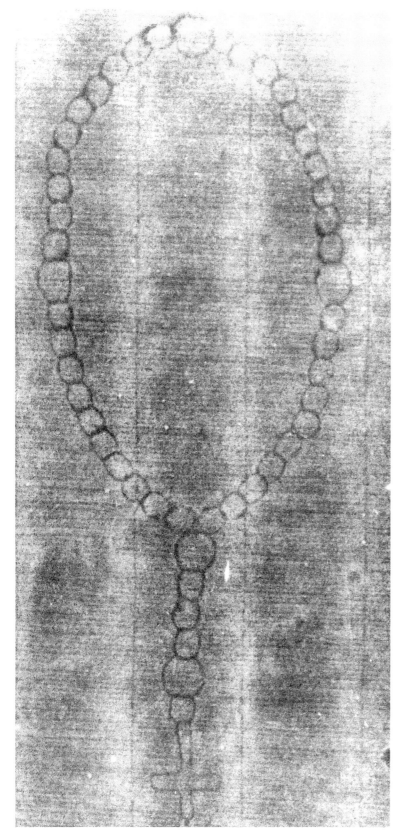

41a   1705   41b

CHAPLET–CIRCLES

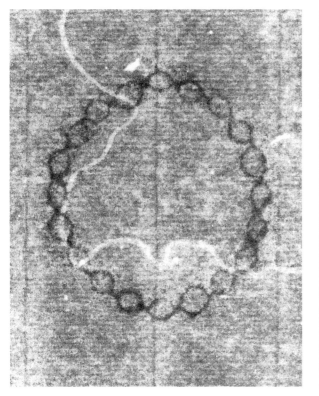

42a   1780   42b

43   1703

44   1670-1710

45   1670-1710

114   CIRCLES

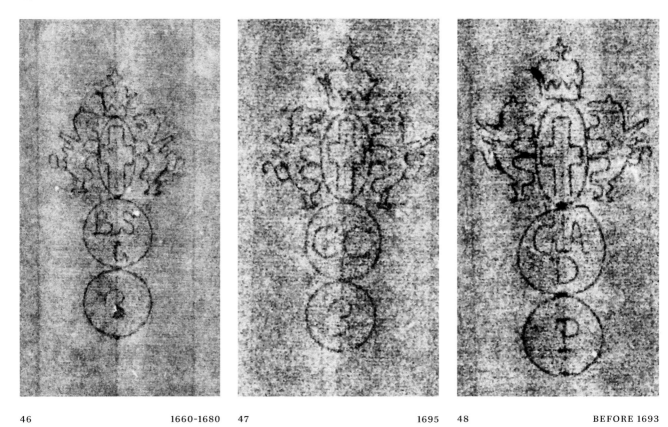

46   1660-1680   47   1695   48   BEFORE 1693

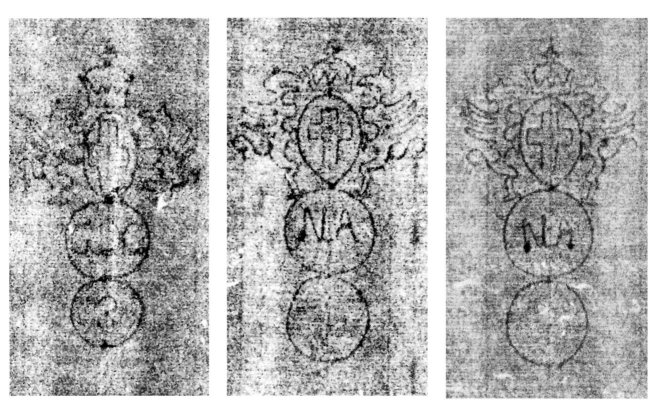

49   1660-1675   50   1660-1700   51   1660-1665

CIRCLES

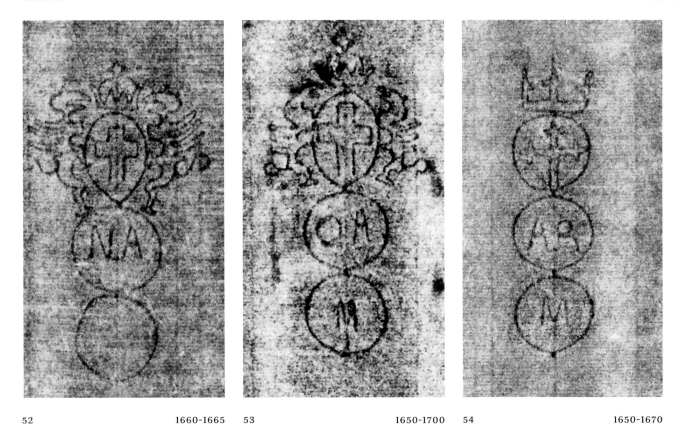

52   1660-1665   53   1650-1700   54   1650-1670

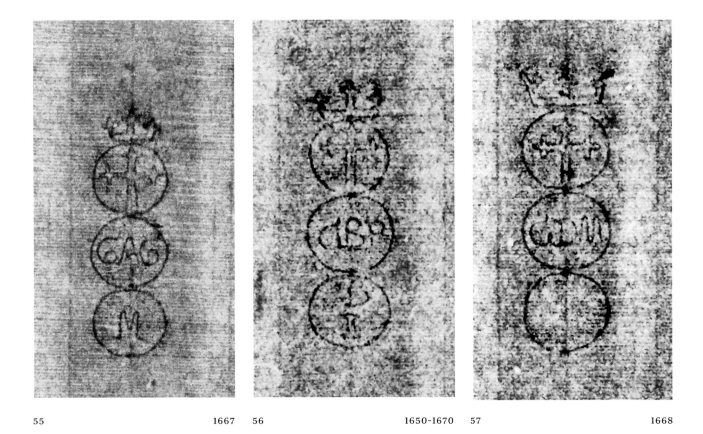

55   1667   56   1650-1670   57   1668

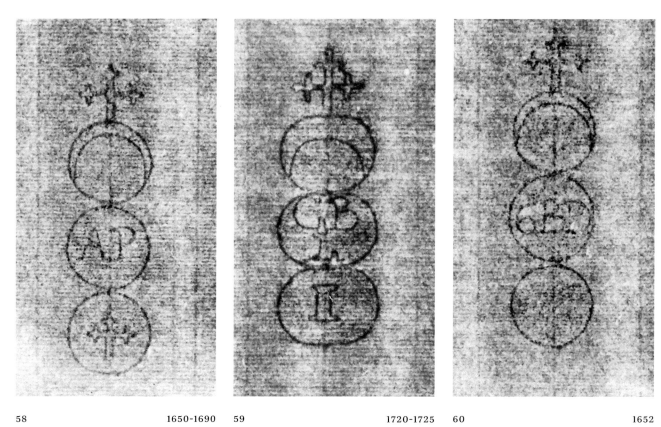

58 1650-1690   59 1720-1725   60 1652

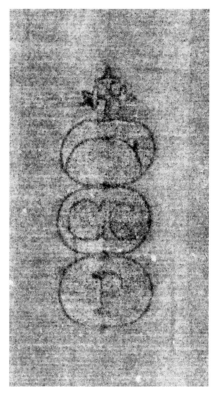  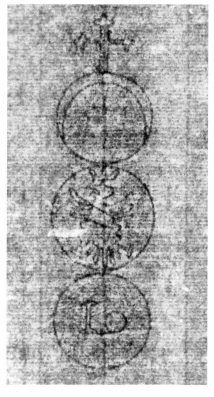

61 1660-1675   62 1660-1675   63 1670

CIRCLES—COAT OF ARMS

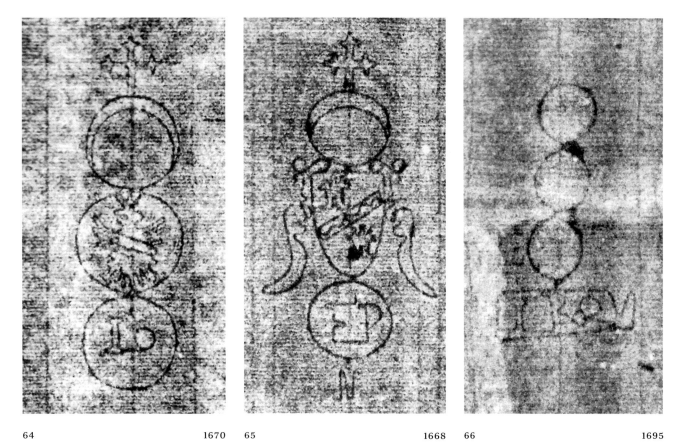

64 1670   65 1668   66 1695

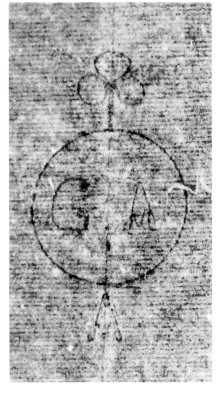 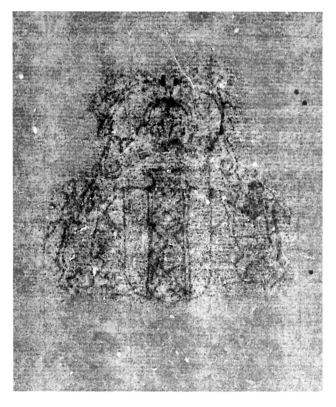

67 1600   68 1716

69   1690-1700

COAT OF ARMS

70   1683-1709

71   1685-1696

72a 1750

72b

COAT OF ARMS

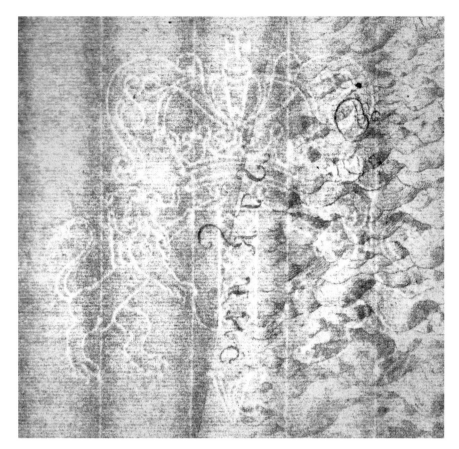

73a   1678

73b

74   1722-1730

COAT OF ARMS

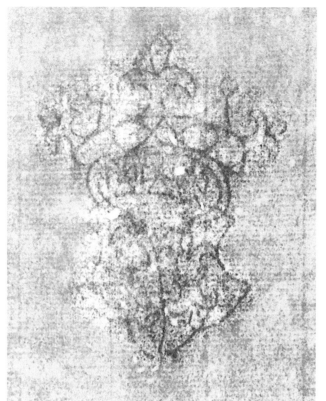

75　　　　　　　　　　　1730-1745

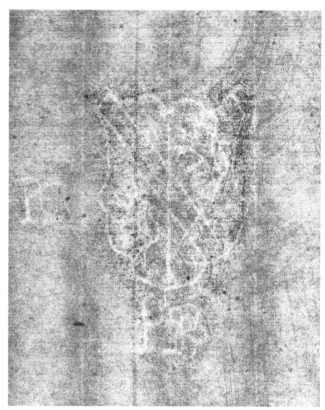

76　　　　　　　　　　　1625

77　　　　　　　　　　　1599-1638

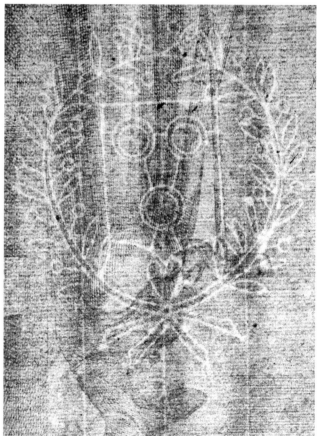

78　　　　　　　　　　　1670-1675

COAT OF ARMS

79   1645-1650

80   1584

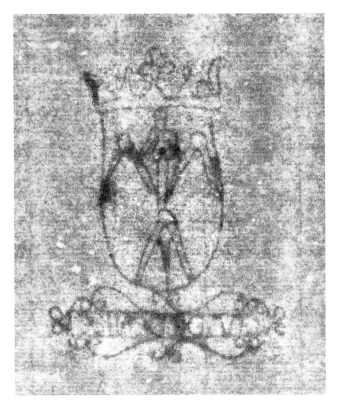

81   1584

82   1584

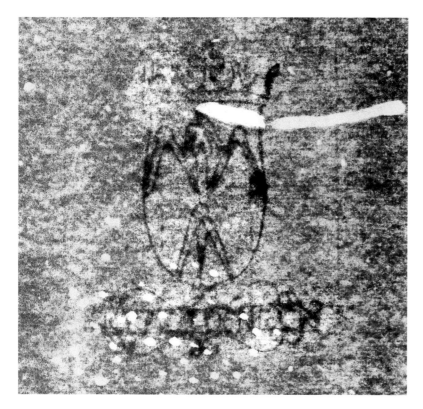

83   1584

 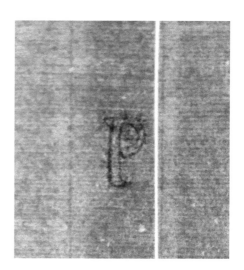

84a   1695-1700   84b

COAT OF ARMS   125

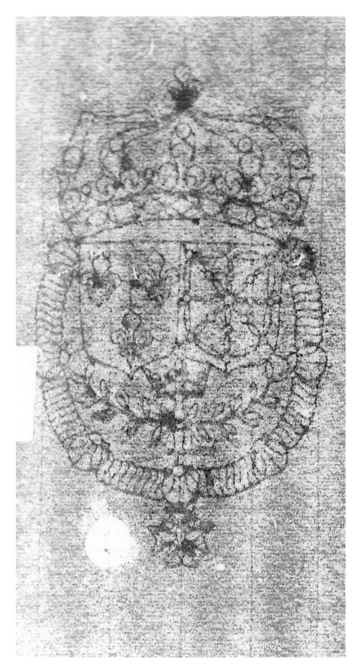

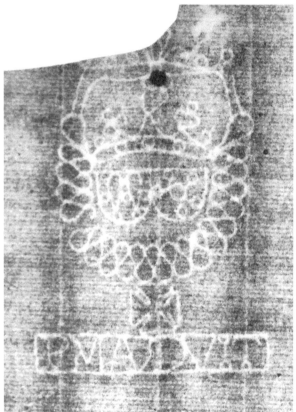

85   1645-1655   87   1677

86 ON NEXT PAGE

126   COAT OF ARMS

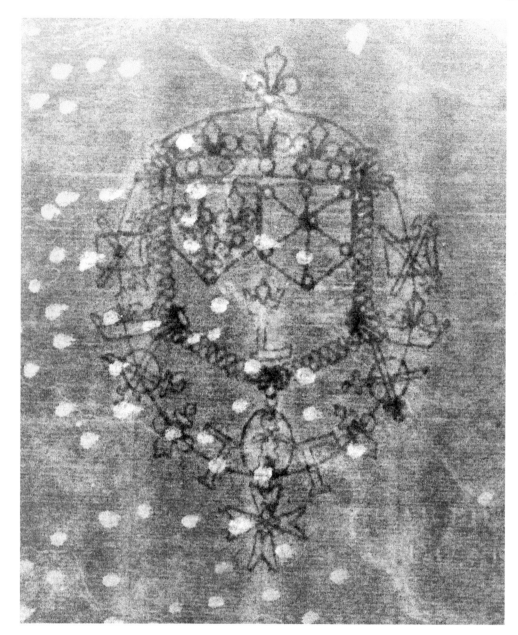

86   1630-1655

COAT OF ARMS

88   AFTER 1644

89a   1655-1691

COAT OF ARMS

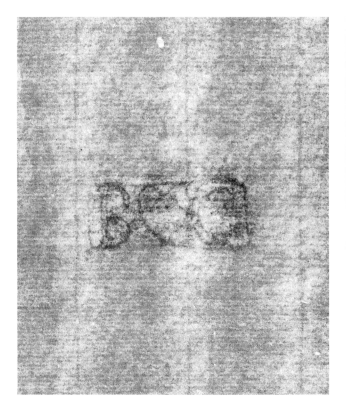

89b

90   1578

91   1559

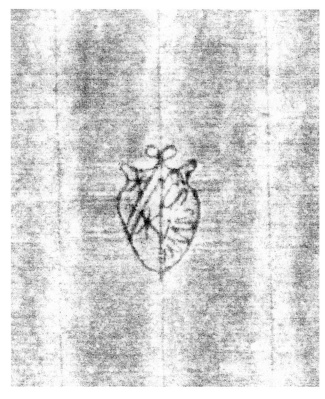

92   1550-1570

130   COAT OF ARMS

93   1550-1570

94   1769

95   1750

96   1595

COAT OF ARMS

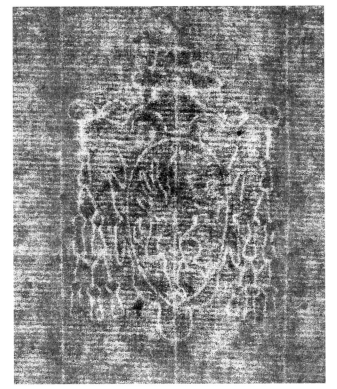

97   1603

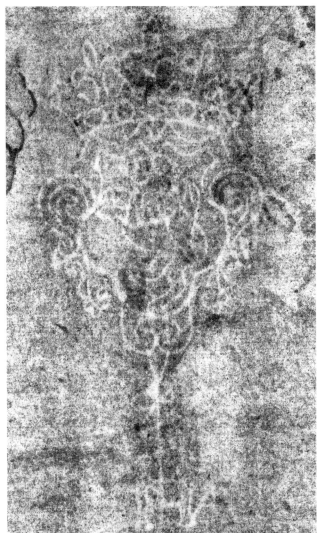

98   1780

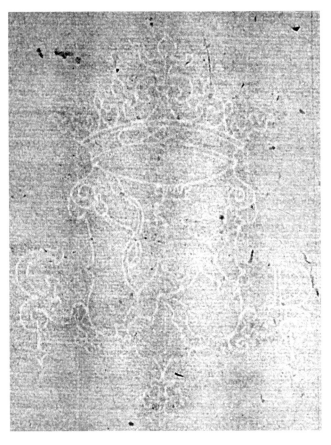

99   1678

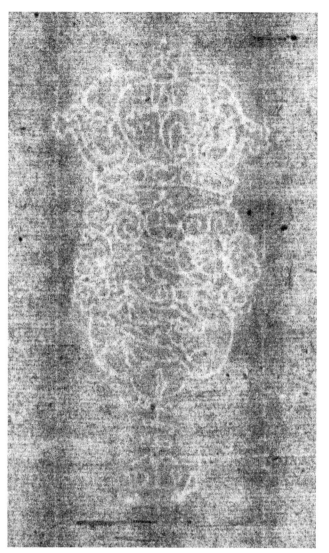

100   1780

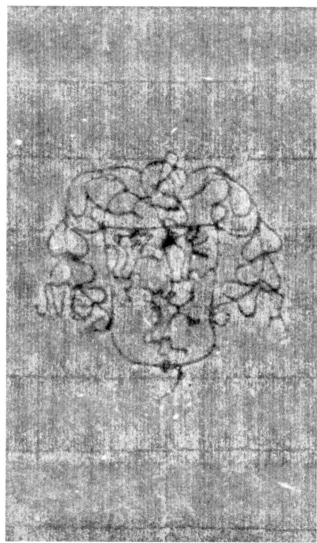

101   1660-1695

COAT OF ARMS

102a   1773

102b

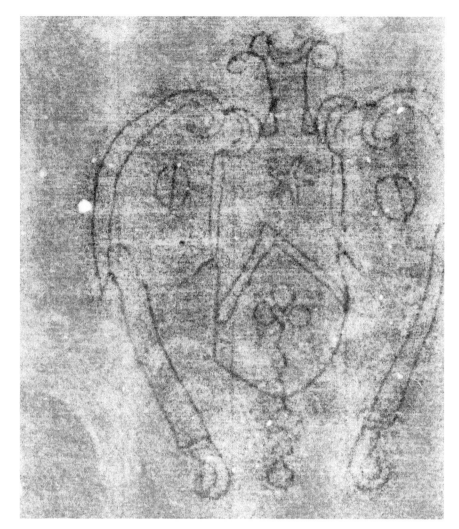

103a   1681

103b

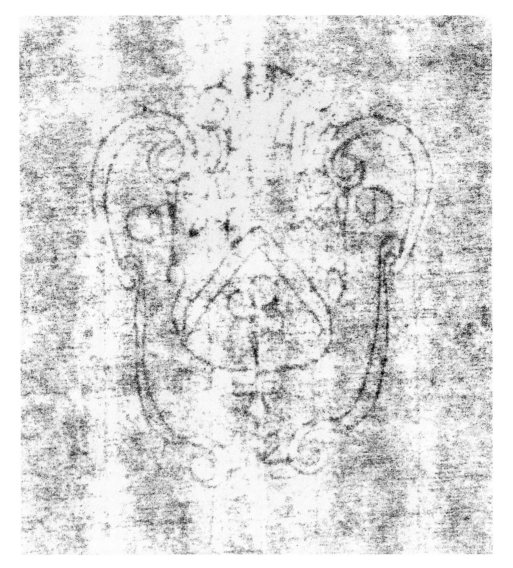

104a   1689

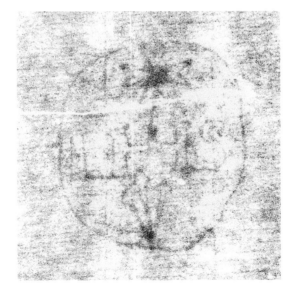

104b

105a 1679

105b

COAT OF ARMS

106 1780-1820

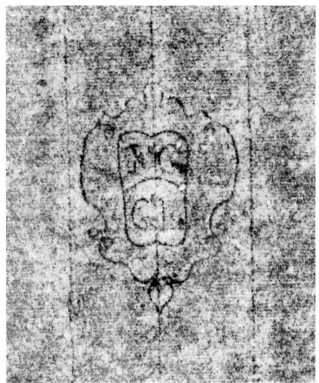

107 1795

108a 1773

138 COAT OF ARMS

108b

109   1580

110   1580

111   1760

COAT OF ARMS

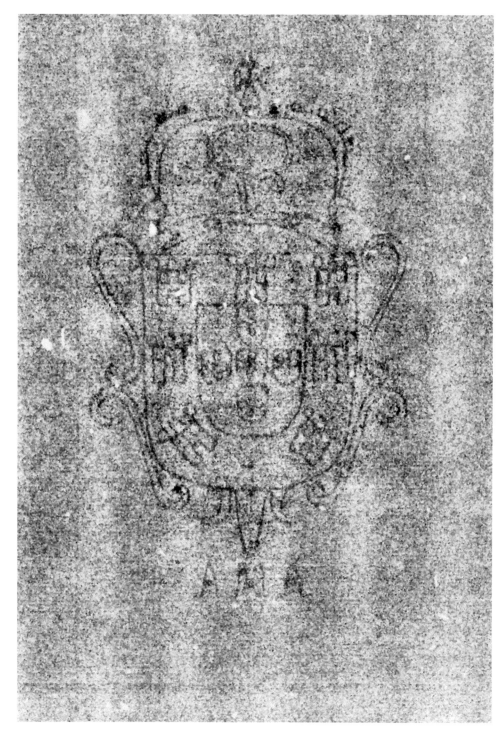

112   1775

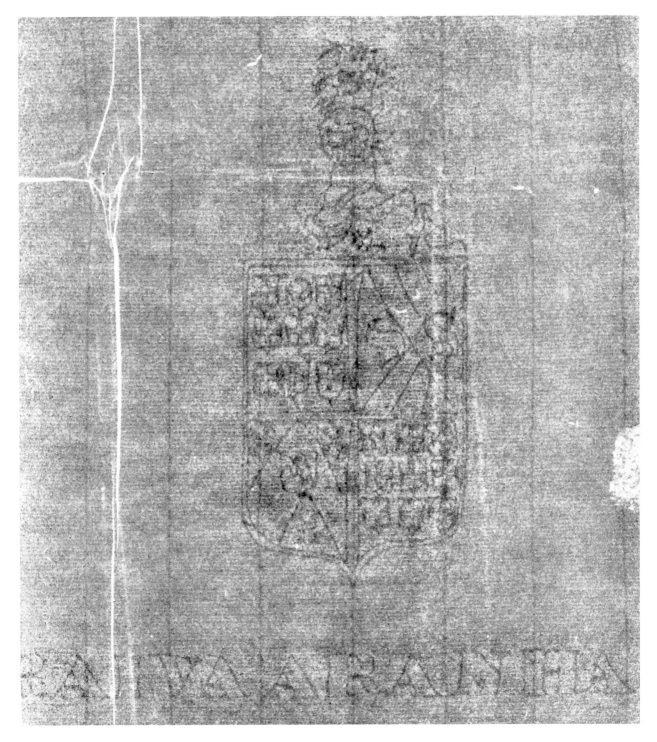

COAT OF ARMS

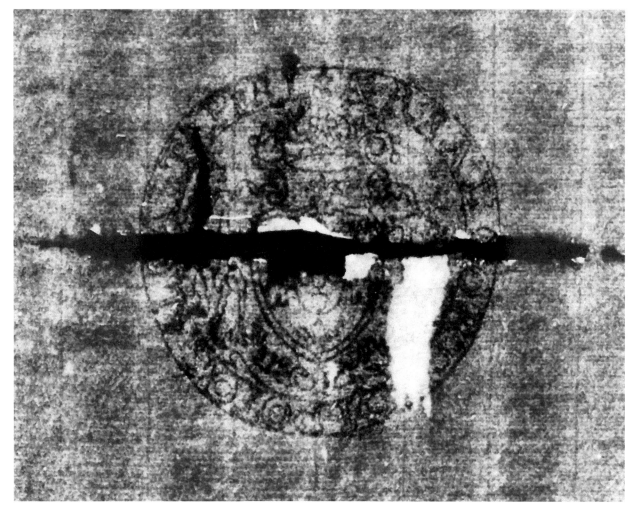

114a   1785

114b

115b   1755

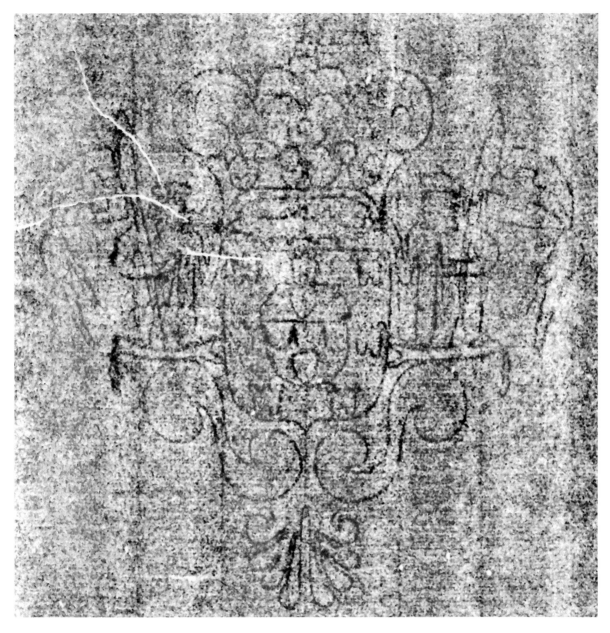

115a 1755

116a 1750

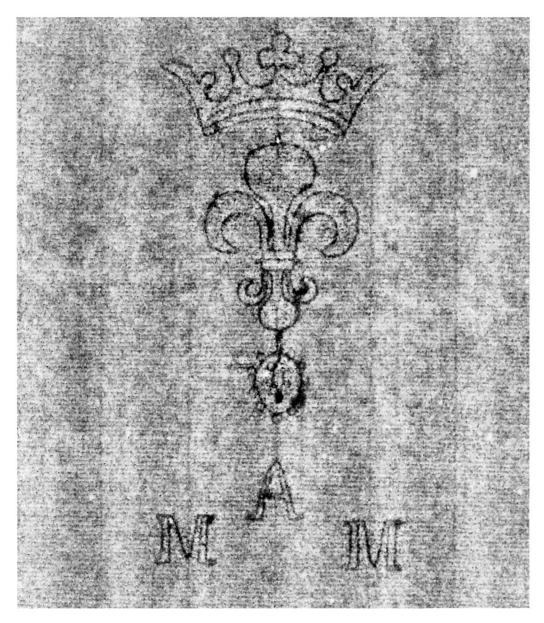

116b

COAT OF ARMS

117a   1750

117b

COAT OF ARMS

118a   1750

118b

COAT OF ARMS

119a   1745

119b

120a   1750

120b

COAT OF ARMS

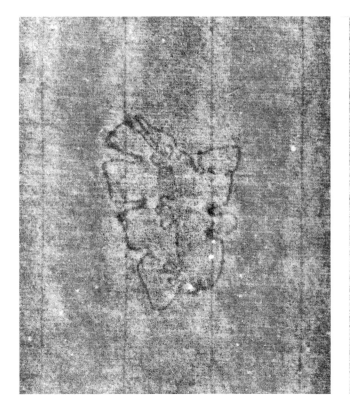

121   1623-1627

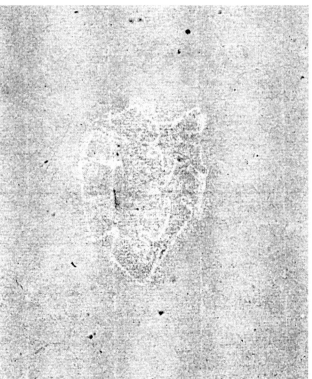

122   1623-1627

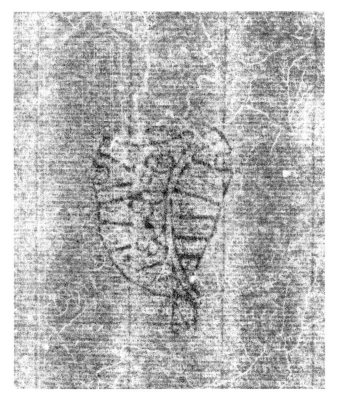

123   1612

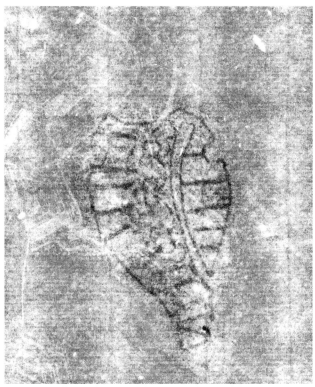

124   1612

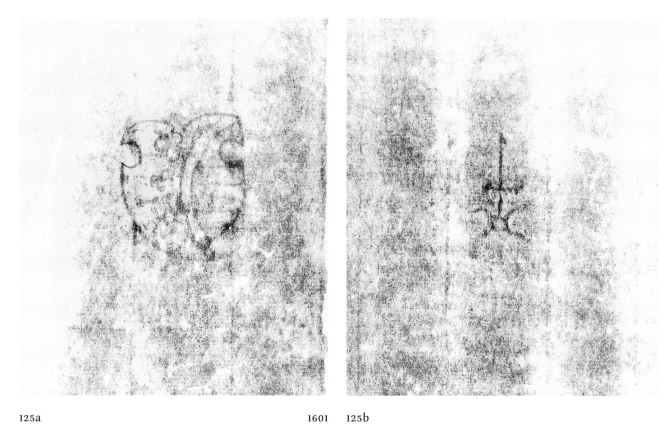

125a   1601   125b

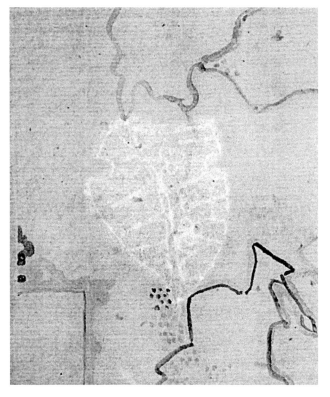 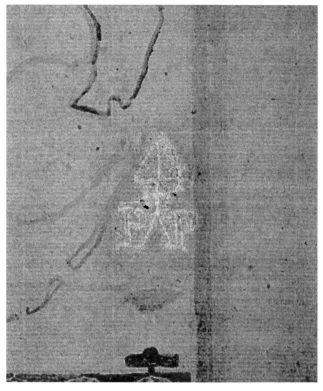

126a   1613   126b

COAT OF ARMS

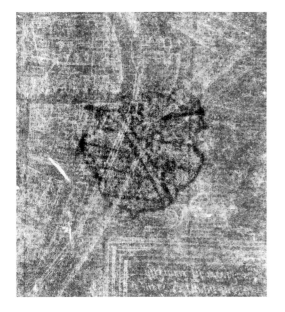

127a   1609

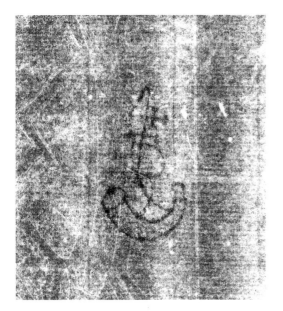

127b

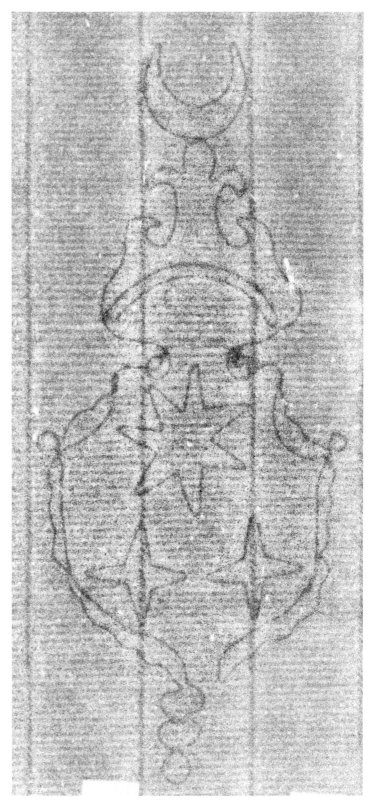

128a   1784

128b

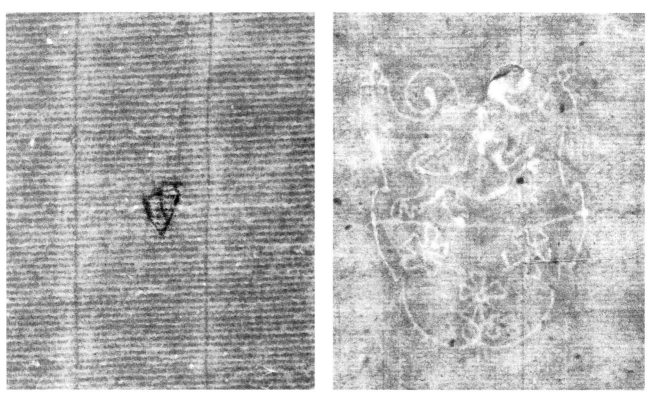

129   1581   130   1615

COAT OF ARMS

131a

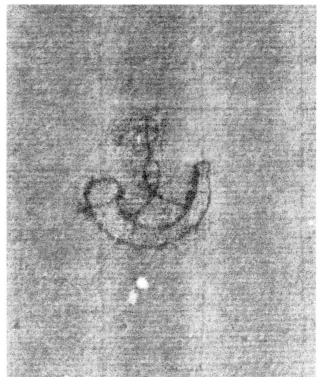

1609   131b

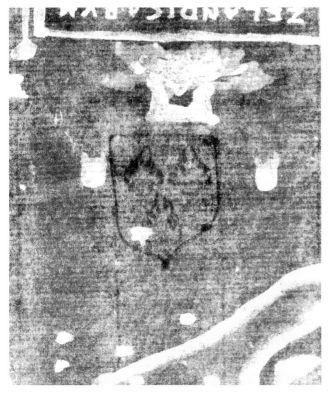

132a

1609-1612   132b

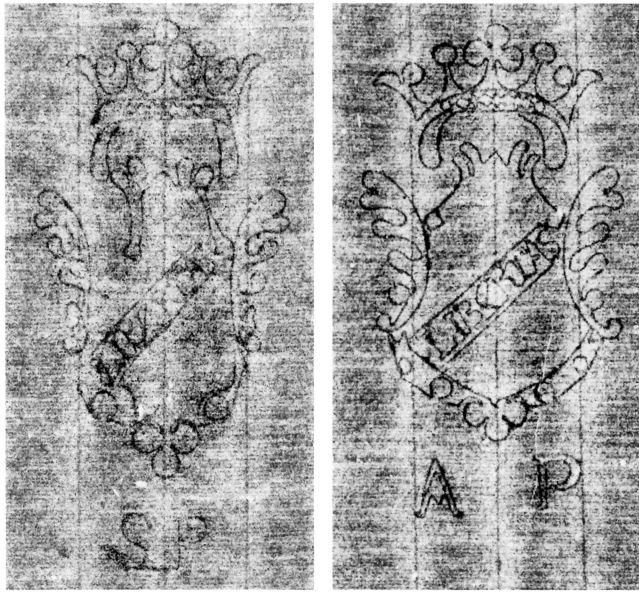

133   1750   134   1750

135   1755

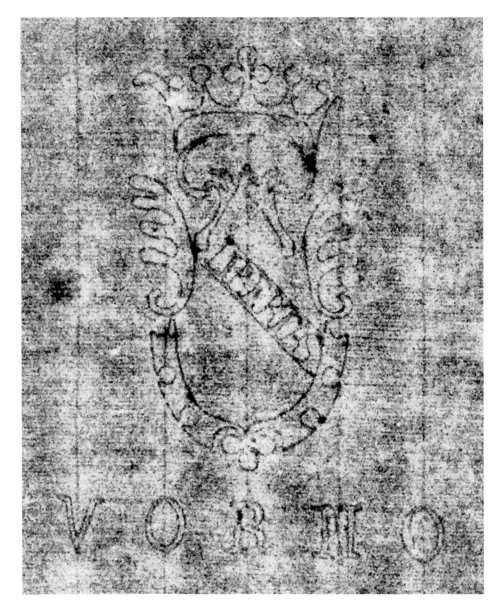

COAT OF ARMS 161

137a   1750

137b

138a   1792

138b

139a   1747

139b

COAT OF ARMS

140 1610

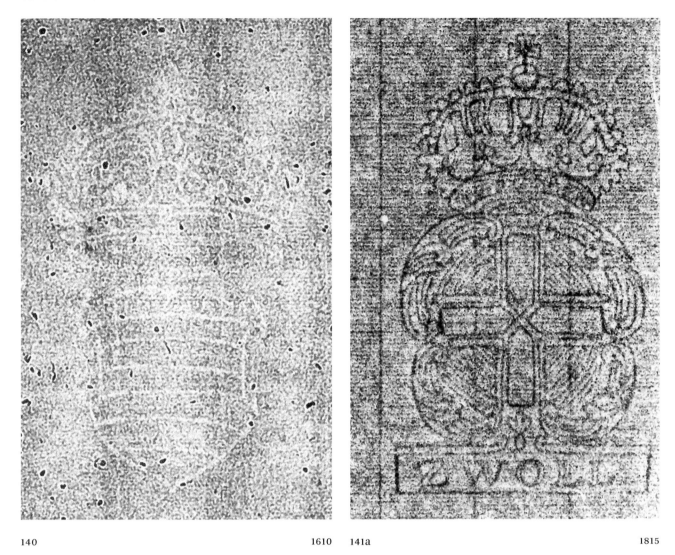

141a 1815

141b

142   1639

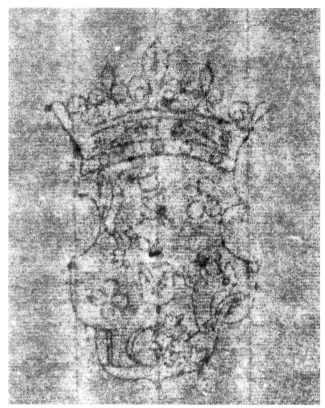

143   1635

144   1673

COAT OF ARMS

145 1673

146 1693

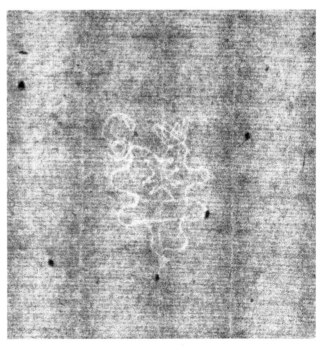

147 1624-1665

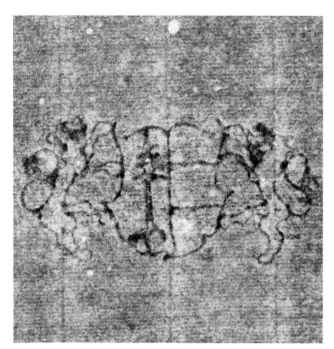

148   1598-1626

149   1520-1540

150   1720

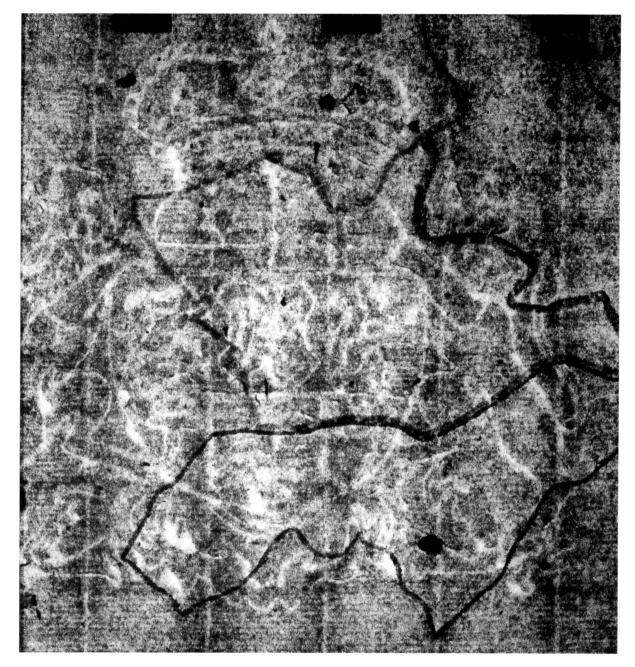

151a 1789

COAT OF ARMS—CRESCENT

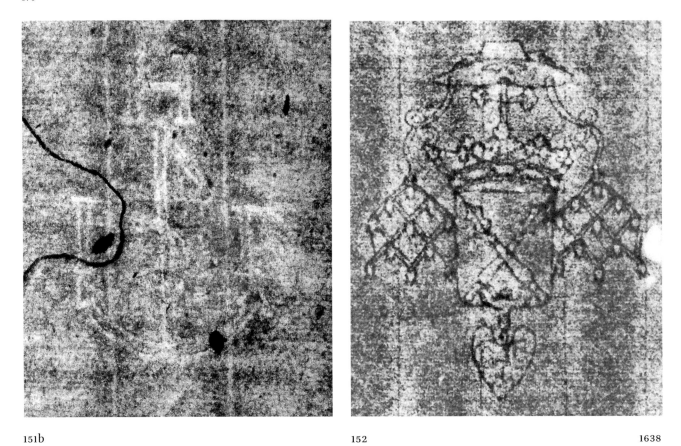

151b

152   1638

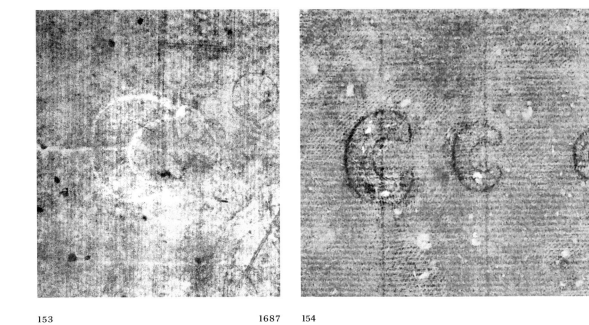

153   1687   154   1595-1620

155a 1778

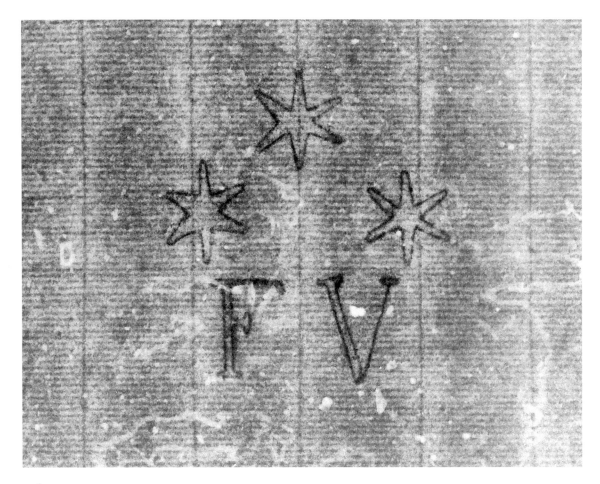

155b

156   1567

157   1551-1562

158   1620

159   1610-1620

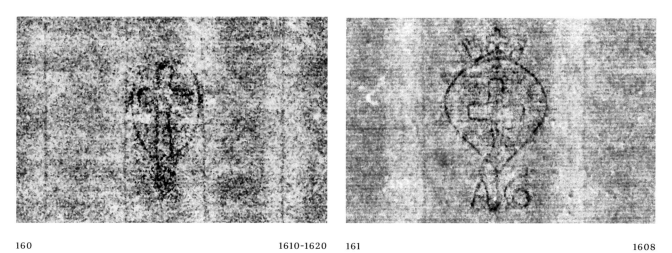

160   1610-1620   161   1608

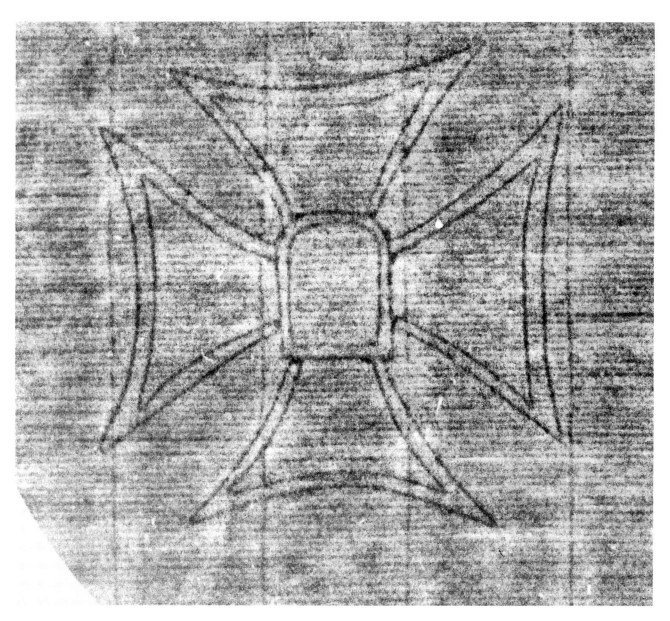

162a   1777

CROSS—CROSSBOW—CROWN

162b

163   1550-1560

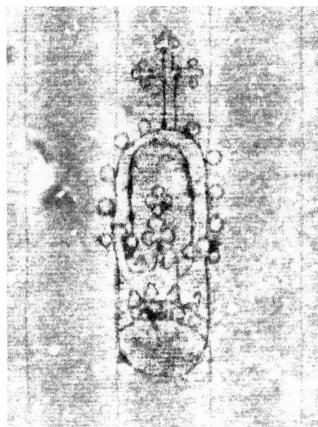

164   1569

CROWN

165   1565-1606

166   1565-1606

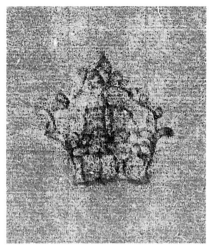

167   1635

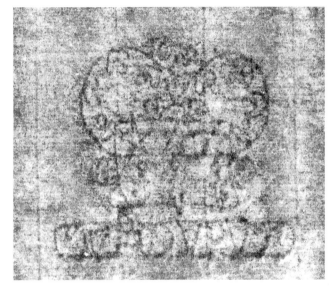

168   1672

169   1578-1600

170   1578-1600

171   1578-1600

CROWN—CROZIER

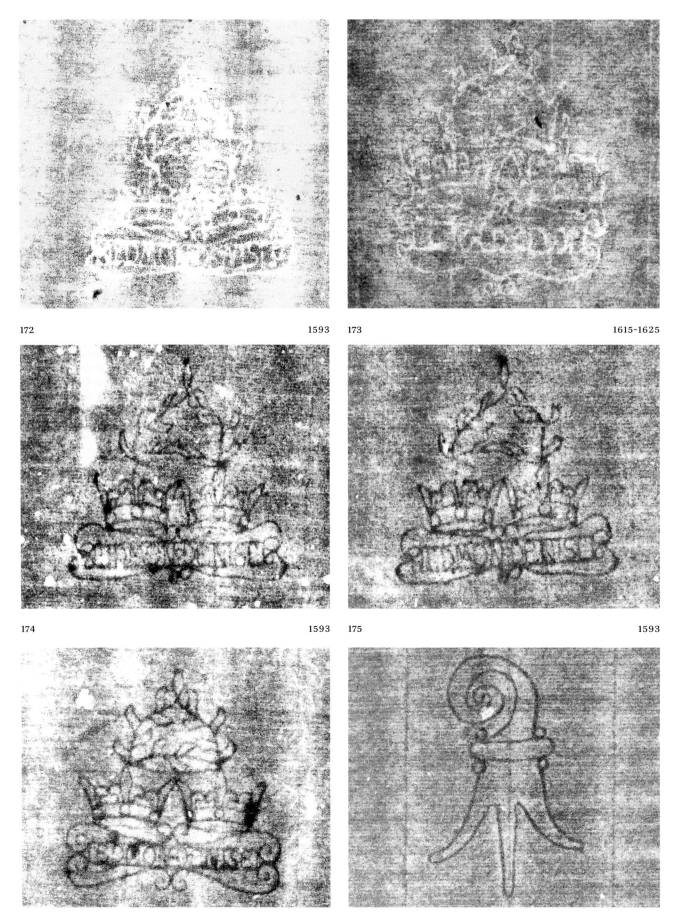

172   1593
173   1615-1625
174   1593
175   1593
176   1596-1597
177   1544

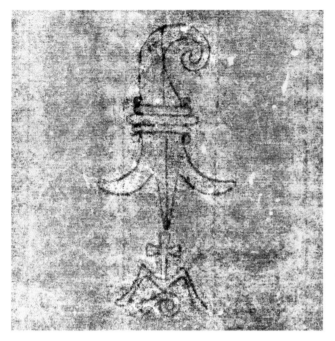

178 1585

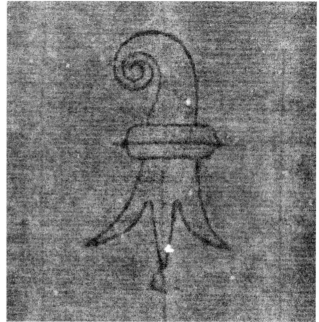

179 1572-1617

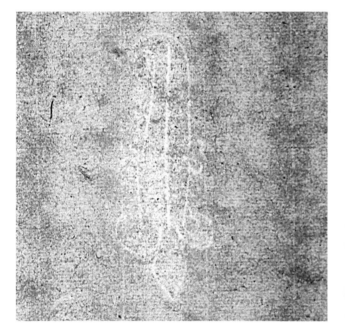

180 1623-1627

181 1630

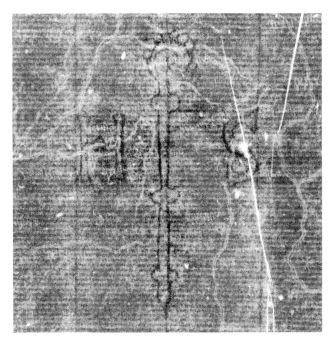
182 1656

183 1808

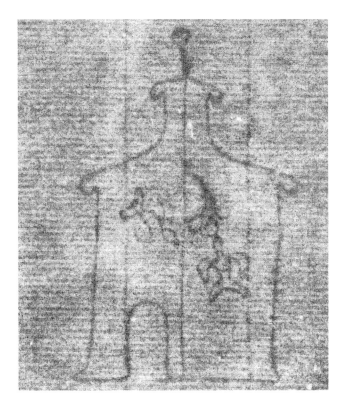
184a 1693

184b

DOVECOT

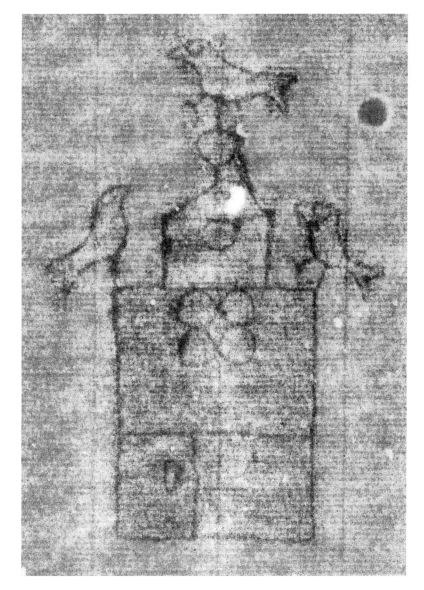

185a   1757

185b

EAGLE

186   1582

187   1579

188   1585

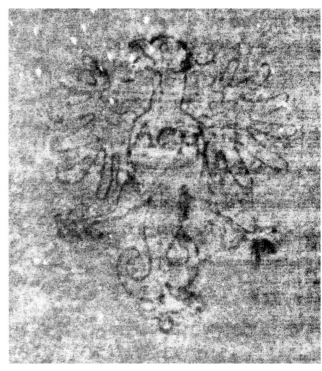

189   1579

EAGLE

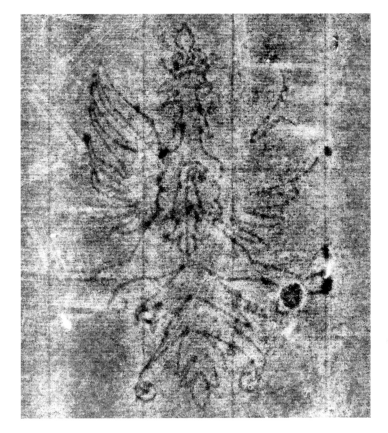

190　　　　　　　　　　　　　　　　　　　1635

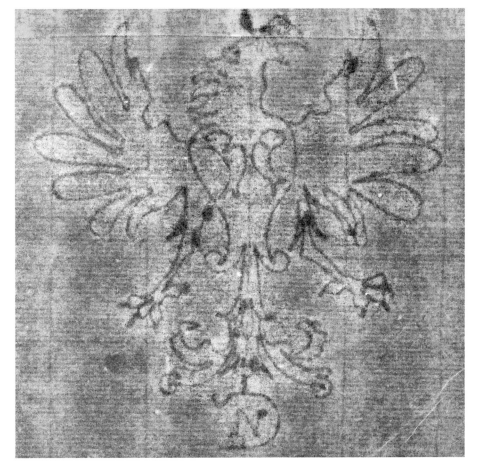

191　　　　　　　　　　　　　　　　　　　1612

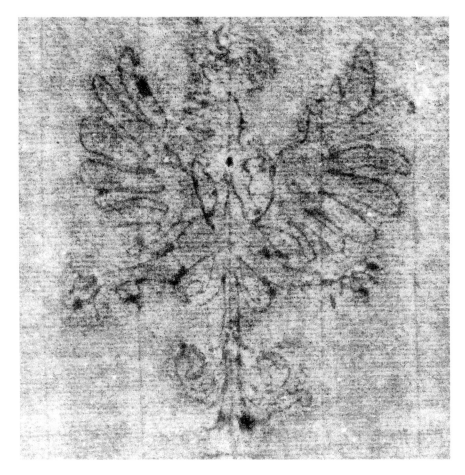

192 1612

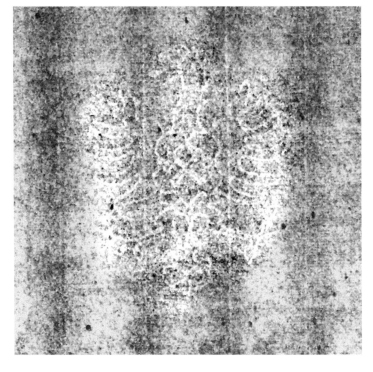

193 1711

EAGLE

194 1572

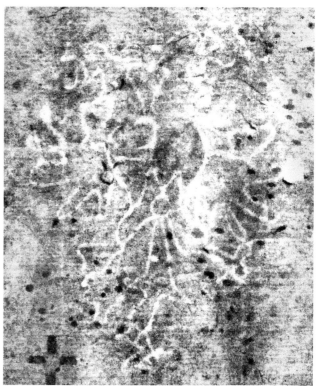

195 1617

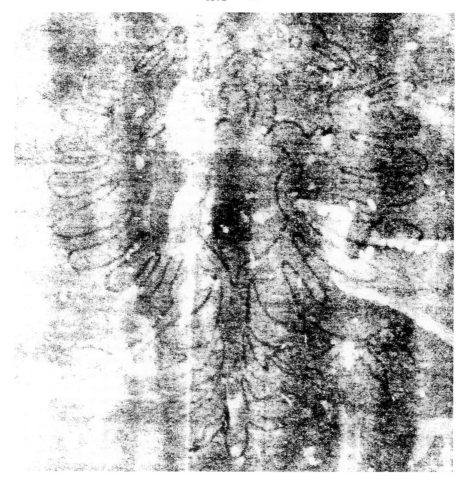

196 1596

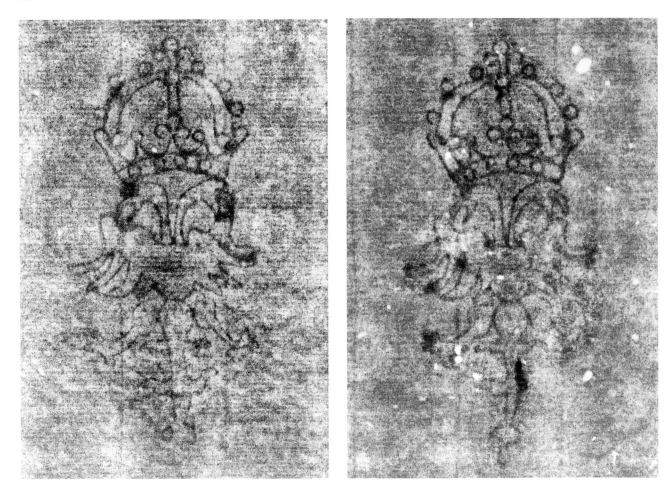

197   1585   198   1583

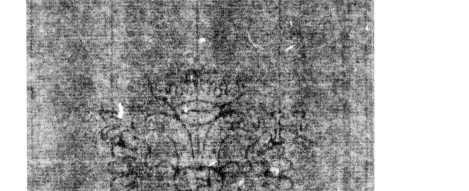

199   1630

EAGLE

200   1700-1725

201   1630

202 1693

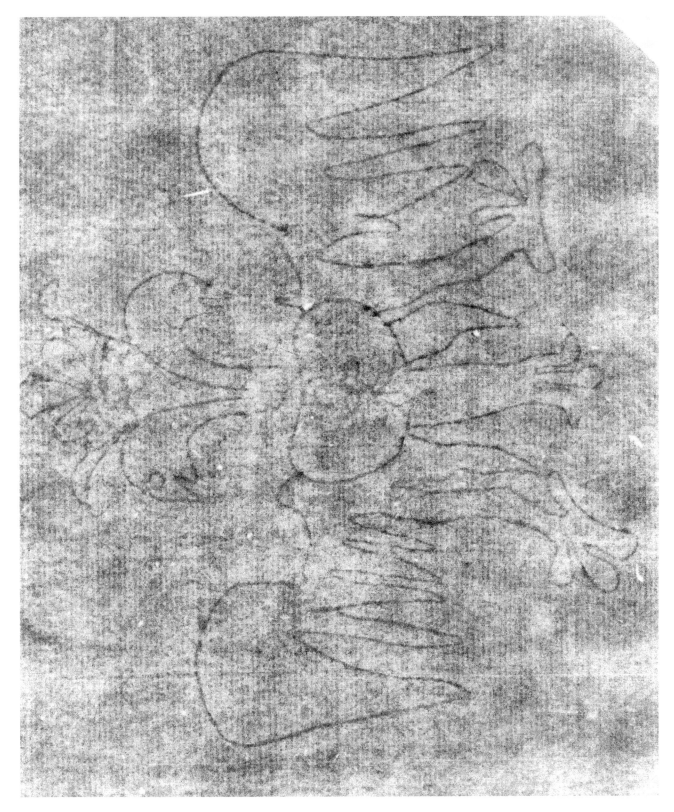

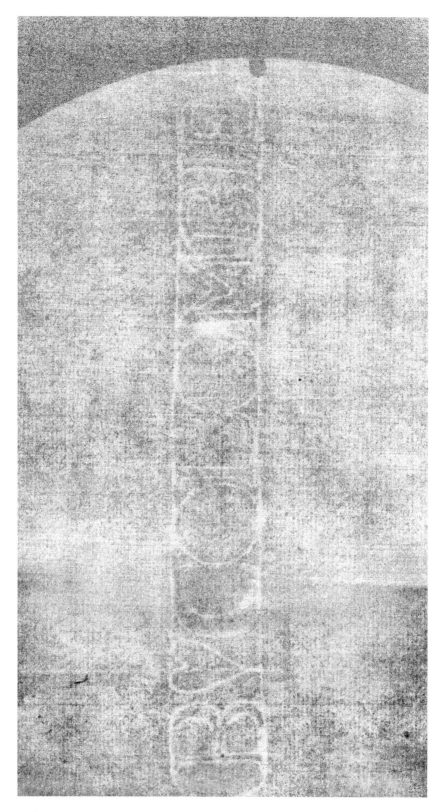

203b

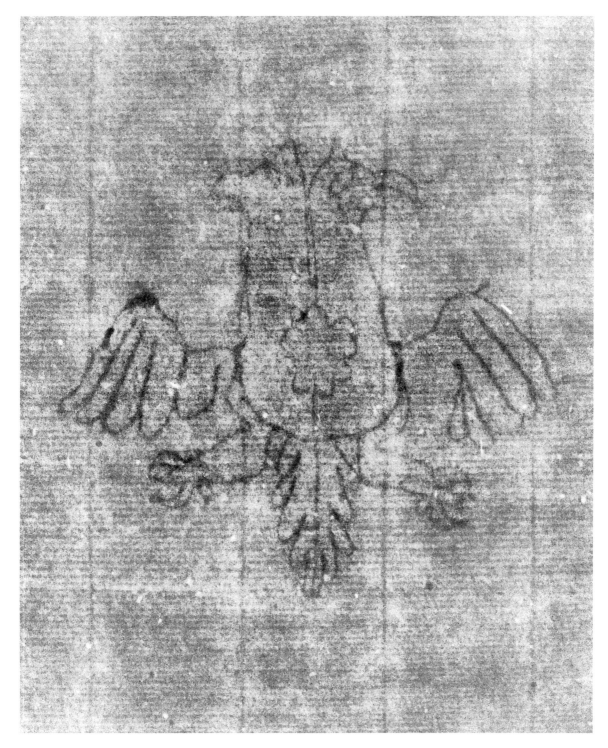

204a 1794

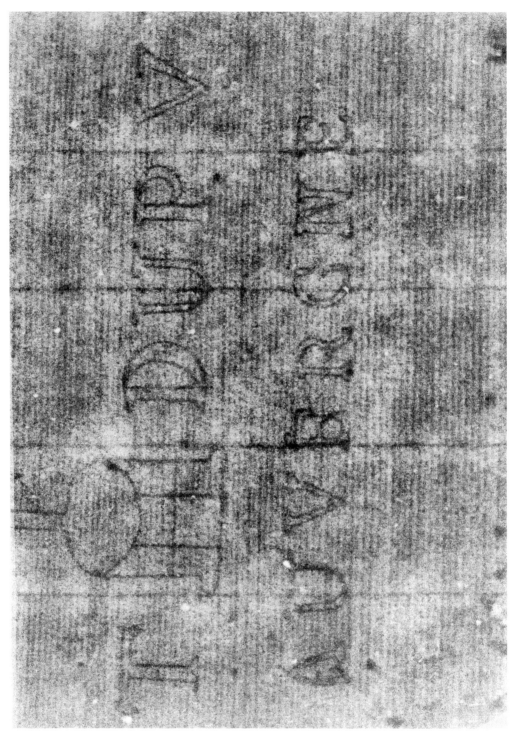

204b

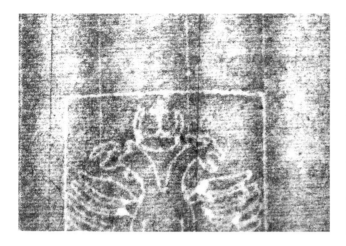

205   1666

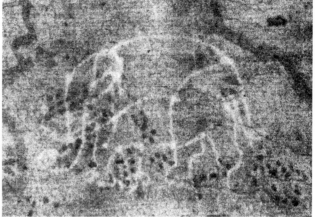

206   1660

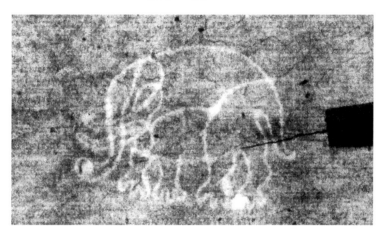

207   1695

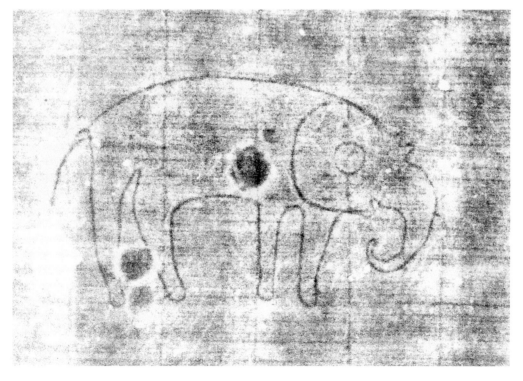

208   1655-1660

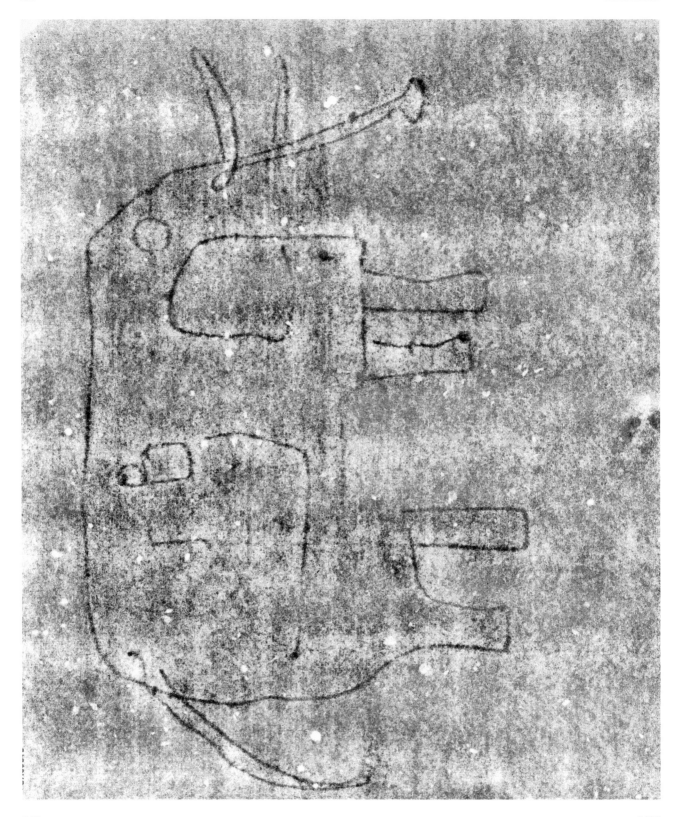

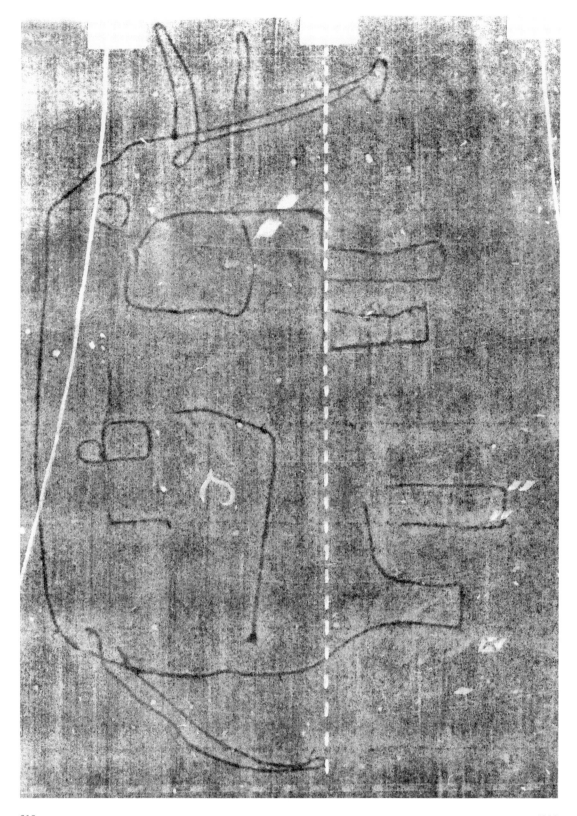

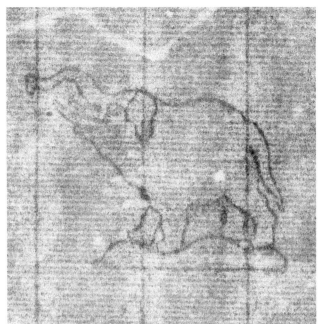

211a

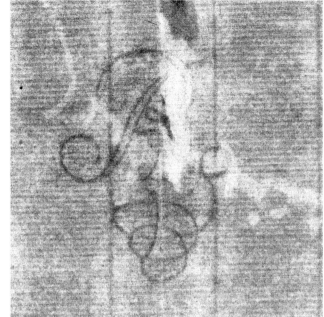

1784-1793 211b

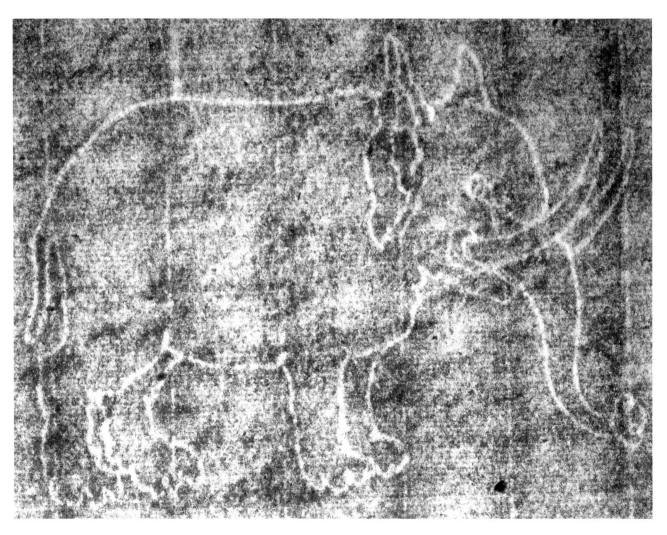

212 1780

FIGURES

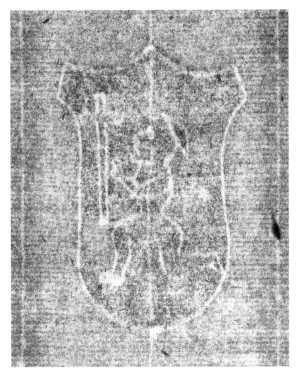

213   1558

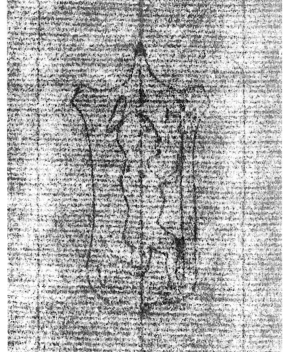

214   1550

215   1609

216   1662

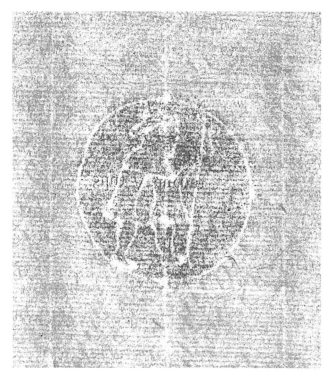

217   1568

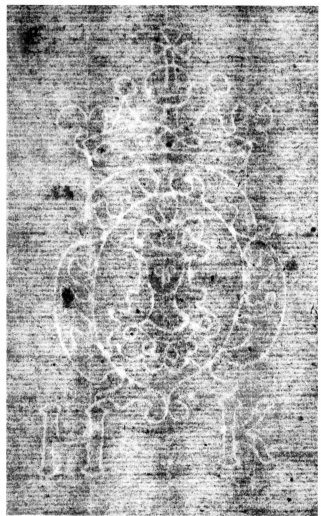

218   1663-1692

219   1740

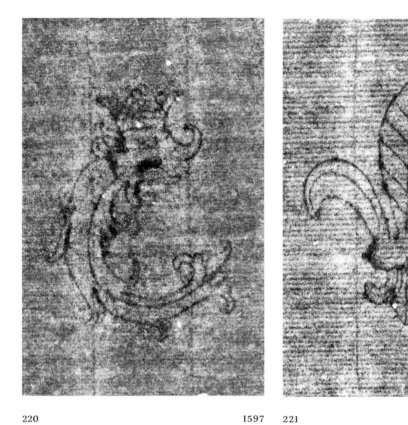

220 1597 221 1659

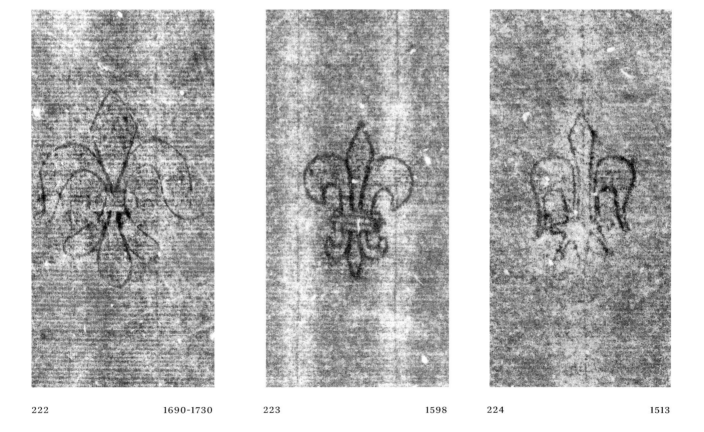

222 1690-1730 223 1598 224 1513

225　　　　　　1617

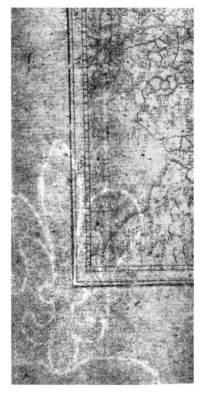

226　　　　　　1613

227　　　　　　1608

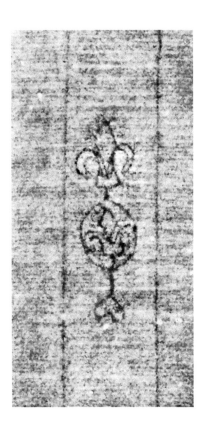

228　　　　　　1601

229　　　　　　1588

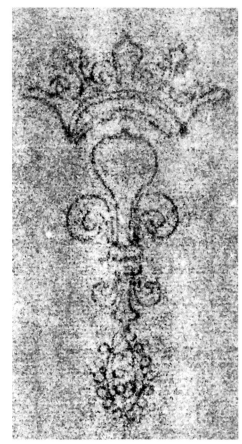

230　　　　　　1750

FLEUR DE LIS

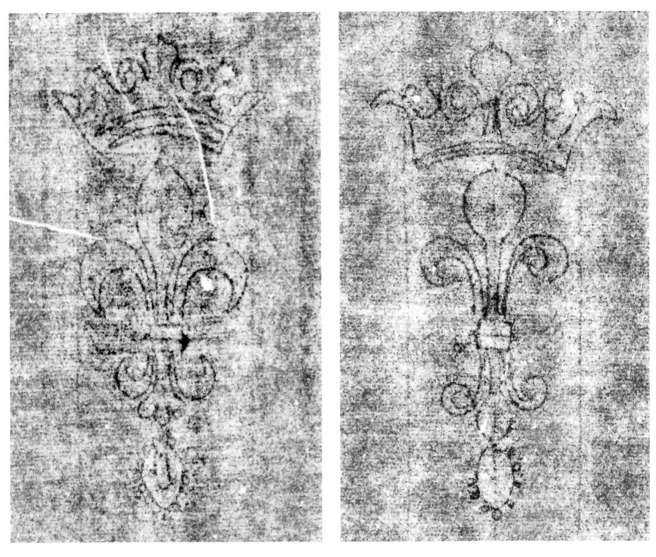

231 1750 232 1750

233   1755   234   1750

FLEUR DE LIS

235   1675

236   1728

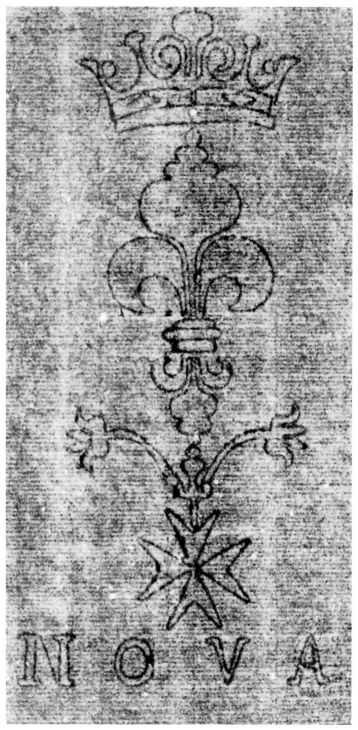

237   1750

FLEUR DE LIS

238   1745-1755

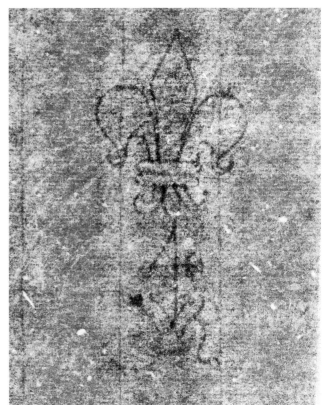

239   1639

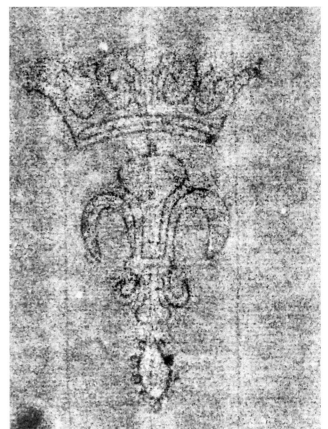

240a   1700

FLEUR DE LIS

240b

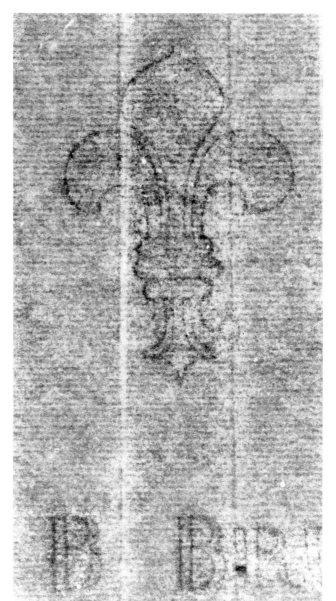

241a 1783

241b

242a 1745

242b

243a

1676

243b

244a

1630

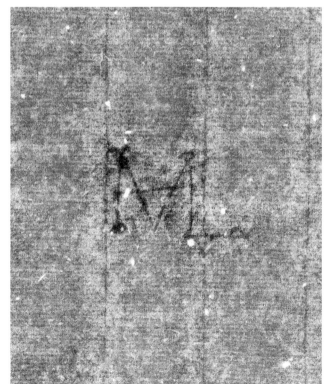

244b

245a   1785

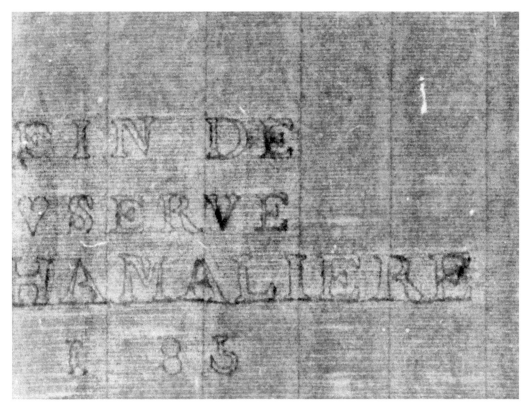

245b

208　　　　　　　　　　　　　　　　　　　　　　　　　　　　　　　　　　　　　FLEUR DE LIS

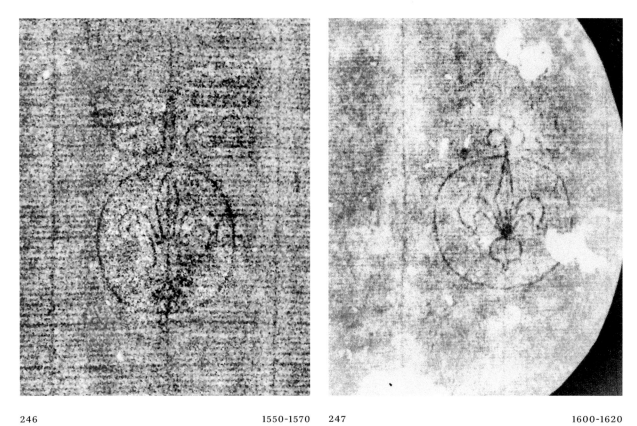

246　　　　　　　　　1550-1570　　247　　　　　　　　　1600-1620

248　　　　　　　　　1750　　249　　　　　　　　　1750

FLEUR DE LIS

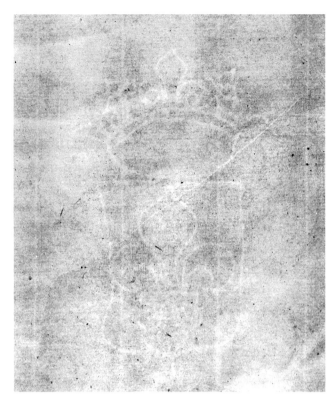

250   1652

251   1652

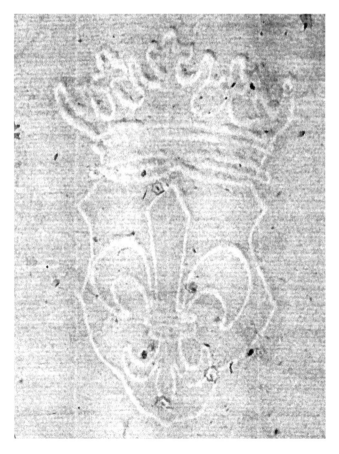

252   1658

253   1730

254a

254b

1726

255 1648

FLEUR DE LIS

257 1654 258 1650

259   1675

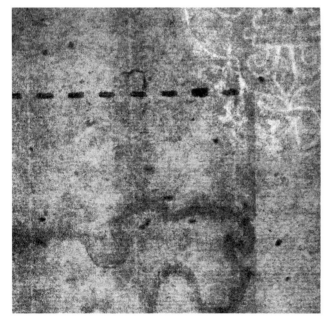

260   1613

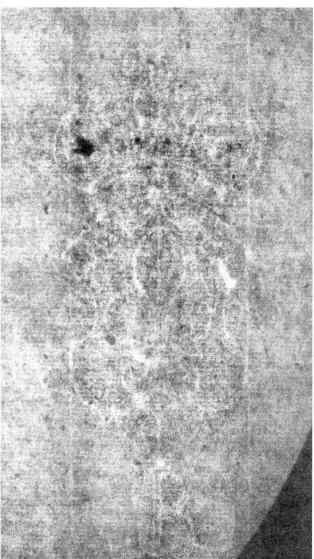

261   1643

FLEUR DE LIS

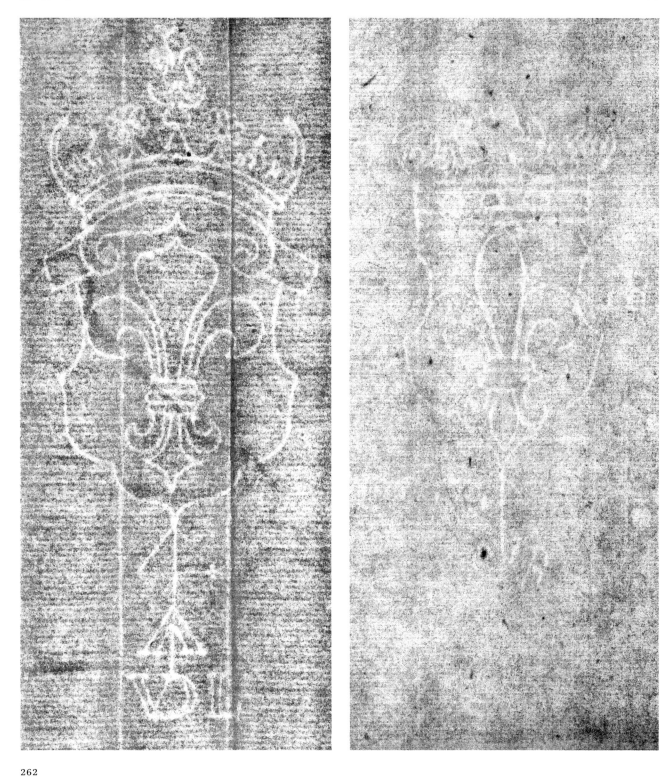

262   1755   263   1625

216 FLEUR DE LIS

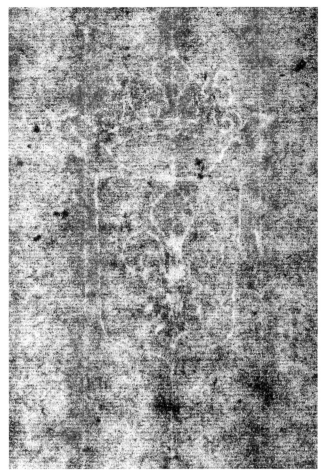

264a 1650

265a 1684

264b

FLEUR DE LIS

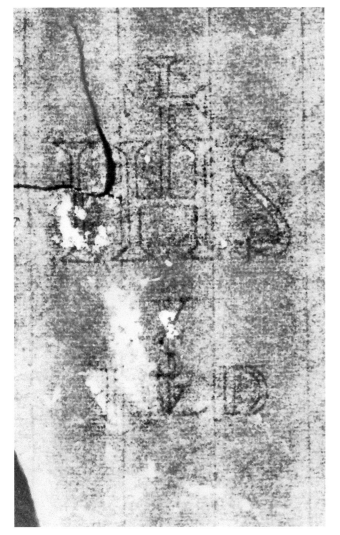

265b

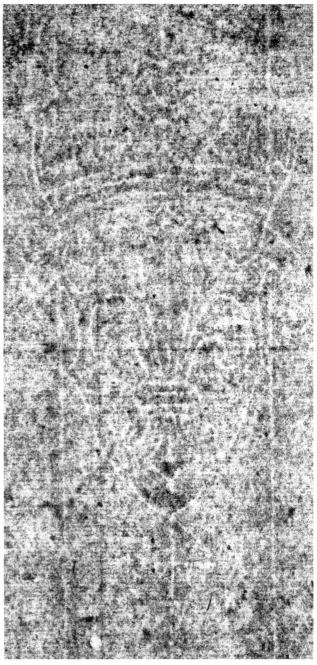

266a 1812

266b

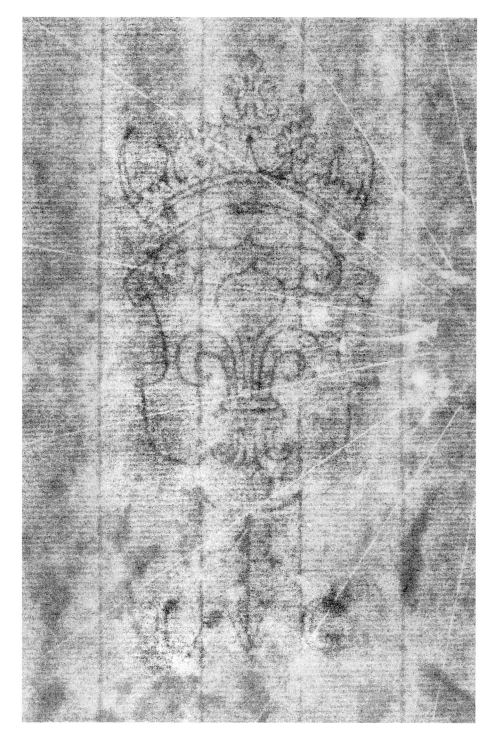

267a   1740

FLEUR DE LIS

267b

268   1570

269   1570

270   1570

271   1573

272a   1636

272b

273   1695

274   1800

275   1685-1700

FLOWER 223

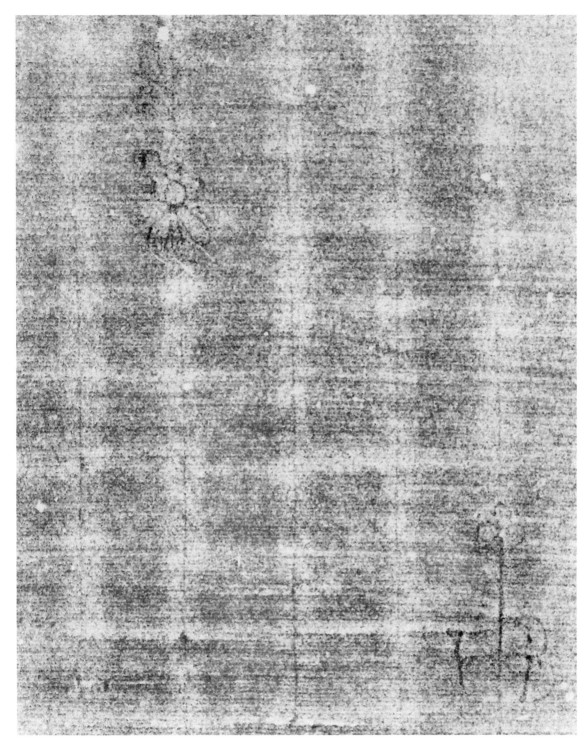

276 1685-1700

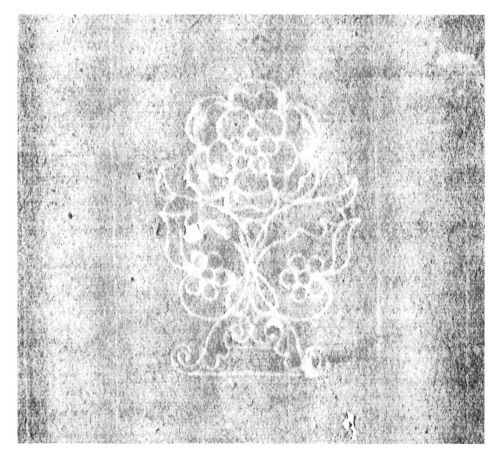

277   1637

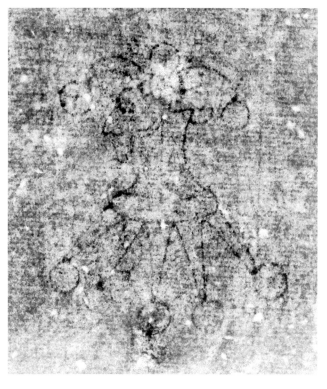

278   1640

FOOLSCAP, FIVE-POINTED

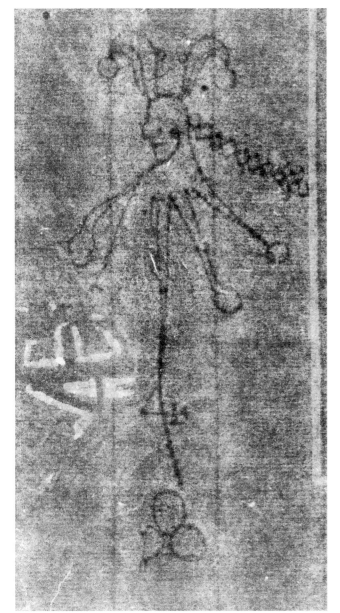

279   1640-1645

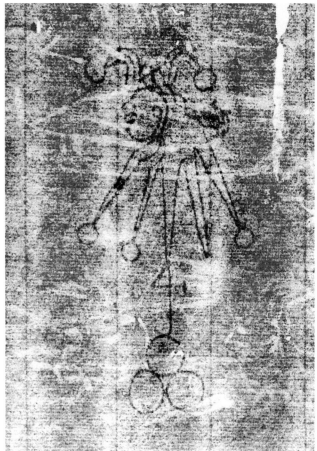

280   1640

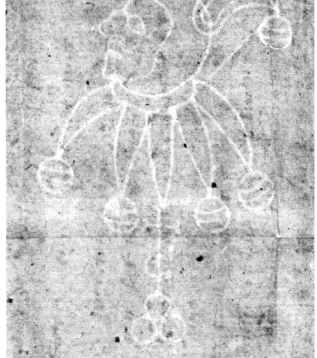

281   1589

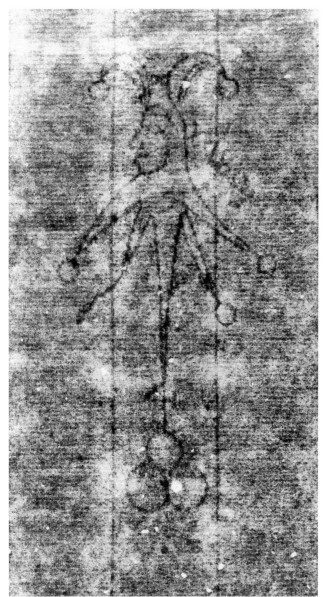

282a 1644

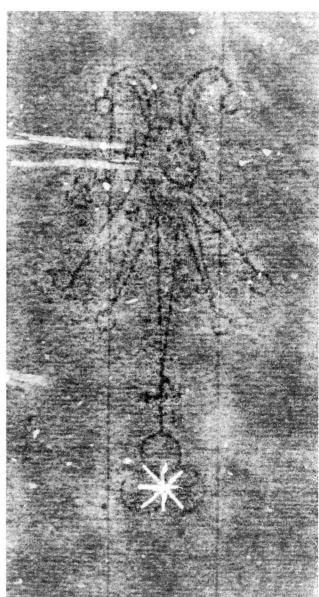

283a 1644

282b

283b

FOOLSCAP, FIVE-POINTED

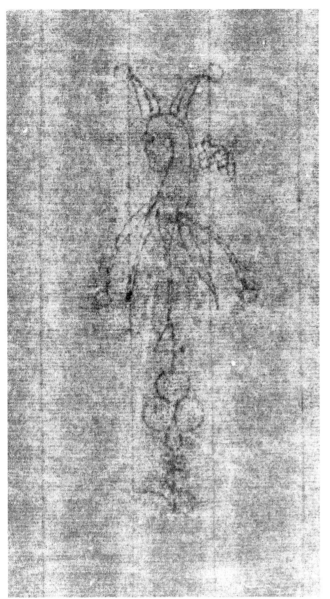

284a   1654

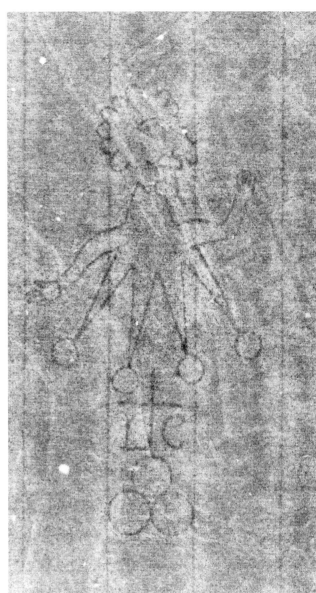

285a   1654

284b

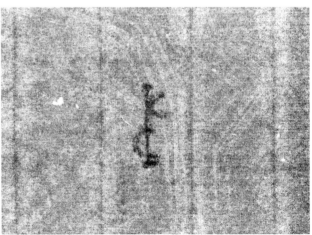

285b

228   FOOLSCAP, FIVE-POINTED–FOOLSCAP, SEVEN-POINTED

286   1654

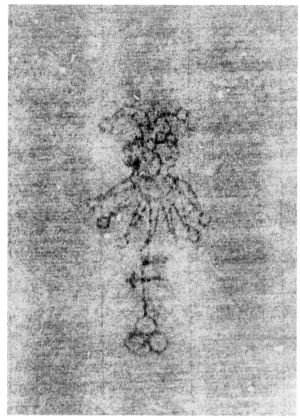

287   1680

288   1685

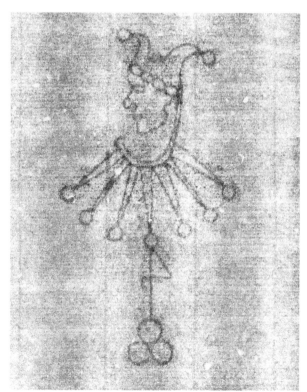

289   1670

FOOLSCAP, SEVEN-POINTED

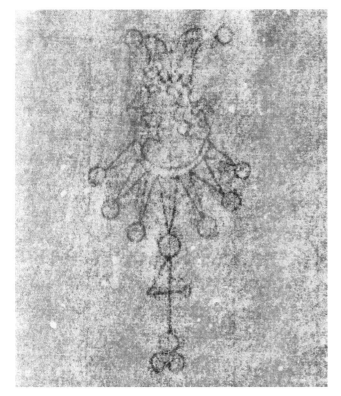

290   1690

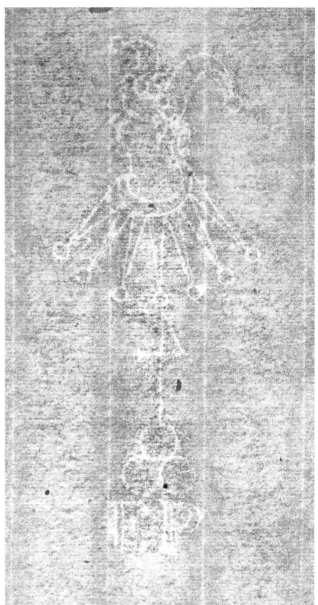

291   1709-1727

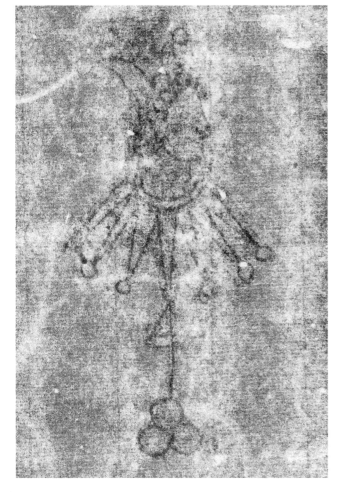

292a   1650-1670

292b

230   FORTUNA

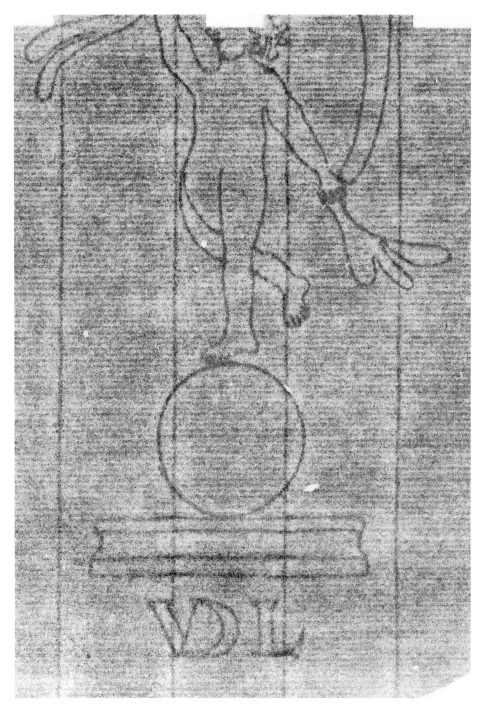

293a   1817

293b

GRAPES

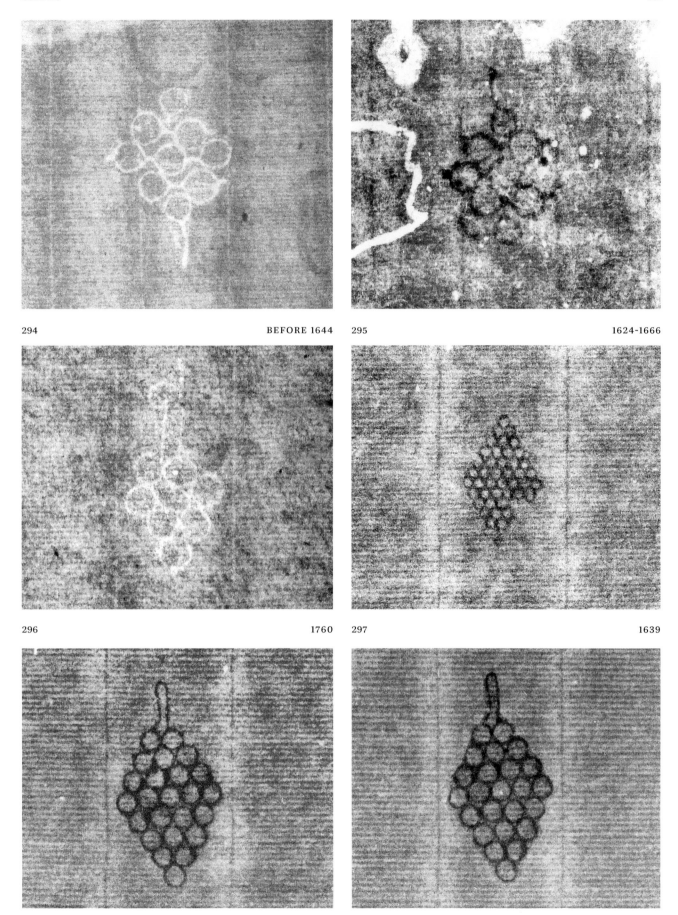

294   BEFORE 1644   295   1624-1666

296   1760   297   1639

298   1684   299   1684

232

GRAPES

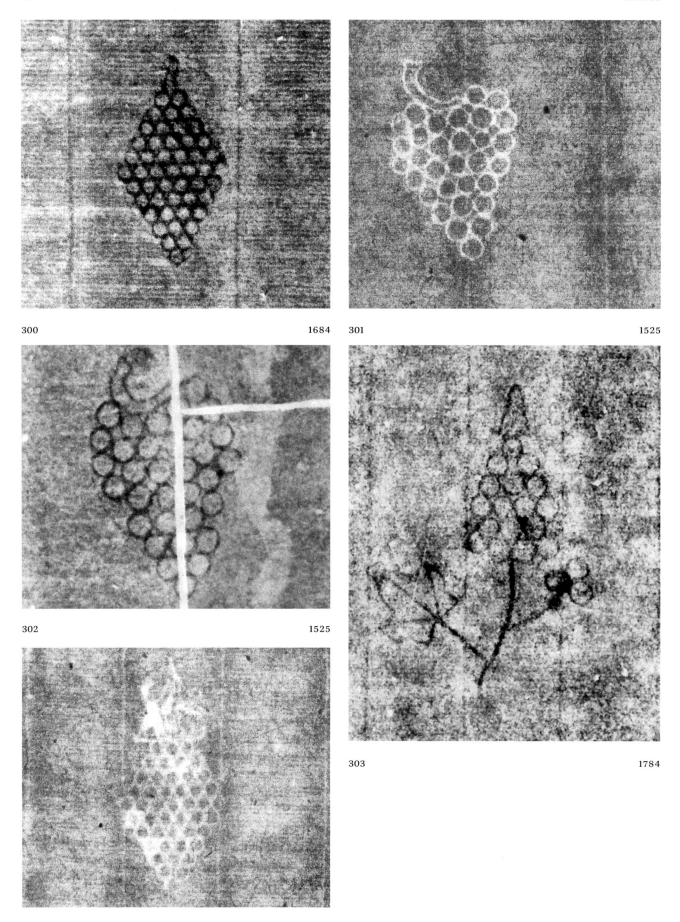

300   1684   301   1525

302   1525

303   1784

304   1584

GRAPES

305 1588

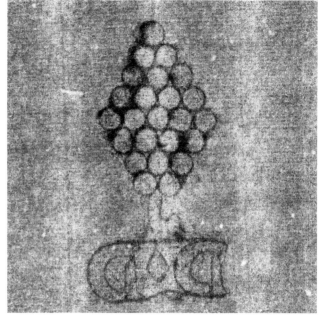

306 BEFORE 1657

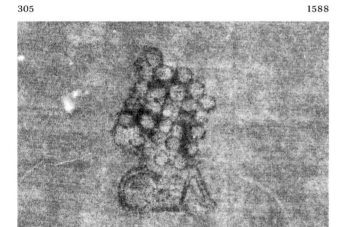

307 1654

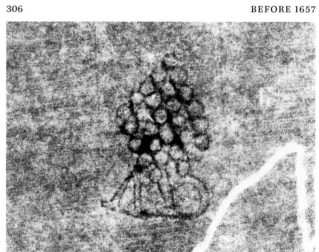

308 1650

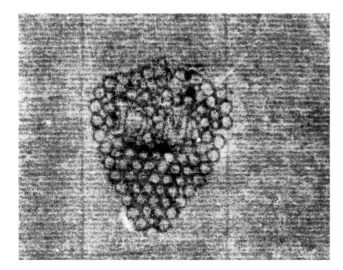

309 1572-1574

GRAPES

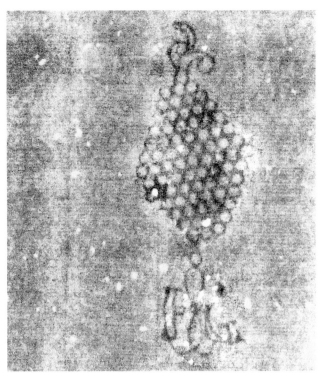

310　　　　　　　　　　　　　BEFORE 1595

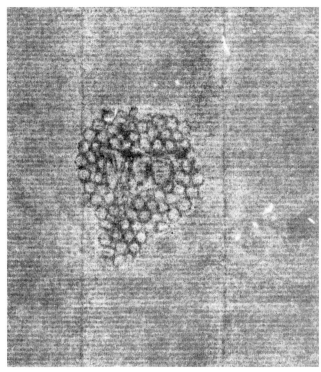

311　　　　　　　　　　　　　1572-1574

312　　　　　　　　　　　　　1575

313　　　　　　　　　　　　　1631

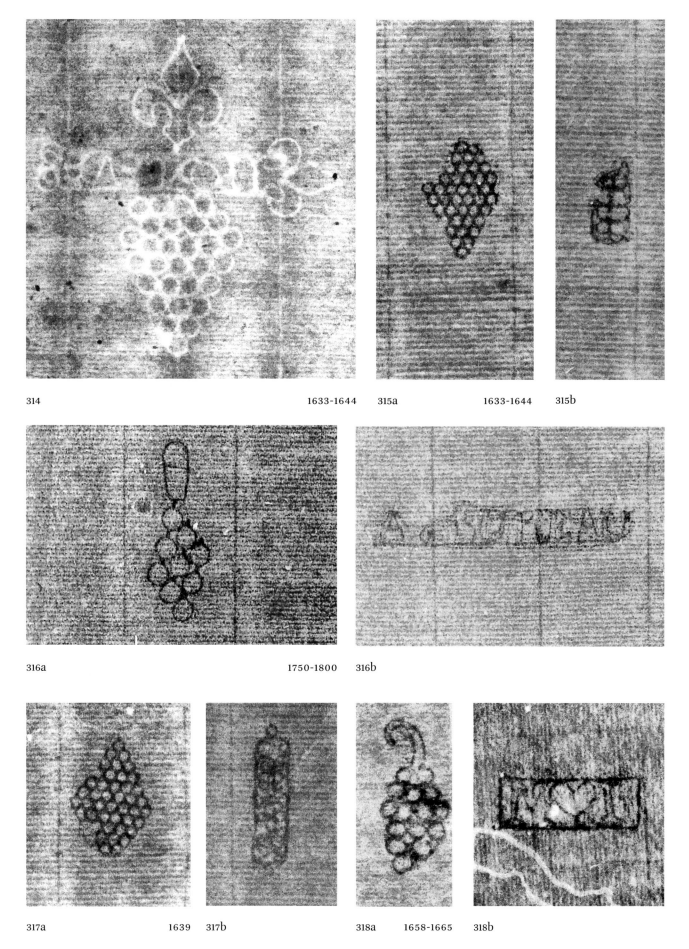

314

315a 1633-1644

315b 1633-1644

316a

316b 1750-1800

317a 1639

317b

318a 1658-1665

318b

319a   1740-1760   319b

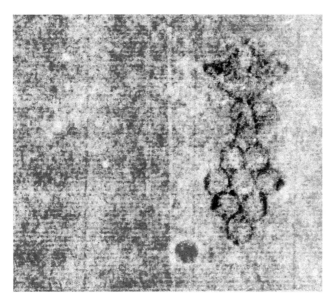

320   1756   321a   1756

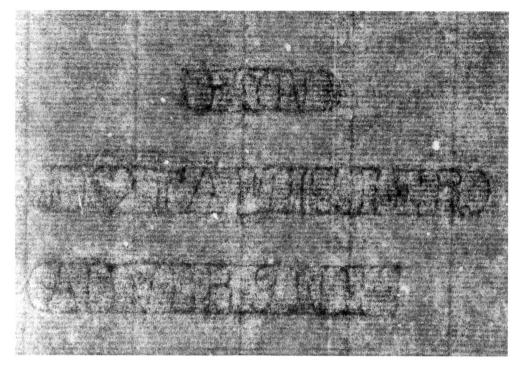

321b

322   1660

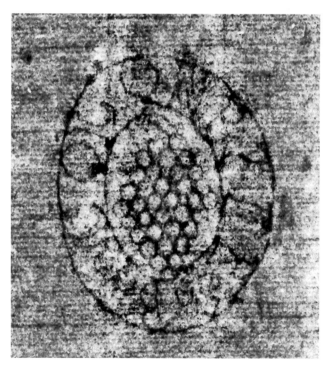

323   1655

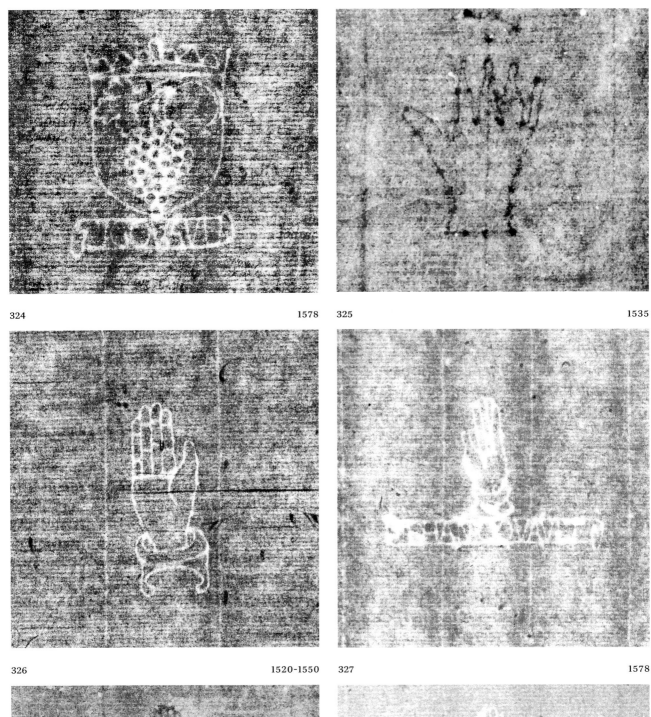

324 1578
325 1535
326 1520-1550
327 1578

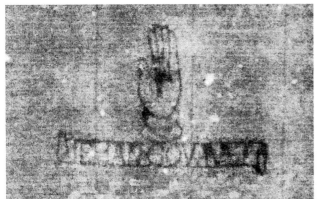

328 1572-1617

329 1572-1617

HAND

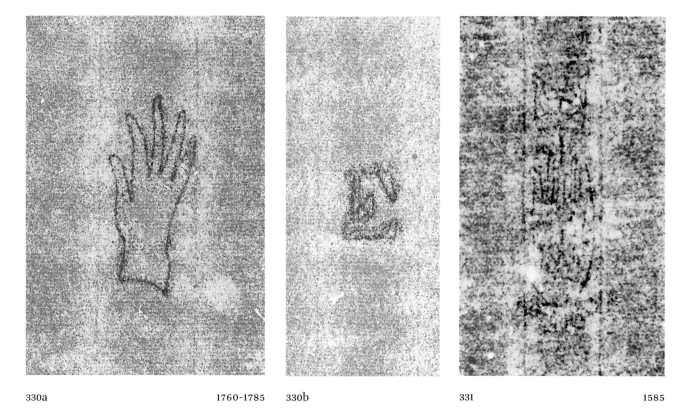

330a   1760-1785   330b   331   1585

332   1575-1580   333   1585   334   1550

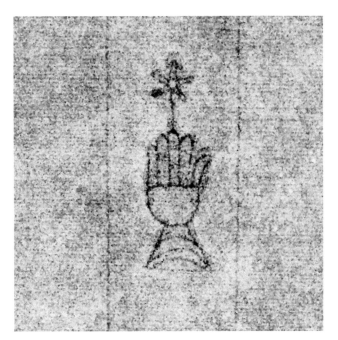

335   1550

336   1555

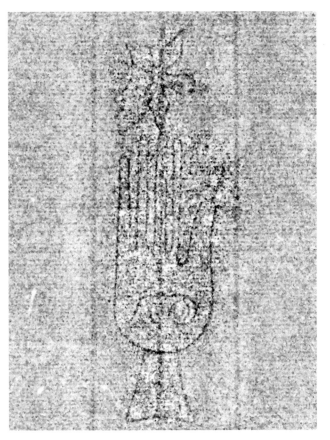

337   1500-1530

338   1560

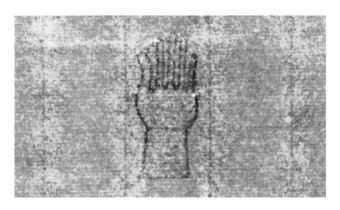

339a	1730

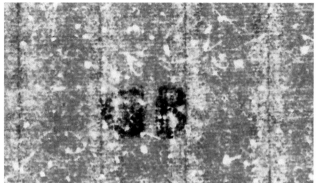

339b

340	1586

341	1685-1695

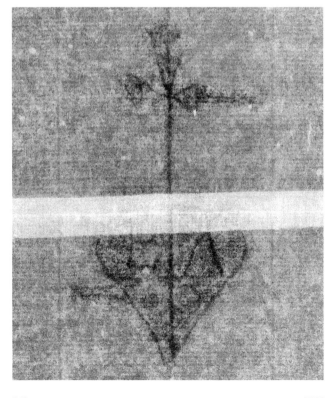

342	1561

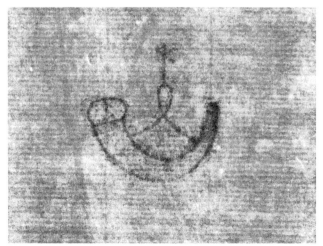

343	1617

242 SUN

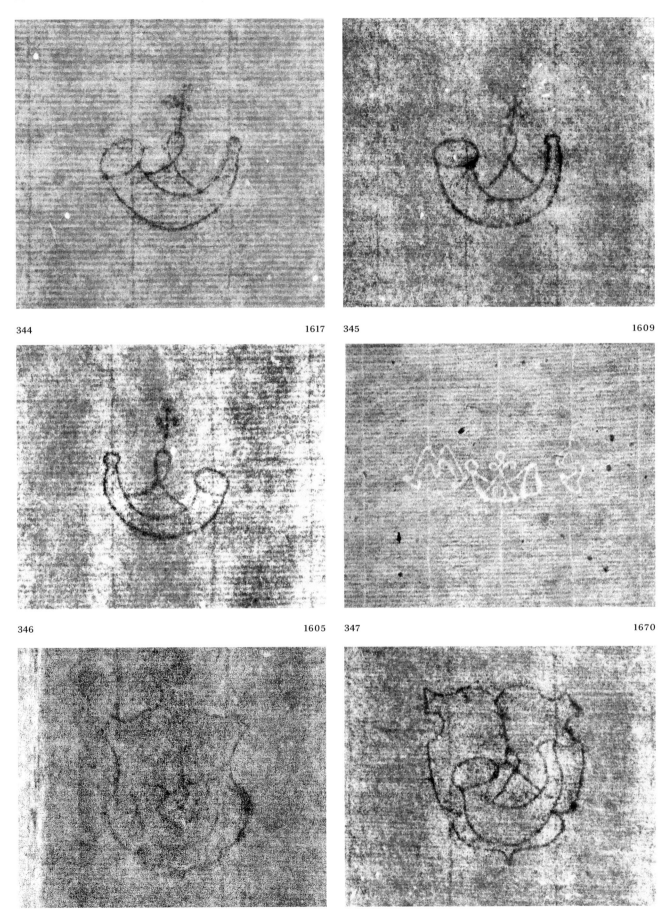

344   1617   345   1609

346   1605   347   1670

348   1593   349   1598-1606

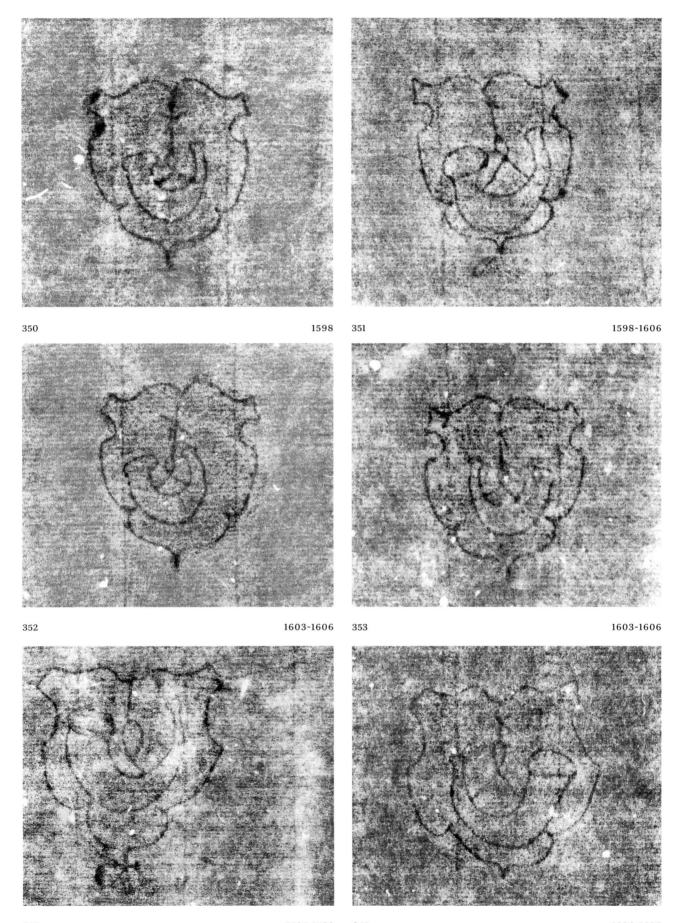

350   1598
351   1598-1606
352   1603-1606
353   1603-1606
354   1595-1599
355   1606-1609

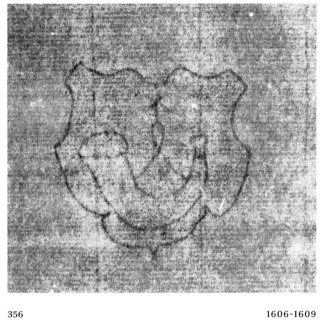

356 1606-1609

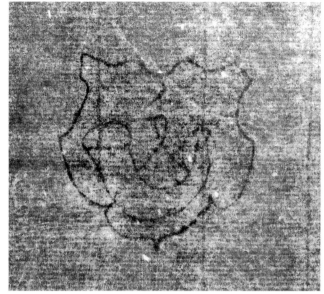

357 1608-1609

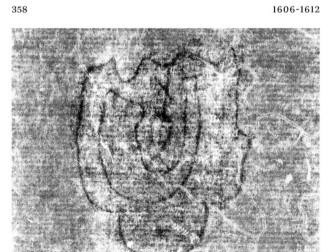

358 1606-1612

359 1601

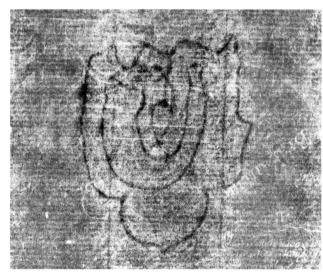

360 1602-1606

361 1606-1612

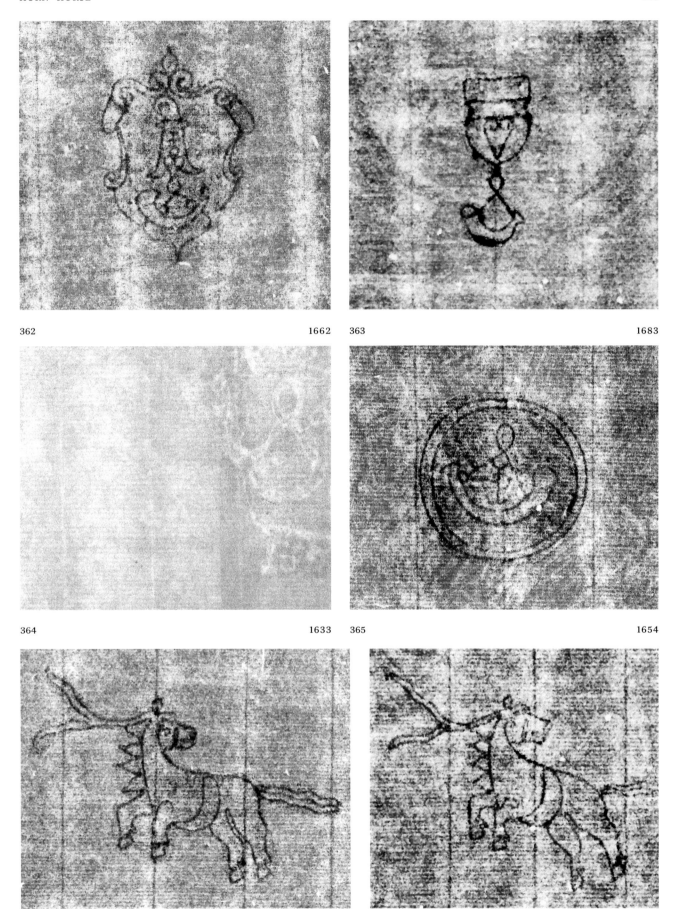

362　　　　　　　　　　1662　363　　　　　　　　　　1683

364　　　　　　　　　　1633　365　　　　　　　　　　1654

366　　　　　　　　　　1783　367　　　　　　　　　　1795

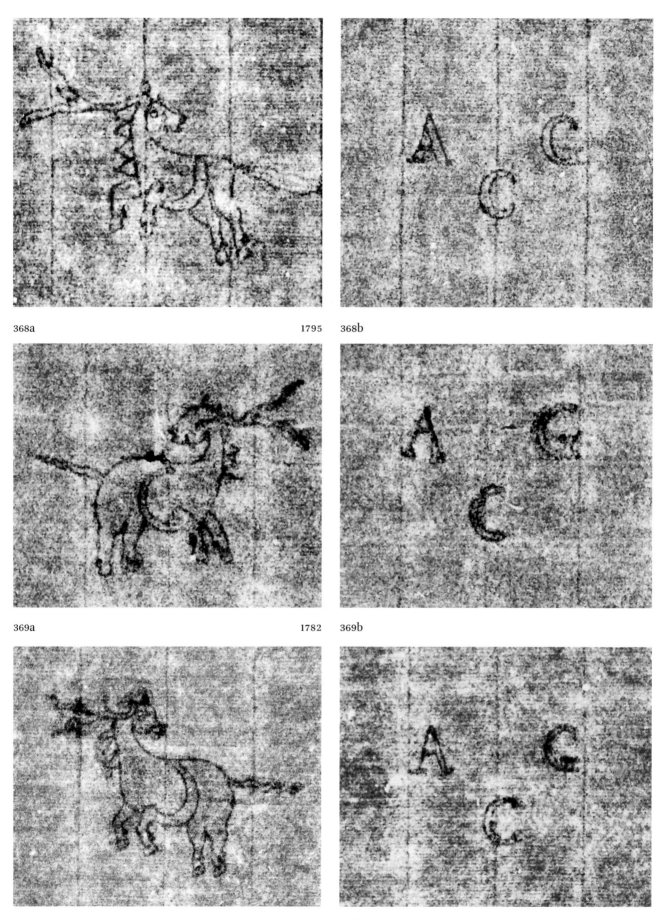

368a   1795   368b

369a   1782   369b

370a   1795   370b

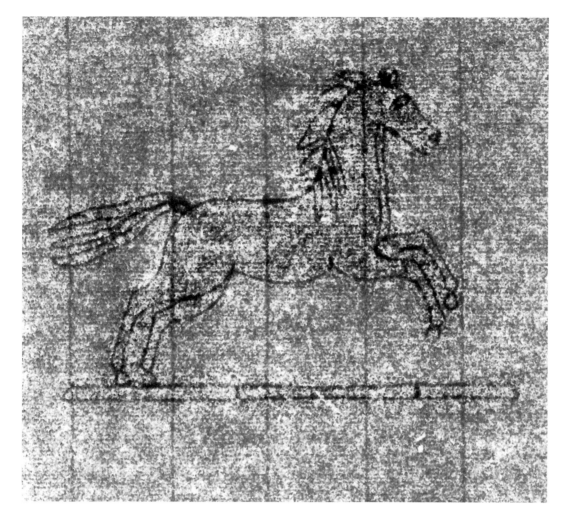

371a   1840

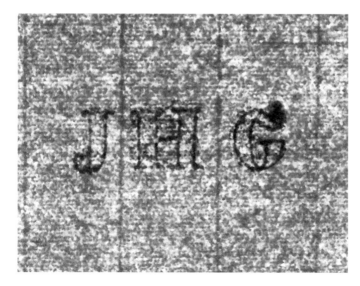

371b

372a   1780-1790

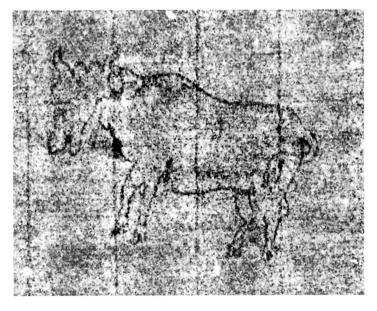

372b

373   1654-1659

LADDER-LETTERS

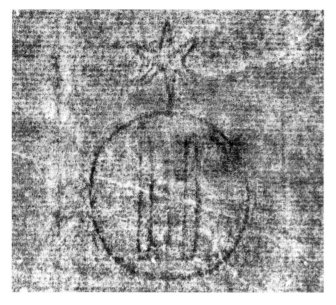

374   1558

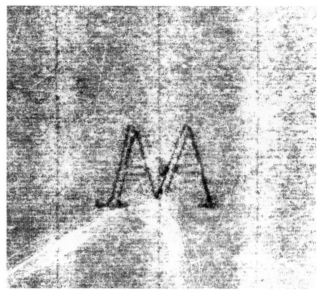

375   1688

376   1688

377   1688

378   1740-1760

379   -

380   1843-1850

381a 1637 381b

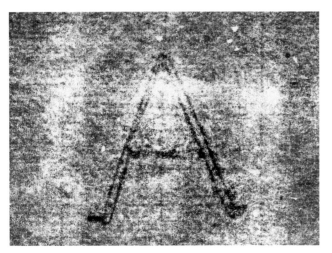

382a 1637 382b

383a 1637 383b

LETTERS

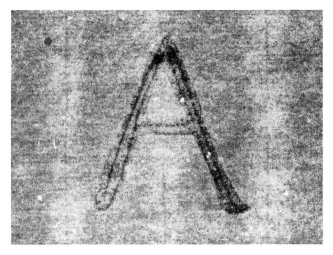

384a   1637

384b

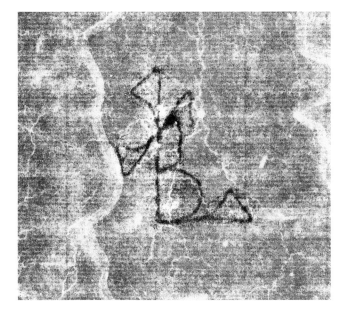

385   1671-1675

386   1630

387   1690-1696

388a 1629 388b

389a 1628 389b

LETTERS

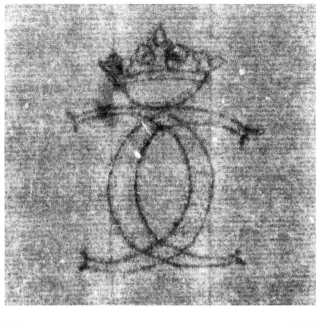

390a   1629

390b

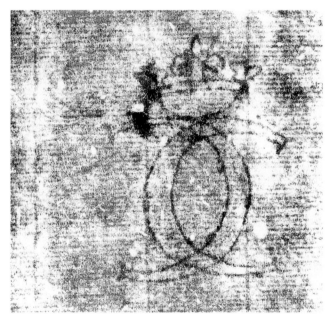

391a   1628

391b

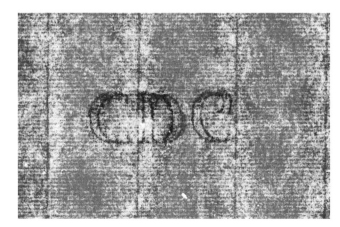

392   1679

393   1685-1693

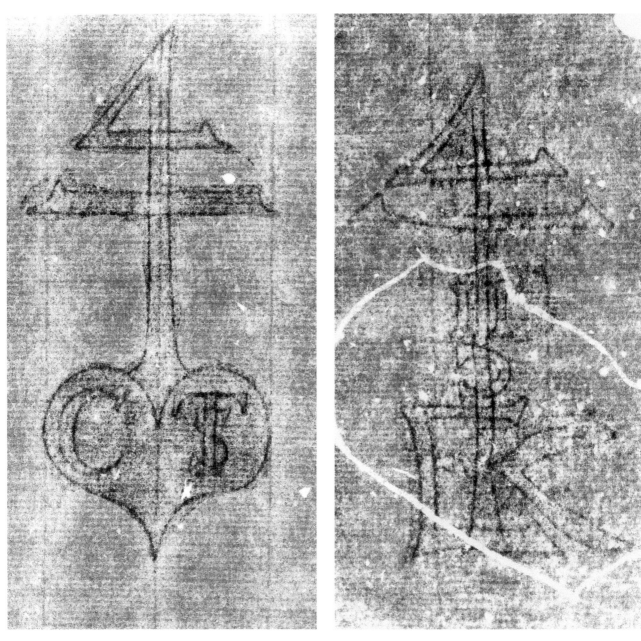

394   1760-1770   396   1741-1756

395   1578

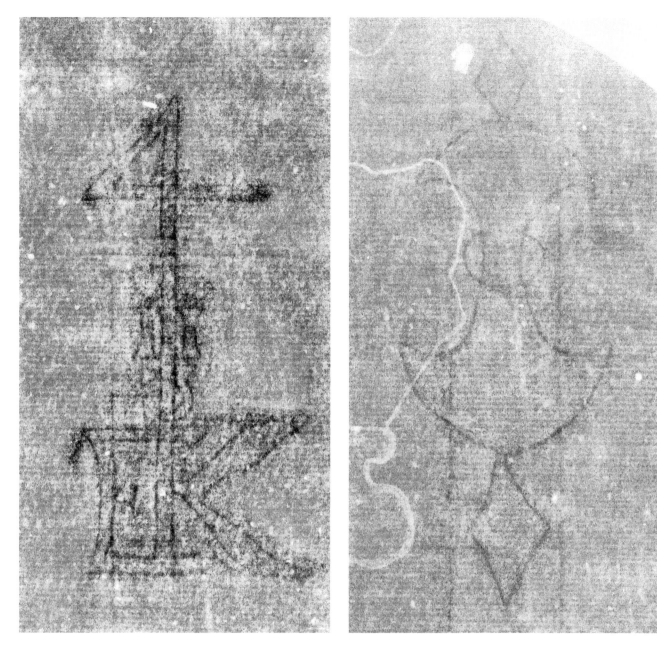

397a   1741-1756   397b

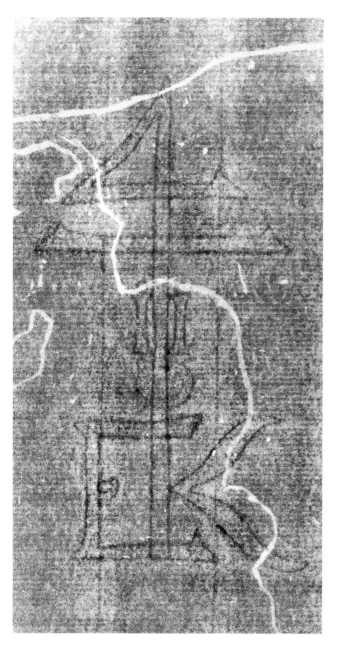

398a

1741-1756 398b

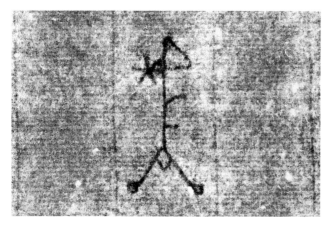

399   1585

400

LETTERS

401   1609

402   1611

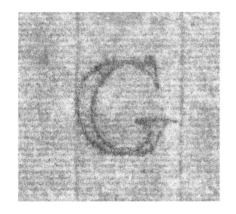

403a   1804-1810

403b

404   1556

405a   AFTER 1651

405b

406   1597-1611

407   1590-1611

408   1643

409   1810

LETTERS

410   1820

411   1572-1594

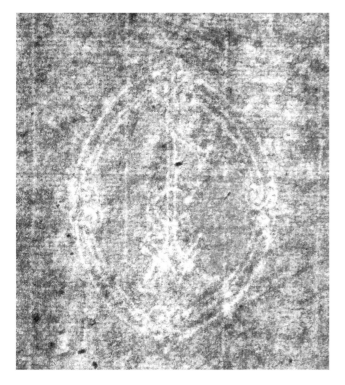

412   1572-1594

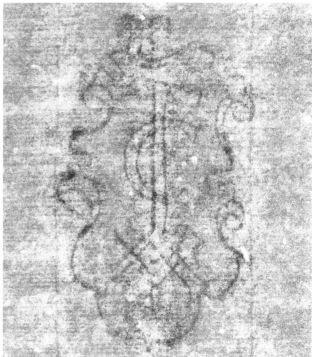

413   1582-1603

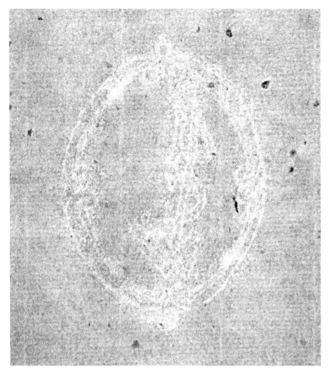

414   1604

415   1791-1815

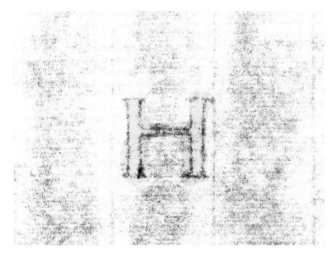

416   1698

417   1628

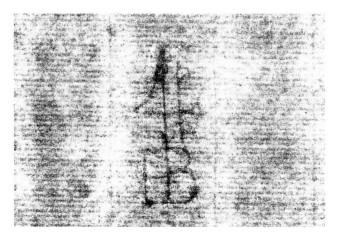

418   1600

LETTERS

419a   1627

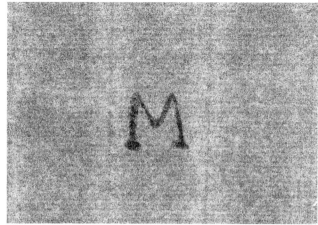

419b

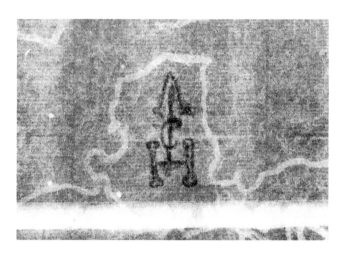

420   1679

421   1690-1700

422   1705

423   1690

424a 1684

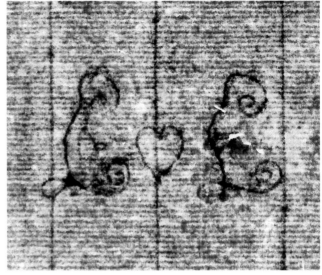
424b

425 1812

426 1638

427a 1770-1780

427b

LETTERS

428   1669

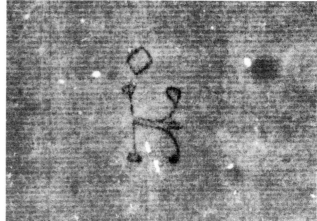

429   1673

430   1662

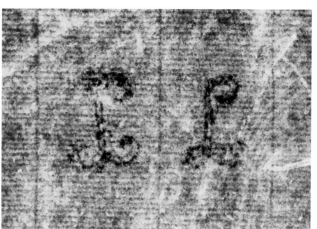

431   1684

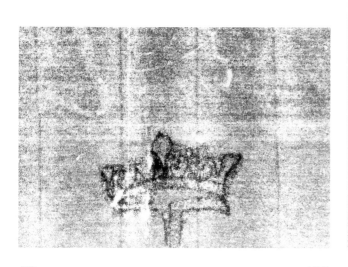

432   1672

433   1660

434   1748-1787

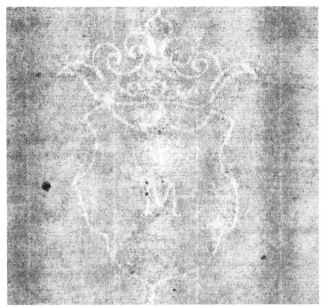

435   1652

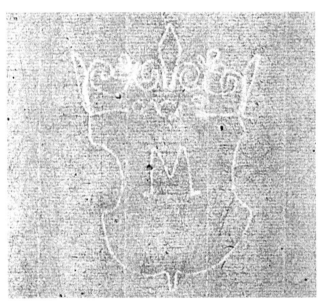

436   1623

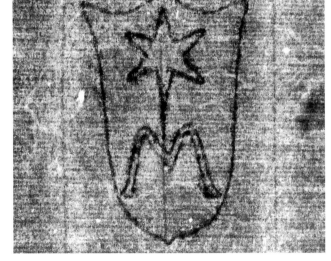

437   1577-1585

438   1730-1745

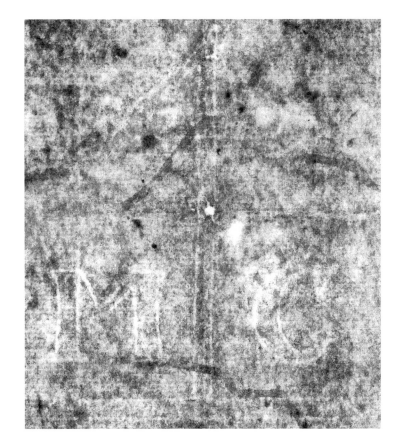

439   1775-1784

440   1784

441   1743-1770

442   1613

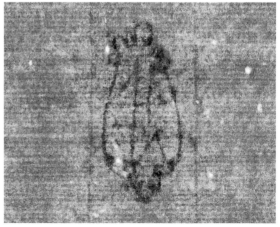

443   1614

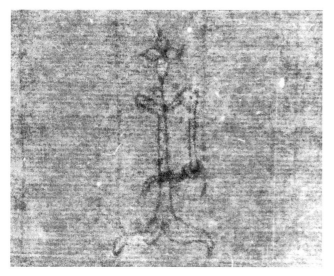

444a 1609

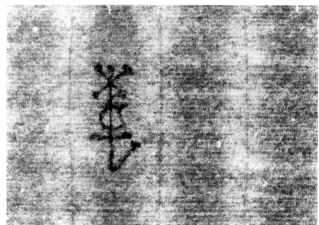

444b

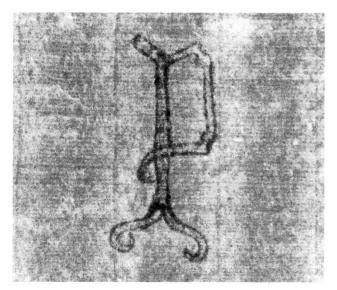

445 1598

446 1596

447 1662

448 1649

449   1780

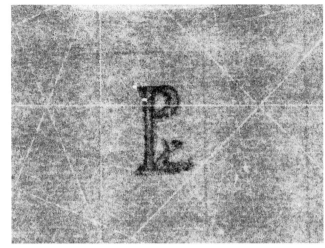

450   AFTER 1675

451   1682

452   1737

453   AFTER 1690

454   AFTER 1690

LETTERS

455   1617-1623

456   1617-1623

457   1617-1623

458a   1645

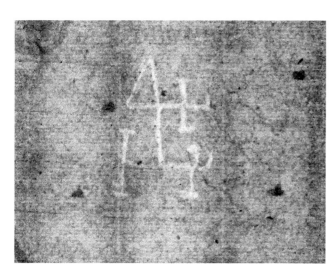

458b

459   1620

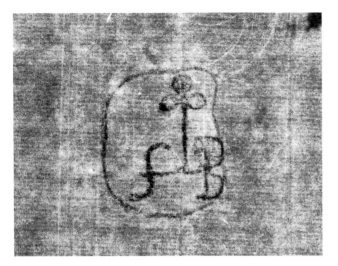

460   1649

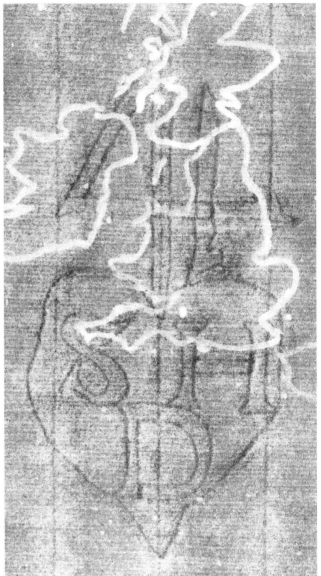

461   1735

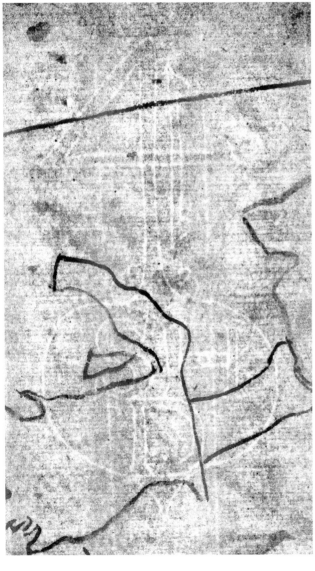

462   1735

LETTERS

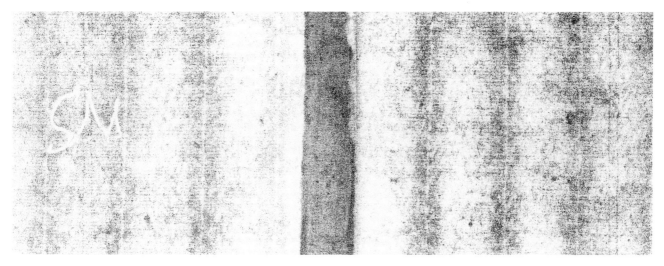

463	1587

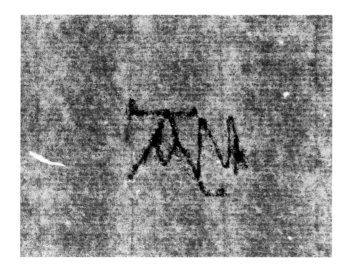

464	1585

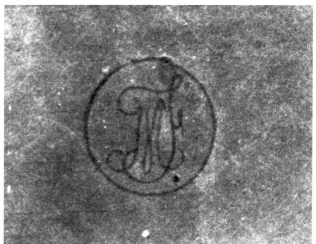

465	1837

466a	1662

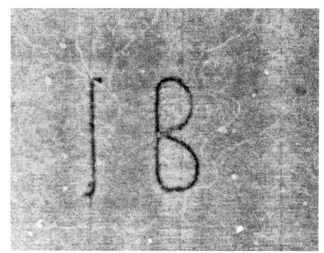

466b

467   1673

469   1800

468   1800

470   AFTER 1751

471   1782

LION—MACE 273

472   1800

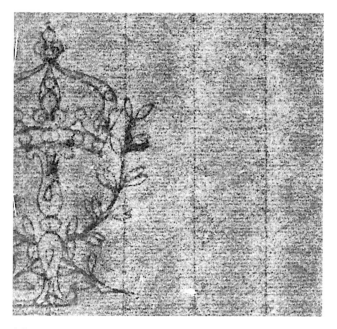

473   1660-1690

474   1622

475   1580

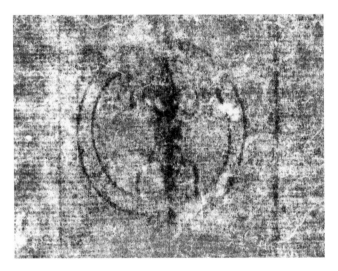

476   1600

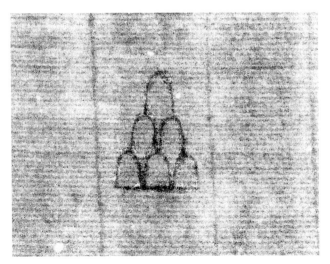

477a   1661

477b

478 BEFORE 1666

479 1788

480 1577-1589

481 1575-1588

482   1582

483   1780-1815

484   1813

485   1820

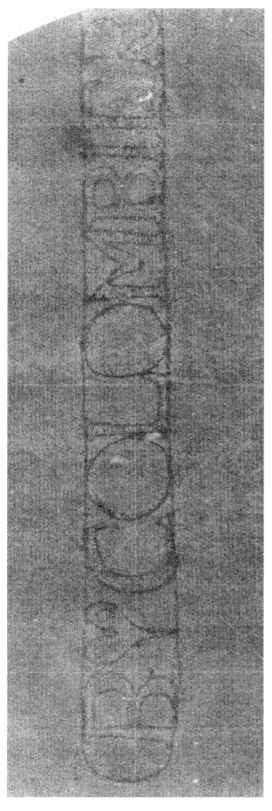

486   1693

487   AFTER 1723

488a 1826

488b

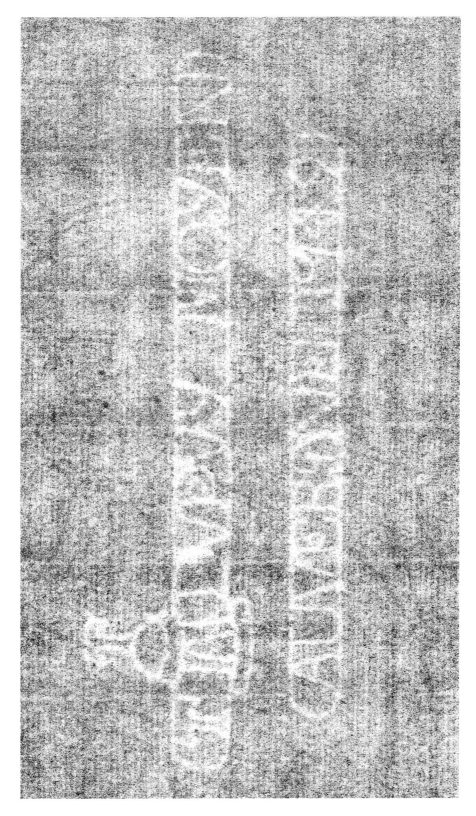

490   1807

491   1867

492   1709

493a   1745

493b

494a   1744

494b

495   1800-1840

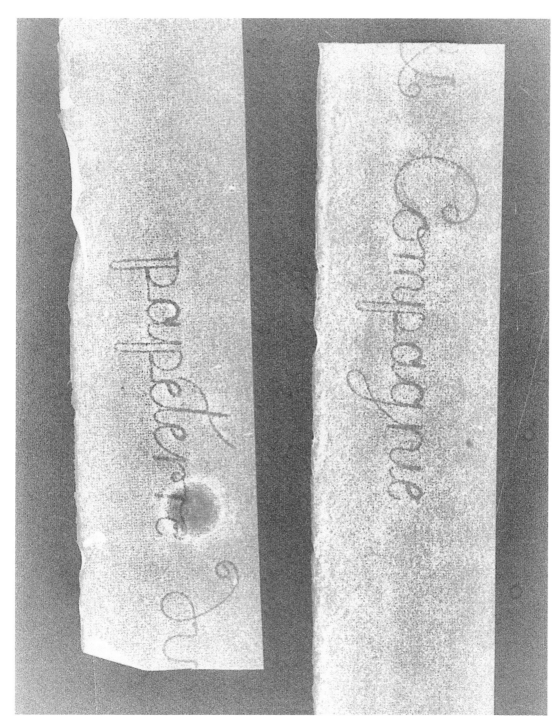

496 1790-1800

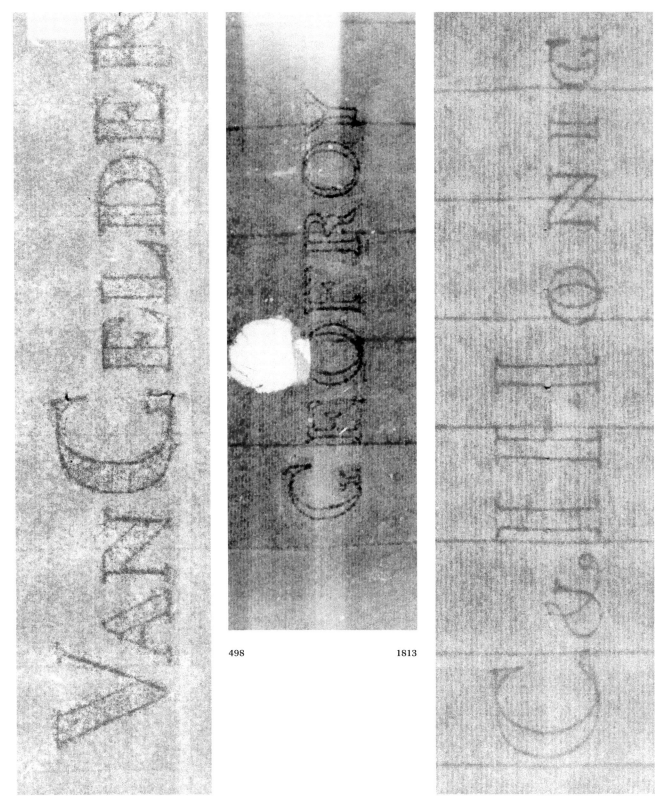

497 AFTER 1816

498 1813

499 1800

NAMES

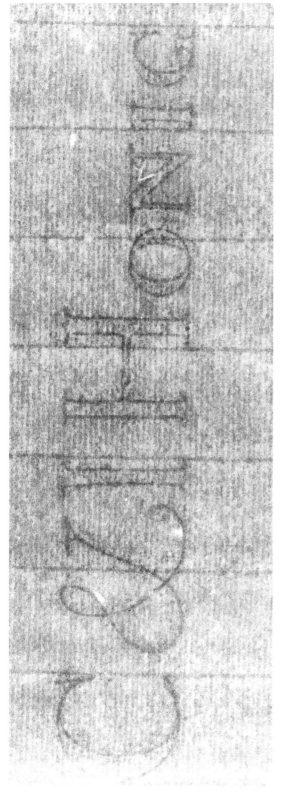

500 BEFORE 1738

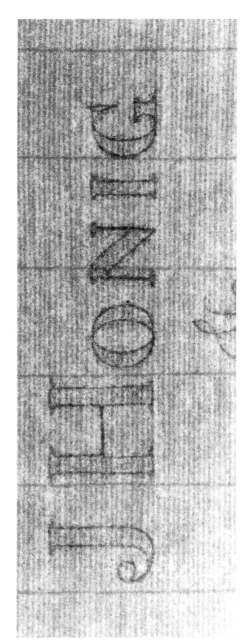

501 AFTER 1830

502a   AFTER 1830

502b

503   1748-1787

504a

1823

504b

505   1780

506   1690

507   1780-1832

508 1750-1765

509 1820

510 1819

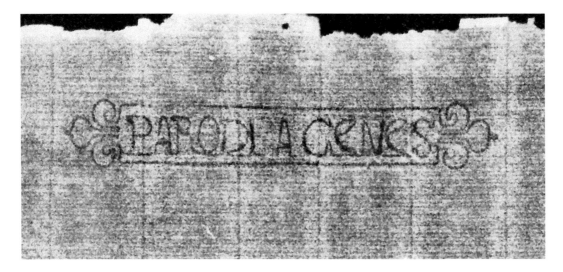

511a 1805-1815

511b

512 1585

513a 1800

513b

514 1690-1700

515a 1745

515b

294 NAMES—OFFICIAL MARKS

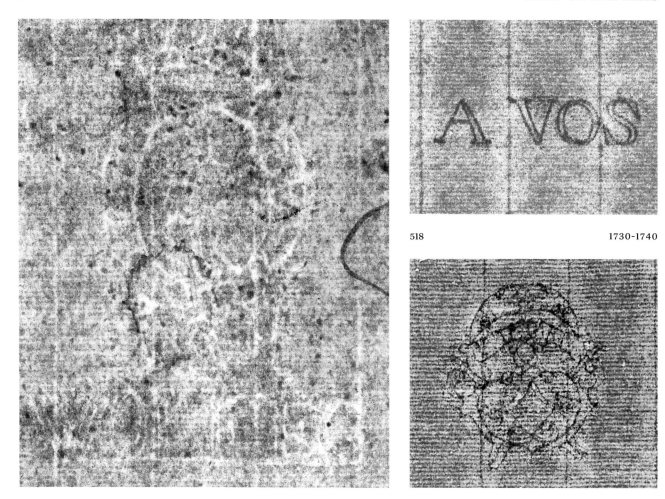

517 1785

518 1730-1740

519 1763

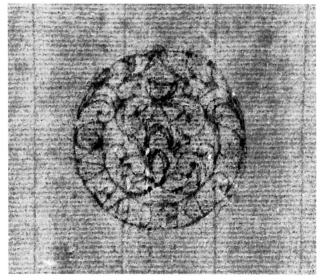

520 1730

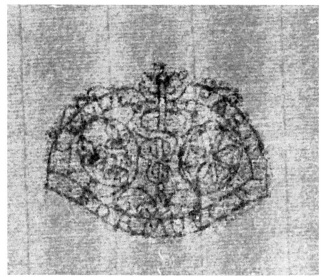

521 1760

523　　　　　　　　　　　　　　1672

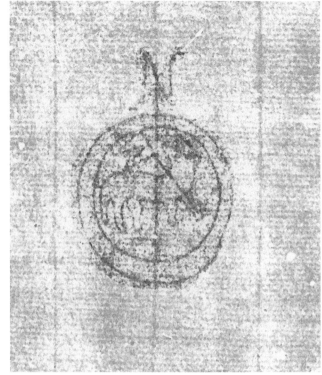

524　　　　　　　　　　　　　　1650-1660

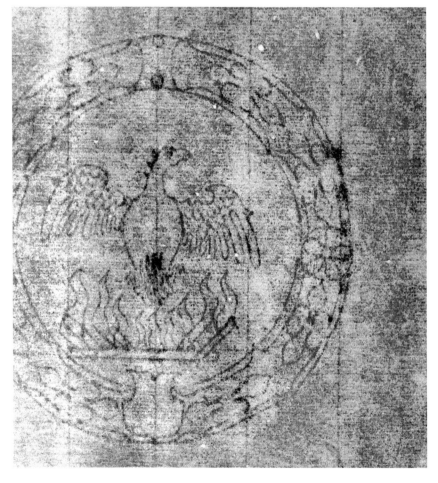

525　　　　　　　　　　　　　　1651

PILLARS

526   1635

527   1690-1695

528   1570-1571

529   1570

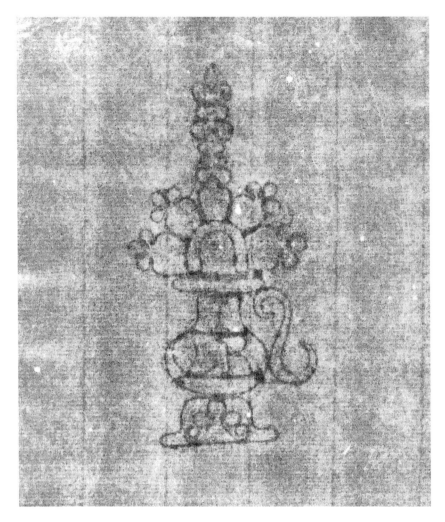

530 1667

531 1618

532 1611

533 1601

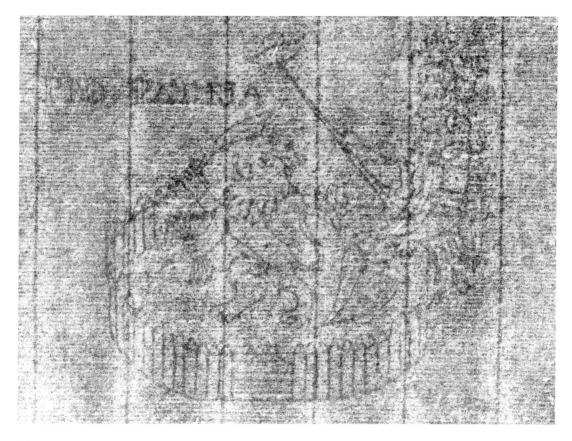

534 1748-1787

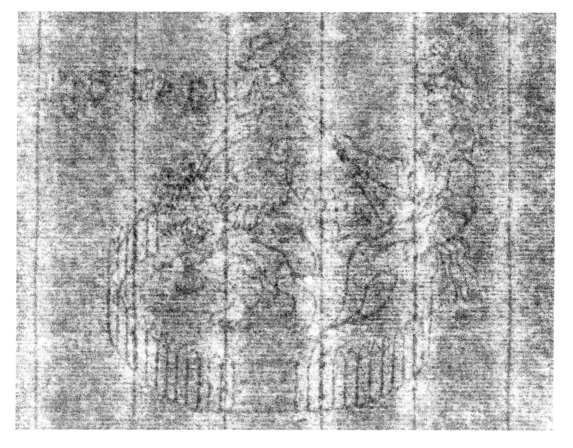

535 1748-1787

536a   1700-1710

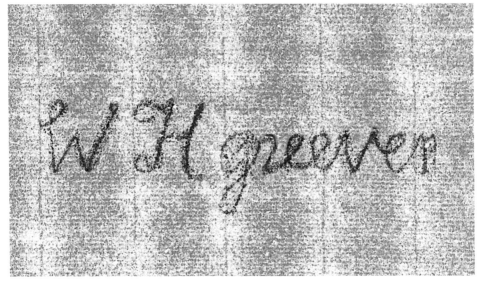

536b

SERPENT

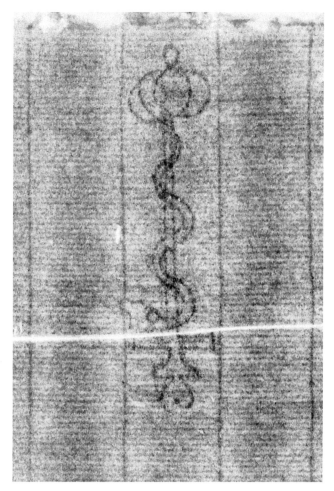

537   1750-1800

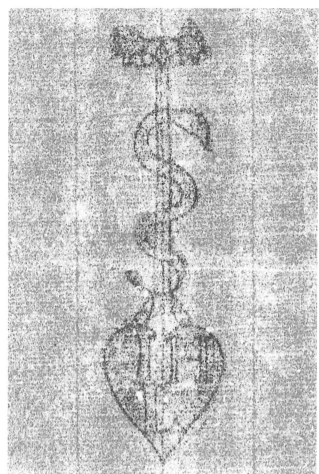

538   1826-1837

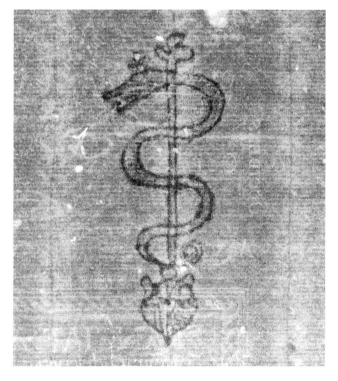

539   1596

540   1635

SHELL–SPHERE–STAR

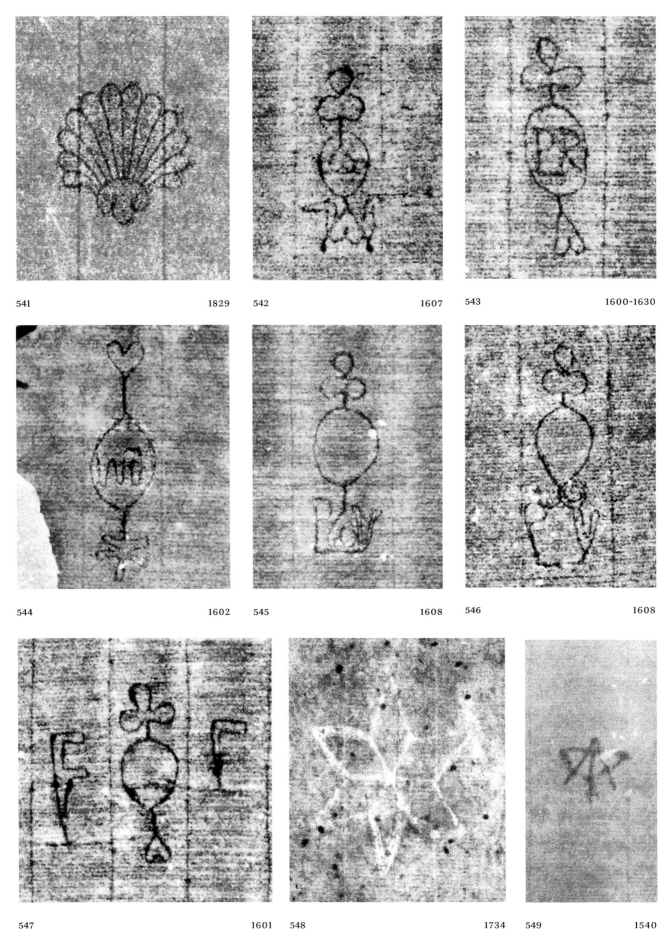

541 1829   542 1607   543 1600-1630

544 1602   545 1608   546 1608

547 1601   548 1734   549 1540

550   1649

551   1640-1660

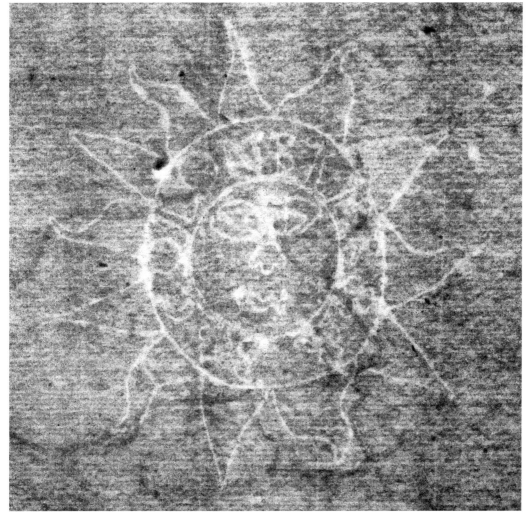

552   1673

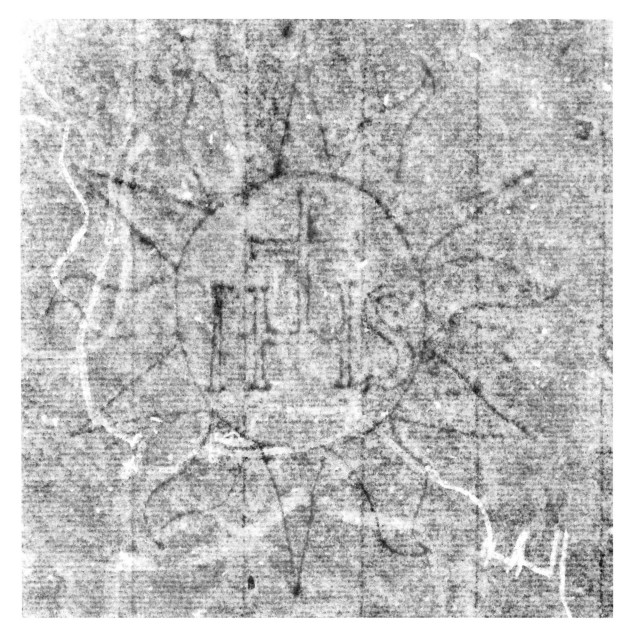

553   1716-1719

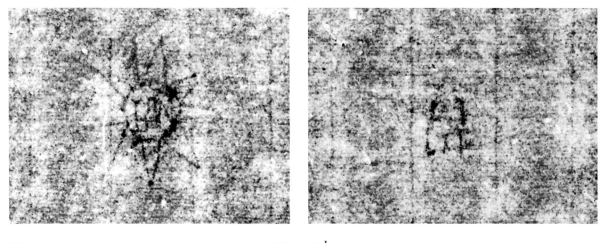

554a   1636   554b

SWORD—TOWER

555   1700-1720

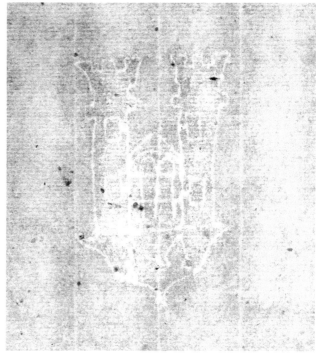

556   1695-1700

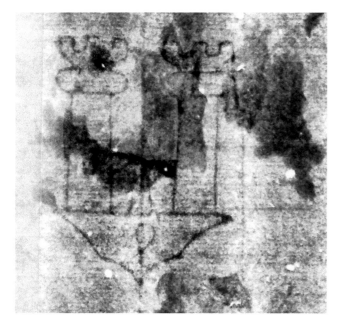

557   1614

558   1676

559　　　　　　　　　　　　　　1685

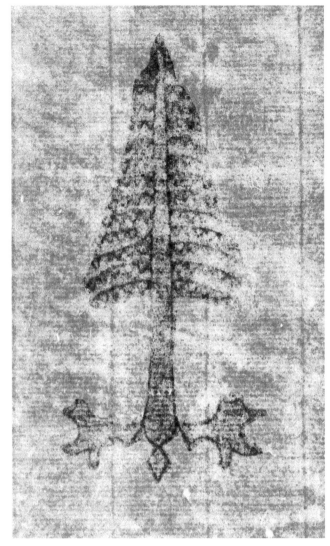

560a　　　　　　　　　　　　1690-1700

560b

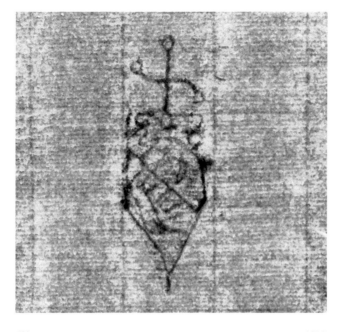

561   1610

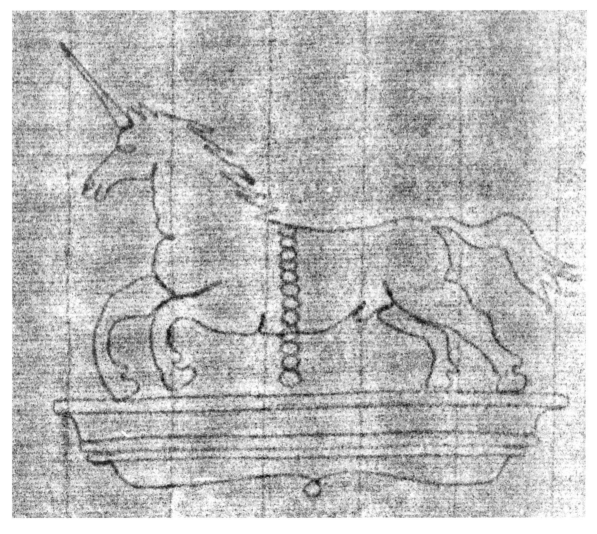

562   1750-1800

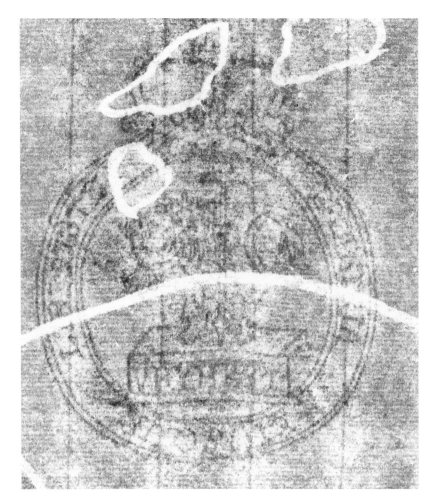

563

564 1556

1740-1750

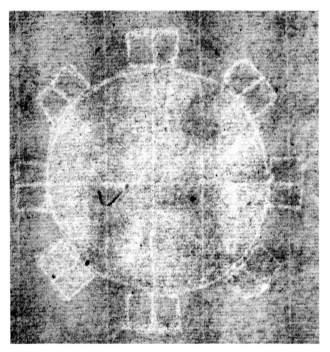

565 1647

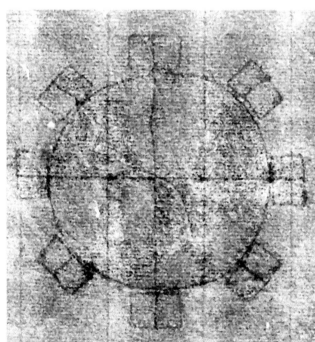

566 1646-1647

567